Religion in Global
Civil Society

Religion in Global Civil Society

EDITED BY MARK JUERGENSMEYER

OXFORD
UNIVERSITY PRESS

2005

OXFORD
UNIVERSITY PRESS

Oxford University Press, Inc., publishes works that further
Oxford University's objective of excellence
in research, scholarship, and education.

Oxford   New York
Auckland   Cape Town   Dar es Salaam   Hong Kong   Karachi
Kuala Lumpur   Madrid   Melbourne   Mexico City   Nairobi
New Delhi   Shanghai   Taipei   Toronto

With offices in
Argentina   Austria   Brazil   Chile   Czech Republic   France   Greece
Guatemala   Hungary   Italy   Japan   Poland   Portugal   Singapore
South Korea   Switzerland   Thailand   Turkey   Ukraine   Vietnam

Copyright © 2006 by Oxford University Press, Inc.

Published by Oxford University Press, Inc.
198 Madison Avenue, New York, New York 10016

www.oup.com

Oxford is a registered trademark of Oxford University Press

Library of Congress Cataloging-in-Publication Data
Religion in global civil society / edited by Mark Juergensmeyer.
p.   cm.
Includes bibliographical references and index.
ISBN: 978-0-19-518827-1; 978-0-19-518835-6 (pbk.)
1. Globalization—Religious aspects.   I. Juergensmeyer, Mark.
BL65. G55R39 2005
201'.7—dc22   2004031125

9 8 7 6 5

Printed in the United States of America
on acid-free paper

To the memory of Claus M. Halle

Acknowledgments

This volume was the product of a two-year series of seminars and conferences on religion in global civil society sponsored by the Claus M. Halle Institute for Global Learning at Emory University, for which I was asked to serve as director. I would like to acknowledge the support of the Director of the Halle Institute, Thomas Remington, who took an active role in the seminars and conferences and was the guiding force behind the project. We were delighted that Claus Halle was personally interested in the project and participated in it, though he did not live to see its completion as a book. In preparing the manuscript, I greatly appreciate the help of the Emory graduate assistant, Chris Noble, and the assistance of John Ucciferri and Ben Schonthal at Santa Barbara. Susanne Rudolph's chapter has been published in a slightly different version in John D. Carlson and Erik C. Owens, eds., *The Sacred and the Sovereign: Religion and International Politics*; parts of my chapter on religious antiglobalism were published in my chapter in Dominic Sachsenmaier, Shmuel N. Eisenstadt, and Jens Riedel, eds., *Reflections on Multiple Modernities: European, Chinese and Other Interpretations*. Harold Berman's article is a revised and expanded version of an article that first appeared in the *Journal of Law and Religion*. Our thanks to all the participants in the seminar and conference for their insights and involvement, and for helping us understand the complexities of thinking about religion and civil society in a global age.

Contents

Contributors

ABDULLAHI A. AN-NA'IM is Charles Howard Candler Professor of Law and senior fellow of the Center for Interdisciplinary Study of Religion at Emory University. He is the author of "Toward an Islamic Reformation" and of numerous articles and book chapters on Islamic law, comparative constitutionalism and human rights, and human rights in cross-cultural perspectives.

PETER BERGER is director of the Institute on Religion and World Affairs at Boston University. His recent publications include *Many Globalizations: Cultural Diversity in the Modern World, The Desecularization of the World: Resurgent Religion and World Politics, The Limits of Social Cohesion,* and *Redeeming Laughter: The Comic Dimension of Human Experience.*

HAROLD J. BERMAN is Robert W. Woodruff Professor of Law at Emory University and former James Barr Ames Professor of Law at Harvard University. He is also a fellow at the Carter Center. His most recent publications include *Faith and Order: The Reconciliation of Law and Religion,* and *Law and Revolution, II: The Impact of the Protestant Reformations on the Western Legal Tradition.*

ELIZABETH M. BOUNDS is coordinator of the Initiative in Religious Practices and Practical Theology at Emory University, where she is also associate director of the graduate division of religion and associate professor of Christian ethics. Along with the volume *Coming Together/Coming Apart: Religion, Community, and Modernity,* she has published various articles on welfare reform, pedagogy, and racism. She is also engaged in a research project in the Atlanta area studying congregational responses to social problems.

JON P. GUNNEMANN is professor of social ethics at Candler School of Theology and the graduate division of religion at Emory University. He has published several articles on theology, ethics, and economics, including "Thinking Theologically about the Economic" and "Capital Ideas." He has received a Christian Faith and Life Sabbatical Fellowship from the Louisville Institute and is currently completing a book on theology and economics.

MARK JUERGENSMEYER is professor of sociology and director of global and international studies at the University of California, Santa Barbara. His most recent books include *Terror in the Mind of God: The Global Rise of Religious Violence* and *Global Religions: An Introduction*. He received the 2003 Grawemeyer Award in Religion and is currently working on several projects on religion, globalization, and violence.

FRANK J. LECHNER is associate professor of sociology at Emory University. He is author of *World Culture: Origins and Consequences* and coeditor of *The Globalization Reader*. His current research includes a project on globalization and national identity in the Netherlands.

BOBBI PATTERSON is a senior lecturer at Emory University's department of religion and director of the Emory Scholars Program in Emory College. She is the winner of collegewide teaching awards and has written on the scholarship of teaching, including "Religion Teaching Portfolio," in *The Teaching Portfolio*, ed. Peter Seldin; and "Practicing Reconciliation in the Classroom," in *Roads to Reconciliation: Approaches to Conflict*, eds. Amy Benson Brown and Karen Poremski. Her research currently focuses on spiritual practices, particularly in relation to wilderness spirituality and social change.

SUSANNE HOEBER RUDOLPH is Benton Distinguished Service Professor Emerita at the University of Chicago. She is editor of *Transnational Religion and Fading States* and author of *Reversing the Gaze: the Amar Singh Diary, a Colonial Subject's Narrative of Imperial India* (with Lloyd Rudolph), and other works on comparative politics and India. She served as President of the American Political Science Association (2003–4) and is currently working on how modes of inquiry affect problems of area studies.

STEVEN M. TIPTON teaches sociology and ethics at Emory University and its Candler School of Theology, where he is professor of sociology of religion. Coauthor of *Habits of the Heart* and *The Good Society*, he is currently at work on a book entitled *Public Pulpits*, a study of moral advocacy by the mainline churches on Capitol Hill.

CARRIE ROSEFSKY WICKHAM is associate professor of political science at Emory University. Her recent book *Mobilizing Islam* examines new trends in Islamic political thought and practice throughout the Middle East.

Religion in Global
Civil Society

Introduction: Religious Ambivalence to Global Civil Society

Mark Juergensmeyer

More than two hundred years ago, one of the leading figures of the European Enlightenment looked back over the preceding centuries and breathed a huge sigh of relief. Voltaire observed that the era of European history known as the Age of the Wars of Religion had finally, with the Peace of Westphalia, come to an end. Religious wars—those "abominable monuments to fanaticism"—had ceased forever.

Would that that were so. At the dawn of a new millennium, religion is once again in the news, and when it is, it is often bad news. The extraordinary changes in world society at the beginning of the twenty-first century have involved religion to a degree that would have surprised the earlier centuries' most sage observers of modernity. Within the past decade religion has been associated with some of the world's most strident forms of social encounter, including the ideologies of transnational movements, the identities of xenophobic political parties, the rhetoric of political leaders, and the motivations of pious militants involved in some of the world's most devastating acts of terrorism.

Religion seems to be trying to tear the planet apart, even as other cultural forces seem to be trying to pull it together. After all, the twenty-first century is also witness to the emerging era of globalization. The technology of the Internet, film, television, cell phones, and other forms of rapid universal communication seems to be knitting the world into a single social fabric. Familiar consumer franchises and the ubiquitous MTV forms of popular culture seem to be making the world a single global city. Religion seems to be at odds with all of this. Is religion the natural enemy of globalization?

Some activists seem to be shouting yes. The "new world order" was the demon that activists like Timothy McVeigh and other Christian militia enthusiasts in the United States imagined to be behind the multicultured popular consumer-driven values of globalization. He and others like him were implicated in a string of terrorist acts against symbols of government power and the acceptance of racial and sexual orientation diversity that were ultimately aimed at a worldview and a vision of global order that they thought were profoundly secular and absolutely wrong. This global clash of cultures—a cosmic war of religion versus antireligion—was also within the imaginations of Shoko Asahara and other members of Aum Shinrikyo in Tokyo who unleashed nerve gas in the Tokyo subways. A similar spiritual battle was in the minds of Osama bin Laden and the nineteen al Qaeda soldiers who were involved in the attacks on the World Trade Center and Pentagon on September 11, 2001. But counter to what sometimes seems to be the impression of many in the United States, Islamic activists have no monopoly on religious terror. There are Buddhist, Christian, Jewish, Hindu, and Sikh terrorists as well. What they all share is a sense of cosmic war, a grand encounter between the forces of good and evil in a globalized world.

Thus, if the globalized world—the world of a homogeneous Westernized secular culture—is becoming a single global city, religion is often identified with the culture and politics of the hostile antiurban village. Religion often appears in the news as part of the angry local tribalism of jihad that Benjamin Barber identified as the opponent to the homogeneous global culture of "McWorld" (Barber 1995).

Yet before we rush to the conclusion that religion naturally adopts an antiglobal stance, it is worth considering the larger picture. It is true that some religious activists have tried to blow things up. But others have tried to smooth things over. Religion plays diverse roles in today's globalized society, just as it has in local communities and transcultural interactions throughout the centuries. The violent religious rebels are just one part of the news.

Even the religious opposition to globalization is nuanced. Some violent activists—like militant Sikh supporters of the Khalistani movement in India—have wanted a new religious state, a sort of Sikh version of Shiite Iran. Others, like Osama bin Laden's al Qaeda network, have envisioned a transnational religious entity, a kind of religious globalization to supplant the secular one.

Still other forms of religious opposition are more positive. Prophetic religious voices, like those of South Africa's Bishop Tutu, have called for moderation, justice, and environmental protection. No less a religious figure than the late Pope John Paul II has joined other concerned global citizens in speaking out against the unbridled excesses of global capitalism and an indiscriminate popular consumer culture. These religious activists do not blow things up, but when it comes to contemporary globalization they do demur: they seek a better world than the one of global consumerism.

So even when religion is the enemy of globalization, its opposition is varied, and its voices are diverse. But religion is not only globalization's foe. It can also facilitate the understanding and tolerance necessary for globalization's multicultural communities, and it can offer alternative visions of global values of its own.

The fact is that religion is a part of globalization in many ways. Whatever globalization is—whether one conceives of it as the homogenizing forces of economic globalization, the diasporas of communities, or the easy mobility of peoples around the world—these trends have led to new cultural patterns and shared values that have affected religion along with everything else. If this global interaction of people and information is leading to something more than just a mixed cultural stew—if there is a new global society emerging—then this emerging syncretic soup will have religious sensitivities and moral values as one ingredient.

This means that the religious factor in globalization is often a puzzling one. Its role—though significant—is frequently contradictory. In some cases it provides the resources for shared values—including a universal sensibility toward spirituality and the elements of a global ethic—that provide the cultural basis for transnational laws and regulations, agencies of economic and social accountability, and a sense of global citizenship. In some cases it helps to ease the cultural difficulties experienced in multicultural societies by providing the shared values that allow peoples of divergent cultures to live together in harmony. In other cases it sounds a prophetic note by warning against the superficial aspects of a homogeneous global culture. And, yes, in extreme cases it also fosters ideologies of rebellion that embolden its proponents to reject globalization and reassert traditional allegiances, sometimes with quite violent methods.

How can one make sense of this religious ambivalence to globalization? This was the question faced by the authors of this volume, all of whom were involved in an extensive project on religion in global civil society sponsored by the Claus M. Halle Institute for Global Learning at Emory University. The chapters in this volume are products of this venture, a two-year interdisciplinary project based in Atlanta, involving scholars from Emory and around the country. The task of the project was to explore the role of religion in an emerging global civil society.

The interdisciplinary team of scholars associated with this project abandoned at the outset any single way of characterizing the religious responses to the emerging transnational sense of world citizenship that is identified with the phrase "global civil society." But in doing so they provided clarity in considering the range of possibilities.

The team explored what they regarded as both the "hard" and "soft" sides of thinking about each of the key terms—"religion," "global," and "civil society"—in the context of contemporary global social change. "Religion," for instance, can mean the expressions of particular organized communities of faith, but it can also imply a more widely shared sentiment of morality and spirituality. Though "global" usual refers to transnational aspects of culture that appear throughout the world, it can also refer to the pockets of cultural pluralism that are found in globalized multicultural societies. The term "civil society" can point not only to nongovernmental service organizations but also to a broader sense of global citizenship.

In all these cases—whether one is speaking about the role of religion in global civil society in the narrow or broad definitions of these terms—there are common elements. In each case one can assume that there are forms of culture that are transnational, that there is a transnational community that in some way serves as a civil society on a global scale, and that religion is a factor in this global culture and its attendant civil society. The team observed that religion in the broadest sense is most conducive to global civil society when it is conceived in the broadest sense of those terms, but the authors of these chapters refused to put the notion of religion's global role into a single mold.

One of the goals of the project was, in fact, to map the diversity of religion's role. One can see the chapters in this volume as providing insights into at least six different ways in which religion plays a role in global civil society.

Globalized Religious Groups

Much of religion's globalization is due to the fact that religious people do not stay put. The remarkable mobility of the world's population in an era of mass tranportation and easy communications means that most religious communities are now dispersed across the planet. The chapters by Peter Berger and Abdullahi An-Na'im explore the difficulties and possibilities of the diversity of religious groups occupying the same civil society. It is fashionable to celebrate the multicultured character of pluralist societies, but Berger and An-Na'im go beyond the superficial acceptance of multiculturalism and inquire into the religious conditions for cultural tolerance in civil society. They suggest that religion, in such changing contexts, will itself have to change.

Global Civil Values

Some of the traditional values of religion—including honesty, justice, fair play, tolerance, and respect for others—are necessary for the maintenance of any society, perhaps even more so for a globalized society that has no single cultural tradition. In a global culture the shared values of different religious traditions can provide a collective sense of virtuous conduct in public life. The civil values of religion are explored in chapters by Steven Tipton, Harold

Berman, and Jon Gunnemann. Tipton shows how the prophetic role of some Christian denominations in embracing a pluralist civic society can be replicated in other traditions. Berman mines the religious roots of shared legal assumptions that are necessary to create a world legal system. Gunnemann shows how religious attitudes toward property and place can be antithetical to global sharing but also in some instances enhance it.

Global Critics

These same values of morality in public life can be marshaled by critics of global society when they perceive that these values are being undermined. Hence religion can be a critic of aspects of globalization that are seen as unjust or immoral. Frank Lechner makes a point somewhat similar to that of Tipton, in showing that religious groups can play a prophetic role in a global world. In Lechner's chapter he focuses on the particular role that socially conscious religious groups have played in assisting developing countries that are often left out of the successes of the liberal economic patterns associated with globalization.

Guerilla Antiglobalists

In extreme cases, religion can support the position of enemies of global society—those who see in some forms of globalization an effort to impose the values and power of one country over the others. Acts of terrorism are often associated with these religiously motivated guerrilla antiglobalists. My chapter focuses on these antiglobal extremists and suggests that, paradoxically, the networks of antiglobalism are themselves global. In this sense the radical religious politics of the contemporary age involves a contest between opposing views of global order.

Alternative Globalization

As noted earlier, the criticism of globalization often contains alternative visions of a just global society. There are, indeed, "many globalizations," as Peter Berger has described these perspectives in a previous book (Berger and Huntington 2002). Religion often conveys the differences among these views. The chapters by Carrie Rosefsky Wickham and the chapter jointly written by Elizabeth Bounds and Bobbi Patterson explore the alternative globalizations of two quite different groups. Wickham shows how some Islamist groups that resist the Americanized version of globalization affirm the values of global civil society in their own Islamic way. Bounds and Patterson focus on an international community school and demonstrate that this microcosm of globalization is not just a Westernized melting pot but a crucible of shared values with its own distinctive globalized features.

Global Religiosity

One alternative vision of globalization is a world in which the shared sense of spirituality and morality forms, in a sense, a new kind of globalized religion. In the final chapter in this volume, Susanne Hoeber Rudolph looks at the spiritual and ethical dimensions of an emerging global culture. She asks not only whether there is religion in globalization but also whether there might be a religious dimension of globalization.

In one sense these chapters offer a map—perhaps menu would be a better metaphor—of the diverse forms that religion takes in responding and relating to globalization. At the same time they probe some of the central issues involved in conceptualizing the problem. Rudolph's optimism in the concluding chapter raises a question that was posed at the outset of this introduction and that ran like a thread throughout the whole project: Is religion good for globalization or its foe?

The easy way of responding is to say that it is both, and of course it is. But the team wanted to know what conditions would make the religious factor conducive to global civil society and what situations would make it antithetical to it. As Abdullahi An-Na'im puts it, the issue is what kind of role religion can play in global civil society—whether it can enter into a kind of "tactical cooperation" or "reluctant partnership," or whether it will resist global civil society and persist in standing outside it. Both An-Na'im and Peter Berger characterize the increasingly multicultural world as one in which religion's role could go either way, depending on the religion and on the perceived character of the social context around it. Religion can foster shared values or become an agent of schism. An-Na'im suggests that civil society will have to mediate between warring religious camps, but both he and Berger observe that religion can play a positive role as well.

Harold Berman sees the necessity for global order as something that might create a vital role for religion. Since the establishment of civil order on a global scale will require a shared moral basis for international law, this implies a kind of universal faith in justice that can be supported by all of the world's faiths. Steven Tipton raises the question of whether such a shared ethnical and spiritual sensibility can provide the basis for a global civil religion and worldwide moral community beyond the limitations of particular religious traditions, and whether the public theologies of particular faiths can address the moral concerns of multicultural societies as well as traditional ones.

This tension between the parochialism of religion and its potentially global reach is at the heart of religion's ambivalence toward globalization. Jon Gunnemann observes that religious attitudes toward property and membership can shape the ability of groups to transcend the defense of particular allegiances and locations and provide the basis for a sense of global community and a shared responsibility for the environment. Frank Lechner points out that religion can play a prophetic role in rejecting the oppressive features of global society. In some instances, he observes, religion can support movements not only for justice but also for mercy, as in the case of the religious support for relief of international debts. My chapter indicates that the religious rejection of globalization is a complicated matter and may, in cases, appropriate visions of a globalization in which religion plays a more dominant role.

Case studies demonstrates that these issues are part of the dynamics of particular communities in which religion plays a role in alternative notions of globalized plural societies. In her study of an Islamic movement in Egypt, Carrie Rosefsky Wickham discovered that religious politics can be transformed into more moderate forms that are compatible with secular democracy through a process of "political learning," and that sometimes these forms point toward a new understanding of globalization. In their study of an international school in the town of Clarkston, Georgia, Bobbi Patterson and Elizabeth Bounds show how a multicultural religious environment can move beyond the superficial homogeneous secular culture and provide a kind of globalized public space.

These chapters therefore provide a nuanced way of giving the yes-and-no answer to the question of whether religion is good for globalization. And they contain some surprises. Wickham's observations about the possibility of the transformation of Islam, for instance, run counter to the assumption that Islamic notions of religious politics do not allow for social change, tolerance, and democratic ideals. This Islamic discussion raises an even larger question, namely, whether it is possible to profile any religion. Do the histories and cultures of religious traditions define religions in predictable ways, or do the diversity of religious strands, the changing interpretations of religious tenets, and the various social settings in which religious communities exist make religions so malleable as to be nigh near unpredictable? Social scientists like to deal with known sets of values, but often—as the chapters in this project show—religious stances are not so easy to predict.

The chapters in this volume advance our understanding of how religion interacts with the various forces of globalization and plays a role in an emerging global civil society. It is fair to conclude, for instance, that when religion is seen primarily in limited organizational terms, and when civil society is viewed primarily as transnational forms of social service, the two may be on different tracks. In the narrow view of religion, the movements of jihad may indeed clash with the cultural assertiveness of "McWorld." But when religion is conceived in its widest sense, as a stratum of spiritual sensibility and shared moral responsibility, it is congenial with the notion of civil society in its broadest sense—the idea of global citizenship.

In this latter case we might envision not a clash of civilizations but the possibility of a coalescence of civilizations. As many of the authors in this volume point out, the world's religious traditions have abundant resources for thinking about tolerance, harmony, and human dignity on a global scale. No one tradition—certainly not contemporary Western consumer-oriented popular culture—has a monopoly on a vision of shared values and the family of humanity. Hence there is every reason to expect that members of all religious traditions are potentially participants in a kind of multicultural world civilization.

This is the interesting possibility raised by Susanne Hoeber Rudolph in her introduction to an earlier book, *Transnational Religion and Fading States* (Rudolph and Pescatori 1997) and in her provocative closing chapter in this volume. It is interesting to speculate, as she does, about the future of religion in the global age. It is a truly prophetic vision that some day the emergence of a global society will lead to new forms of shared morality, spirituality, and social values. Perhaps, if she is right, a future generation of global citizens will look back on such widely venerated figures of today as Mohandas Gandhi, Mother Teresa, Bishop Tutu, and the Dalai Lama and see them as global saints. They may be viewed in the future as the harbingers of a global spirituality shared by peoples of diverse cultural traditions.

Hence it is safe to conclude that although all the options are open—from religion as supportive of guerrilla antiglobalization to religion as a harbinger of a new global religiosity—there is reason for hope. As the world changes, the role of religion in global civil society also evolves, often in innovative and surprising ways. It is not inconceivable, then, that one religious response to globalization will be a new form of global religion, as religion continues to be shaped anew in a global age.

BIBLIOGRAPHY

Barber, Benjamin. 1995. *Jihad vs. McWorld: How Globalism and Tribalism Are Reshaping the World*. New York: Random House.

Berger, Peter L., and Samuel P. Huntington, eds. 2002. *Many Globalizations: Cultural Diversity in the Contemporary World*. New York: Oxford University Press.

Juergensmeyer, Mark. 2003. *Terror in the Mind of God: The Global Rise of Religious Violence*. 3rd ed. Berkeley: University of California Press.

Rudolph, Susanne Hoeber, and James Piscatori, eds. 1997. *Transnational Religion and Fading States*. Boulder, CO: Westview Press.

I

Religion and Global Civil Society

Peter Berger

It is always tedious to begin with a clarification of terms. It is also
the case that terms are understood differently by different people. And
this, for my sins, is certainly so with the term "civil society." The
question to be addressed is whether there is such a thing as a global
civil society and, if so, how religion relates to it. Let us assume that
we are reasonably clear about what is meant by "global" and by
"religion." But what about "civil society"? Minimally I must clarify
in what sense I will be using this term.

The 1968 edition of the *International Encyclopedia of the Social
Sciences*, with its imposing sixteen volumes, could rightly claim to be
a compendium of the state of these disciplines as of that date (Sills
1968). It contains no entry under "civil society." The omission is
telling. The term has a long history, but by the 1960s it was rarely if
ever used to describe contemporary realities, though it was recognized as a term important for the understanding of a number of
thinkers in the eighteenth and nineteenth centuries. If asked about it
in 1968, I would have recalled the term as occurring in undergrad-
uate courses in the history of philosophy, but probably not in any
part of my graduate training in sociology.

This is not the place to go into the development of the term "civil
society" in the history of Western thought, and in any case I am
not the right person to do so. As far as I know, the term has its roots
in the ideas of the Enlightenment, of such thinkers as Locke and
Rousseau, and it was further developed by German thinkers, notably
by Hegel and Marx, with the somewhat different meaning of
"bourgeois society" (*buergerliche Gesellschaft*). Whatever the place of

the term in the theoretical systems of the various thinkers who employed it, it clearly referred to an emerging social reality—namely, the rise of institutions that occurred outside the official hierarchies of church and state—precisely those institutions that were the carriers of the turbulent reality of nascent modernity. And, of course, the rising bourgeoisie was at the center of this phenomenon. At that point, the institutions of the new capitalist economy were, quite plausibly, subsumed under the same term—something that today, I think, is not very helpful.

It is rather telling how the term "civil society" returned into our discourse. As far as I know, this renascence of the term occurred in Eastern Europe, in the opposition to Communist totalitarianism, and then was picked up again in the West—John Locke, as it were, returned with a Polish accent. This intellectual trajectory is revealing. Just as the notion of "civil society" had a hopeful and potentially revolutionary significance in the opposition to the rigid hierarchies of the ancien régime, it had a similar significance in the opposition to the Communist project of creating a new, all-embracing hierarchy in which the party took the place of the church. This political function, of course, could not be carried over *tout court* as the term migrated back to the West. But the term "civil society" has continued to have a positive tone. "Civil society" is generally assumed to be a *good thing*. It is associated with social vitality, with pluralism and democracy—all deemed to be *good things*. And the same association continues in the notion of "global civil society": the *good thing* is now supposed to become a worldwide reality in the making.

Let me give the assurance that I, too, think that vitality, pluralism, and democracy are good. However, as an orthodox Weberian in sociology, I prefer conceptualizations that are less value-laden. My own working definition of the term "civil society" consists of two parts, one structural, the other cultural. Structurally, the term refers to the ensemble of institutions that stand *in between* the private sphere (which notably includes the family), on the one hand, and the macro-institutions of the state and the economy, on the other hand. (Contrary to what was plausible in an earlier phase of modern capitalism, it is confusing today if, say, General Motors is understood to be an institution of "civil society.") And culturally, the term refers to those "inbetween" institutions that are indeed *civil*—that is, institutions that mitigate conflict and foster social peace. (The Mafia, say, also stands between the private sphere and the macro-institutions of the state and the economy, but it is certainly confusing to think of it as belonging to "civil society.")

This is a working definition—no more, no less. But one more comment on it is in order here, important if the term is to be used cross-nationally: in the West, especially in America, the notion of "civil society" has been generally associated with *voluntarism*—citizens coming together voluntarily to carry on this or that collective agenda. Alexis de Tocqueville's interpretation of American democracy embodies such an understanding. I have no quarrel with this understanding as it applies to Western societies. But one should be careful if one insists on it as a criterion of "civil society" worldwide. This has been an ongoing concern in the work of our research center at Boston University. In this context my colleague Robert Weller (1999), in his studies of intermediate institutions in Chinese societies, has coined the useful term "alternate civilities." Along the same lines another colleague, Robert Hefner (2000) has analyzed Muslim institutions in Indonesia. I would even argue that, under modern conditions, caste in India—a nonvoluntary institution if there ever was one—could be understood as a component of "civil society."

One more definitional comment before I leave this tedious exercise: the concept of "civil society" resembles another term, one that, unlike it, has been much used in sociology—that of "intermediate institutions." In classical sociology, for example, Durkheim thought that it is those institutions that make modern society possible after the demise of traditional solidarities. They, too, have been deemed to be a *good thing*. In my own work of a few years ago I referred to them as "mediating structures" in the little book I wrote with Richard Neuhaus, *To Empower People* (Berger and Neuhaus 1977). We argued, in the context of debates over social policy in America, that these institutions could be better utilized in the delivery of human services as compared with the unwieldy agencies of state bureaucracy.

I have not changed my mind about this. But I would now say that the identification of the adjectives "intermediate" and "mediating" was overly optimistic: Some intermediate institutions mediate; some do not (again, vide the Mafia). This was clarified in my own mind during the large cross-national study on the mediation of normative conflicts that I conducted for the German Bertelsmann Foundation (see the English version of the report on the study, *The Limits of Social Cohesion* [Berger 1998]). In thinking through the results of the study, an analogy occurred to me: there was a time when doctors thought that all cholesterol was bad for you. Then the distinction came to be made between bad cholesterol and good cholesterol. Ditto with "intermediate institutions." Applied to the present topic: some intermediate institutions foster civil society; some do not. Or, if you will: *civil society is as civil society does.*

At a time marked by the intense discussion of the phenomenon of globalization, it is hardly surprising that the concept of civil society has also been globalized. And, as in earlier usage, "global civil society" is also generally proposed as a *good thing*. Nongovernmental organizations (NGOs) in particular have prided themselves on being the vanguard of this allegedly emerging global civil society. Is there such a thing? And is it good?

Globalization means, among other things, a quantitative and qualitative jump in the capacity of just about anybody with the necessary technical equipment to communicate globally. The political and economic macro-institutions do it, of course, and their capacity to do so has had enormous consequences throughout the world, as we are reminded by events every day.

But even individuals are doing it. The teenage nephew of a colleague of mine, who apparently is something of a computer nerd, has set up his own Web site to communicate his opinions to the entire world, and he excitedly reports whenever anybody "visits" the site. And, naturally, intermediate institutions, good or otherwise, can do the same. NGOs headquartered in the United States or Western Europe can link up with kindred organizations all over the globe, and this enables them to stage cross-national campaigns in a way that could not be done just a few years ago. The antiglobalization movement, too, is dependent on this globalization of communicative capacity. This globalization of intermediate institutions, however, may or may not be civil, in the afore-mentioned sense. The global reach of, say, Amnesty International, may be stipulated to be civil. But the same global capacity is shared by terrorist net-works or clubs for the promotion of pedophilia, which are intermediate in their social location but hardly civil in their practical effects. Again, one must be careful to distinguish between good and bad cholesterol.

To hail the global reach of all NGOs as the advent of a global civil society strikes me as highly questionable. It seems to me that the practical effects of the activities of some NGOs are quite nefarious, and I would be very reluctant to endow them with the nimbus of civil society. However, the globalization of some other intermediate institutions, including some NGOs, can legitimately be seen as fostering an emerging global civil society. For example: Daniele Hervieu-Leger, who conducted the French portion of the aforementioned Bertelsmann project, used the phrase "the ecumenism of human rights" (Berger 1998). By that she meant a growing cross-national consensus about some basic human rights, a consensus that is expressed through specific organizations (such as Amnesty International) but that also exists in less institutionalized forms in the spread of values shared by people across the world—a *culture* of human rights, if you will, which can properly be under-stood as contributing to an emerging global civil society. Again, civil society is as civil society does. If there are institutions and cultural developments that enhance civility across borders and continents, then one can indeed speak of a global civil society in the making. NGOs can be part of this. But it is important not to lose sight of the fact that there are other globalizing institutions, movements, and cultural diffusions that are highly uncivil. And NGOs can be part of this, too.

And now to religion. Under modern conditions, which bring about a very high degree of institutional differentiation, religious institutions typically be-come intermediate, in the sense that they are located neither in the private sphere exclusively nor in the structures of the state or the economy. When there is religious liberty, in addition to modernity, religious institutions also acquire the character of voluntary associations, which has very important consequences both for the institutions and for the place of religion in the lives of individuals. I cannot develop this point here, but, briefly put, religious liberty tends to produce a market situation. Maximally, when there is a high degree of religious pluralism, religious institutions must compete with each other for an uncoerced clientele. Minimally, even if a single religious institution continues to be preeminent, it must still compete for the adherence of people who now have the choice of ignoring it. And the fact that religious affiliation now becomes an option rather than a necessity means that religion changes its place in individual existence: from being a destiny determined at birth it becomes the subject of a deliberate choice—indeed, in the pregnant American phrase, it becomes a "religious preference."

These considerations leave open the question of whether religion, under these modern conditions, does or does not contribute to civility. It seems to me that even the most cursory examination will lead to the conclusion that it can do either. I suspect that, in the aggregate, religion is more likely to have negative consequences for civility—that is, that religion, more than not, tends to create conflict both within and between societies. What is more, conflicts are typically aggravated when they are religiously legitimated. Take an obvious case—the conflict between Israel and the Palestinians over the small territory ominously called the Holy Land. This is a conflict over political sovereignty and economic interests that can be replicated elsewhere. It becomes enormously aggravated when all or parts of this territory are understood to be a divinely mandated patrimony. Sometimes, to be sure, religious symbols are used instrumentally, rather than out of profound conviction, to legitimate a political agenda. Thus P. J. O'Rourke (2004), commenting on the conflict in Bosnia, said that it involved three groups of people who looked alike, were of the same race, spoke the same language, and were divided only by religion— in which none of them believed.

Such a comment would obviously not apply to a suicide bomber who confidently expects to wake up in paradise the moment after he has blown himself up in an Israeli bus station. Be this as it may, whether religion is or is not contributing to civility can only be determined case by case, empirically rather than a priori (though I will repeat my suspicion that the empirical record provides little comfort to those who see religion as a powerful force for tolerance and peace).

Whether civil or uncivil, there can be no doubt that religion today is being globalized to an unprecedented degree. I will mention only a few dramatic instances. The American Evangelical organization that has produced the so-called Jesus Project has translated the sound track of a film about Jesus into more than one hundred languages and is showing it in every part of the world. And as the Jesus movie is being shown in numerous Indian villages with synchronized sound tracks (Jesus preaching the Sermon on the Mount in Hindi, Gujerati, Tamil, and so forth), devotees of Krishna are dancing and chanting in major cities all over the Western world. An estimated 800,000 Americans are converts to Buddhism. Weekly attendance in mosques in

England is higher than weekly attendance in Anglican churches. There are an estimated ten million Muslims in Europe, and hard-to-count (because illegal) millions of converts to Pentecostalism in China. The same offshoot of American Protestantism has gained tens of thousands of adherents among, of all people, Gypsies in Europe. Not long ago I visited Buenos Aires for the first time. I arrived full of anticipation in the city that, in my mind, was associated with the magical prose of Borges and the languid sensuousness of the tango. As my taxi left the airport, the first thing I saw was a huge Mormon temple, topped with a gilded statue of the angel Moroni. Now a historian will quickly note that religion spreading from one country to another has happened many times before. After all, Buddhism was an Indian religion that transformed all of eastern Asia, Christianity was a Jewish sect that transformed Europe, and Islam thundered out of Arabia to create a civilization that eventually stretched from the Atlantic Ocean to the China Sea. True. But the speed of modern transport and communication has created a situation in which religious messages are diffused worldwide in an unprecedented way. Globalization means that everyone is in a position to address everyone else, and religion is an important ingredient of this universal conversation. The tones of the conversation vary. Some are indeed civil, promoting peace, tolerance, and democratic values. Others are strident, aggressive, even homicidal. It is disingenuous to look at only one sort.

What the preceding considerations suggest is a case-by-case analysis of every religious tradition in every part of the world. Something like this, stretched out over many years, is pretty much the agenda of our research center at Boston University, but it can hardly be undertaken in this essay. All I can attempt to do is to give a rapid overview of some major cases—if you will, a *tour d'horizon*.

The two most dynamic religious movements in the contemporary world are what can loosely be called popular Protestantism and resurgent Islam. The latter, for obvious and most unfortunate reasons, is very much in the public eye. The former was almost invisible for a long time, but it has now reached such massive proportions that even the most secular journalists and social analysts have been forced to pay attention to it. Both movements are enormous in size and global in outreach. Their relation to civil society, I would propose, is significantly different.

The term "popular Protestantism" is deliberately flexible. It can most easily be defined negatively: it refers to religious groups other than the historic denominations deriving from the Protestant Reformation—the ones that in America have been called "mainline denominations." By far the largest part of this assemblage of religious groups is made up of Pentecostals. Indeed, one would not go far wrong if one said, quite simply, that Pentecostalism *is* this vast and dynamic movement. However, there are other groups that are quite different from Pentecostalism in their beliefs and practices, but that bear a family resemblance to it and which in all likelihood have similar social effects. There is non-Pentecostal Evangelical Protestantism in its more free-flowing versions (see the previously mentioned purveyors of the Jesus movie). There are charismatic groups maintaining a formal connection with historic denominations, and indeed with the Catholic Church, but which act independently and resemble their Pentecostal "cousins" in outlook and behavior—the term "Pentecostalization" has been applied to them. There is further the huge phenomenon of the so-called African Initiated Churches, which combine a vaguely Protestant Christianity with traditional African religion. And then there are very active groups that one would hesitate to call Protestant but that, again, evince Protestant outlooks and behavior; notable here are the Mormons and Jehovah's Witnesses. It is significant that most of these groupings have their origins in America, a fact that has had a lasting impact on them. More important, though, is the further fact that the practical values in play here (as distinct from theology or types of worship) bear a striking resemblance to what Max Weber many years ago called the "Protestant ethic"—a morality that encourages individualism, discipline, hard work, self-denial, and (last but not least) education.

I will limit myself to Pentecostalism here. David Martin (1999), the British sociologist who is the foremost expert on this phenomenon, estimates that there are at least 250 million Pentecostals worldwide and possibly many millions more (China is an important case in point—we know that Pentecostalism has been spreading rapidly there but is illegal and hard to enumerate). Pentecostalism, in addition to a healthy existence in its American home base, has been spreading throughout Latin America (an estimated 50 million Pentecostals south of the Rio Grande), sub-Saharan Africa, large areas of eastern Asia (notably in the Chinese diaspora and in the Philippines), in some areas of ex-Communist Eastern Europe, and in scattered marginal groups (such as European Gypsies and tribal populations in northeast India). Martin uses the term "explosion" for this diffusion, and it certainly fits.

The phenomenon has been most fully studied in Latin America, where its expansion has been most dramatic. There, at any rate, one could confidently assert that Pentecostalism functions as a "school for civil society." Its great success in attracting and retaining converts can be explained by both its religious and moral qualities. Religiously, Pentecostalism combines an experience of immediate access to divine reality (understood as the ongoing presence of the Holy Spirit), an emotionally cathartic worship, and the strong solidarity of its congregations. These qualities provide psychological and collective support for people in the midst of turbulent social change—people who are mostly very poor and, mainly as a result of migration, are deprived of traditional sources of support. Morally, precisely because of the "Protestant ethic," Pentecostalism fosters values that are functional for social mobility or, minimally, survival under conditions of great poverty (Martin [1997] uses the term "betterment" to

describe this feature). But probably the most important reason that Pentecostalism is favorable to the development of civil society is its grassroots
character. Pentecostal churches are *indigenous institutions*—dramatically different from, for example, so-called base communities in Latin American Catholicism, which are initiated and led from above. Pentecostal churches are
created and maintained by ordinary people (commonly by women), their
pastors come out of the same people and are not dependent on any outside
hierarchy, and the ongoing life of these churches creates an autonomous space
for people who otherwise lack such space. What is also very important is that
Pentecostalism, while committed to fervent missionary activity, is invariably
peaceful: it has no violent segment, and it does not seek to impose itself on the
larger society. Here, of course, is a sharp contrast to Islam. I would hypothesize
that Pentecostalism in other parts of the world replicates these Latin American
characteristics. More cautiously, I would hypothesize that most of the non-
Pentecostal expressions of popular Protestantism have similar effects.

The Islamic picture is very different. Resurgent Islam also is global in its
reach, not only in the Muslim world stretching from the Maghreb to Southeast Asia but also in the growing Muslim diaspora in Europe and America.
Here, though, is already an important difference from popular Protestantism:
the latter has been exploding in parts of the world where it is completely new,
while the Islamic resurgence has been occurring in the main in populations
that have been traditionally Muslim. And then, of course, Islam has a violent
element, something that is completely alien to popular Protestantism.

We have been urged not to identify Islam as such with its most violent
element, and rightly so (though, alas, this element has been gaining in
strength). But it seems to me that Islam, even in its moderate forms, has
certain characteristics that are unfavorable to the development of civil society.
I would particularly emphasize two aspects—the understanding of religious
law and the role of women. Traditionally there are no limits to the reach of
religious law. All of society is supposed to be subject to the sharia. Thus there
is no separation of religion from the state, and, more important, no social
space for the development of autonomous institutions. This almost certainly
impedes modern economic development, but is also impedes the development of civil-society institutions. As to women, they have been traditionally
defined as having an inferior status in society (along with tolerated unbelievers and slaves), which again is an impediment in terms of both economic
development and civil society. And, despite all the useful cautions to the effect
that jihad can also be understood in nonviolent ways, it has mainly been
understood throughout Muslim history as involving the extension of Islamic
sovereignty through warfare. It hardly needs emphasizing that this is an
understanding inimical to civility.

This does not mean that (to use Hefner's [2000] term) a "civil Islam" is impossible. Moderate Muslims are arguing that none of the previously mentioned

features are intrinsic to Islam—not the all-embracing place of the sharia, not the inferior status of women, not the violent understanding of jihad. Nor are such assertions completely new in Muslim history. There were periods in that history, such as in Muslim Spain and in India under some of the Moghul emperors, when Islamic civilization was peaceful and tolerant. Serif Mardin (1962), a Turkish political scientist, has written about "Ottoman civility." And Hefner (2000) has shown how the largest Muslim movement in Indonesia today propagates the separation of the state from the sharia, the equality of women, tolerance toward other religions, and generally pluralism and democracy. It is accurate to say that there is now an ongoing struggle over the soul of Islam. The outcome of this struggle will decide the relation between Islam and civil society.

I can only comment briefly on the relation of the Catholic Church to civil society. It is arguably the oldest global institution, and it continues to act globally in important ways. I think it is fair to say that for most of its history official Catholicism held views on the relation between religion and society that were not favorable to the development of civil society (though, of course, one can point to Catholic thinkers and movements that held different views). Also, despite the official views, civil society developed in Catholic Europe as a result of other factors. Clearly, however, Vatican II brought about an important change. As recently as the 1930s, during and just after the Spanish civil war, the church supported an ideology and then a regime fervently opposed to civil society. Such a stance has become unthinkable since Vatican II. The latter's endorsement of tolerance and religious liberty has not just been a theoretical exercise but has been expressed in the political activity of the church globally. Samuel Huntington (1991), writing about the "third wave of democracy," has correctly identified the Catholic Church as a major actor in the struggle against authoritarianism, and in favor of human and political rights, in many parts of the world—such as Eastern Europe as it freed itself from Communism, in Latin America, in the Philippines, and in several African countries. I think it is accurate to say that Catholicism, where it is politically active, is today a force in favor of civil society.

Can one summarize the relation of religion to global civil society? I can only repeat that no general answer is possible. There are cases where religion polarizes societies and makes them less civil—probably the majority of cases. There are cases where religion has served to "civilize," or at least tried to do so.

The list of polarizing cases is long, and no major religious tradition (however pacific its official theology) escapes being included. Islam has been polarizing in very uncivil ways in many countries. Huntington (1996) coined an apt phrase when he wrote about the "bloody frontiers of Islam"—not only in the Middle East but also in the Balkans, on the Indian subcontinent, and in Southeast Asia. Judaism has shown its capacity for incivility in Israel. Both Catholics and Protestants have amply demonstrated the same capacity in Northern Ireland. Hinduism and Buddhism have often advertised themselves as religions of tolerance, supposedly different in this respect from "Abra-hamic" monotheism. Yet they, too, have demonstrated, in India and Sri Lanka, that they are capable of murderous incivility. The less said about Orthodox Christianity in this respect, the better. As one looks at this depressingly long list of cases, one is sorely tempted to agree with those Enlightenment phi-losophers who thought of religion as an infamy that must be destroyed if there is to be progress in human civilization.

I will allow myself a personal reminiscence here, of an experience that sharply instructed me as to the polarizing and civilizing potential of religion. My first full-time job in academia was in the 1950s, at what was then the Woman's College of the University of North Carolina. Within a few weeks I attended two events—a meeting of the National Association for the Advancement of Colored People (NAACP) addressed by Martin Luther King, and a rally of the Ku Klux Klan. Obviously I was favorable to the first and very much opposed to the latter, but qua sociologist I thought that it was important for me to observe both. What impressed me at the NAACP meeting, which took place in a church, was the dominating presence of the symbols and habits of Evangelical Protestantism—in King's style of speaking (or, precisely, preaching), in the demeanor of the assembled audience, in the prayers, and in the hymns that were sung, all hymns often heard in revival tents, including "The Old Rugged Cross." The KKK rally took place in an open field on the outskirts of Greensboro, at night, with several hundred people in attendance. I stood on the edge of the crowd, with some trepidation. What again impressed me, among other things, was the predomi-nance of Evangelical culture—in the rhetorical style, the give-and-take between the speakers and the audience (all those "amens"), the prayers, and above all the hymns. After a good deal of "speechifying," finally, a large wooden cross was set ablaze. My hair stood on end (I still had hair at that time) when the participants intoned what, I suppose, they thought was the appropriate hymn at that point in the proceedings. It was "The Old Rugged Cross."

Religion legitimating hatred and violence; religion legitimating tolerance and civility—there *are* instances of the latter. The Community of San Egidio in Rome has a program of quiet conflict resolution in situations where the voice of a Catholic institution can make an impact. A number of American centers devoted to conflict resolution have begun to look on religious institutions as resources in particular cases. Both Protestant and Catholic clergy and agen-cies have valiantly struggled to mediate the interreligious conflict in Northern Ireland. In the wake of World War II, German Protestantism has created a unique institution with the express purpose of mediating both domestic and, to a lesser degree, international conflicts—the so-called Evangelische Akade-mien (the German word *evangelisch* simply means "Protestant" and does not have the implications of the English term "Evangelical"). There are now more than twenty centers with that name, and ever since 1945 they have played an important role in public discourse and sometimes in off-the-record conversations between parties in conflict. The three largest of these centers, the academies in Bad Boll, Tutzing, and Loccum (affiliated, respectively, with the Lutheran provincial churches of Württemberg, Bavaria, and Hannover), have been helpful in the formulation of a number of important policy initiatives (mostly domestic, occasionally foreign) in the Federal Republic—a major religious contribution to civil society. Both Catholic and Protestant clergy and institutions helped along the peaceful transition from Communism in Eastern Europe. The Hartmann Institute in Jerusalem, explicitly identified with Orthodox Judaism, has been working steadily to mediate conflicts within Israeli society as well as between Israel and the Palestinians. In a number of Indian cities, committees of Hindu and Muslim notables have been successful in avoiding communal violence.

The civilizing role of religion is not necessarily embodied in organizations expressly formed for this purpose. I believe that there is an as yet largely untold story about the role of religion in the transition to nonracial democracy in South Africa. There is reason to think that the fact of South Africa being an intensely religious country, in all ethnic groups, had much to do with the surprisingly violence-free collapse of the apartheid regime. An interesting case here is the changing stance of the Dutch Reformed Church—from theologically legitimating apartheid, to stating that apartheid could not be biblically justified, to declaring it to be a sin. It is likely that this shift had an important influence on the decision by the Afrikaner elite to reach an accommodation with the resistance movement. I remember visiting a very impressive individual, Johan Steyn, in the late 1980s. Steyn, a Dutch Reformed professor of theology, was president of the synod of his church when it took the final step of renouncing apartheid. He was an important influence in bringing about this change. When speaking with him in his study in Pretoria, I noticed a tablet on the wall with an inscription from Genesis 26:24, quoting a blessing given by God to the patriarch Isaac: "Fear not, for I am with you and will bless you" (the inscription was in German—Steyn had studied theology in Basel). A few years later Steyn was murdered by an Afrikaner nationalist who saw him as a traitor to his people. The murder took place in Steyn's study, as he was playing with his grandchildren.

I would like to end these considerations with a quasi-theological postscript. There are people (not necessarily on the liberal end of the ideological spectrum) who view religion primarily in terms of this or that political or social agenda. One may agree with such an agenda, as I certainly do with the agenda of fostering civil society, without sharing this view of religion. The great majority of religious believers disagree with this view. They understand religion as being concerned primarily with realities that transcend the political and social problems of the day. In that understanding the most important question to ask about religion is not whether it is useful but whether it is true.

BIBLIOGRAPHY

Berger, Peter, ed. 1998. *The Limits of Social Cohesion: Conflict and Mediation in Pluralist Societies: A Report of the Bertelsmann Foundation to the Club of Rome.* Boulder, CO: Westview Press.

Berger, Peter, and Richard Neuhaus. 1977. *To Empower People: The Role of Mediating Structures in Public Policy.* Washington, DC: American Enterprise Institute for Public Policy Research.

Hefner, Robert W. 2000. *Civil Islam: Muslims and Democratization in Indonesia.* Princeton, NJ: Princeton University Press.

Huntington, Samuel P. 1991. *The Third Wave: Democratization in the Late Twentieth Century.* Norman: University of Oklahoma Press.

———. 1996. *The Clash of Civilizations and the Remaking of World Order.* New York: Simon and Schuster.

Mardin, Serif. 1962. *The Genesis of Young Ottoman Thought.* Princeton, NJ: Princeton University Press.

Martin, David. 1999. "The Evangelical Protestant Upsurge and Its Political Implications." In *The Desecularization of the World: Resurgent Religion and World Politics,* edited by Peter Berger 37–50. Washington, DC: Ethics and Public Policy Center.

O'Rourke, P. J. 2004. *Peace Kills.* New York: Atlantic Monthly Press.

Sills, David L., ed. 1968. *International Encyclopedia of the Social Sciences.* 16 vols. New York: Free Press.

Weller, Robert P. 1999. Alternate Civilities: *Democracy and Culture in China and Taiwan.* Boulder, CO: Westview Press.

2

The Politics of Religion and the Morality of Globalization

Abdullahi A. An-Na'im

The thesis I wish to examine in this chapter is that globalization can facilitate the politics of religion. It can do this in ways that enable the latter to infuse some moral restraints on the dynamics of economic globalization in the interest of social justice. Because such synergy and mediation would need to be initiated and promoted by human agency, as explained later, I propose that an emerging global civil society can play that role. This thesis is premised on three propositions:

1. Religious doctrine and practice are influenced by dynamic processes of change and adaptation within and among communities of believers, in response to a variety of internal and external factors.
2. The forces and processes of economic globalization are unlikely to be responsive to social justice concerns without the influence of some moral frame of reference.
3. There is an emerging global civil society that is partly motivated by religion and facilitated by globalization, which can promote the transformation of exclusive tendencies of religious communities and thereby enable them to infuse moral constraints on economic globalization through transreligious solidarity and consensus in the interest of social justice.

I will begin with brief working definitions of "religion," "globalization," and "global civil society" in terms of aspects of each paradigm that are problematic for my thesis. Through further elaboration on my working definition and the tripartite premise of my analysis, I will argue that those problematic aspects can be transformed through the proposed synergy and mediation among all three paradigms.

From this perspective, though not necessarily for other purposes, religion can be defined as a system of belief, practices, institutions, and relationships that provides the primary source of moral guidance for believers. Religion also commonly serves as an effective framework for political and social motivation and mobilization among believers. These general features of at least the major religious traditions would make them good candidates for infusing moral restraints on economic globalization if the necessary interreligious and intrareligious consensus and solidarity can be generated and sustained.

But religion is unlikely to play this role to the extent that religious communities perceive the doctrine of their faith in orthodox and exclusive terms that suppress dissent within the tradition and diminish solidarity and cooperation with those deemed to be nonbelievers or heretics. Such hegemonic and exclusive tendencies will properly undermine the emergence of a dynamic global consensus on social policy within and among religious communities that is capable of checking the excesses of economic globalization.

However, as I will argue later, this tendency can and should be resisted within the context of each religious community, which is usually more heterogeneous and pluralistic than claimed by the advocates of religious exclusivity. As I attempt to illustrate with reference to Hinduism and Islam later in this chapter, it is possible and desirable to interpret religious traditions in more inclusive ways that enhance possibilities of interreligious solidarity and cooperation. This is particularly true, I suggest, under current conditions of accelerated and intensified globalization. But the possibility of contesting dominant religious doctrine though the viability of alternative understandings of each tradition is contingent on a variety of factors, both internal and external to the religion in question. This process of contestation is what I call the "politics of religion," which can have different outcomes, including the possibility of bringing moral restraints to bear on economic globalization.

By "economic globalization" I am referring to an increasing assimilation of economies through international integration of investment, production, and consumption that is driven by market values. The primary purpose of globalization in this sense is the achievement of rapid and endless corporate growth, fueled by the search for access to natural resources, new and cheaper labor, and new markets. From this perspective, economic globalization is a means to reduce barriers to corporate activity, without regard for social justice, environmental, or public health concerns (International Forum on Globalization [IFG] 2002, 19–20). The question is therefore whether it is possible to adjust the operation of economic globalization in favor of greater social justice. By making this definition specific to "economic" globalization, I mean to suggest that there is a "social" dimension to the concept that can be used to promote the social responsibility of economic actors. This is what I call the morality of globalization. The question is, who is going to moderate the harsh social consequences of economic globalization, and how can that be realized?

It seems to me that there is an emerging global civil society (GCS) that is manifested in an underlying social reality of networks of transnational, national, and local actors who are engaged in negotiations about civil matters with governmental, intergovernmental, and transnational business actors at various levels. This network has become "thicker," stronger, more durable, and more effective over the last decade of the twentieth century (Anheier, Glasius, Kaldor 2001, 4). GCS feeds on and reacts to economic globalization, while seeking to expand its scope to include interconnectedness in political, social, and cultural spheres. These additional dimensions of globalization tend to promote and enhance a growing global consciousness of shared human vulnerability to political violence, poverty, and disease. The follow-up question for the purposes of the thesis of this chapter is, under which conditions can GCS effectively check the exclusivity of religion and lack of social concern in economic globalization?

Upon incorporating these tentative working definitions, the thesis of this chapter is that there are possibilities of synergy and mediation, whereby the exclusivity and intolerance of some religious communities can be moderated by the impact of economic globalization, while the latter's lack of concern for social justice can be redressed through the moral guidance of religion. In other words, GCS can play a mediatory role within and among religious traditions, as well as in relation to economic globalization. GCS can stimulate the internal transformation of religious communities to promote consensus on universal values of social justice and pluralism, as well as influence the forces of economic globalization in favor of these values. In short, I am calling for a tripartite process of mutual influence and transformation within and among all three paradigms.

As already indicated, this thesis and analysis are dependent on the critical role of *human agency* in realizing and sustaining the transformative possibilities of each of these paradigms. By "human agency" I mean that human actors can conceive and realize the sort of religious transformation that can pursue the accountability of various actors in economic globalization for the social consequences of their actions. The term is also intended to emphasize that only human actors can achieve the mediatory potential of GCS. In other words, all aspects of the tripartite processes of mutual influence and transformation are dependent on the choices people make, as well as how they act on the choices they make.

In emphasizing the centrality of human agency in this context, however, I am not assuming that it would necessarily work in favor of the transformations, synergy, and mediation I am proposing. Indeed, my analysis is premised on the expectation that the human agency of some actors will surely be opposed to such objectives, but that it can be countered by those in favor of the proposed synergy and mediation. Accordingly, the question is how to secure the best possible conditions for human agency to operate within and among religion, globalization, and GCS in favor of the thesis of this chapter. Before discussing this and related questions in the last section of this chapter, it may be helpful to further elaborate on each of these three paradigms.

Politics of Religion

For the purposes of this analysis, the premise of what I call the "politics of religion" is that religion everywhere is *socially constructed*, dynamic, and embedded in socioeconomic and political power relations, always in the particular context of specific religious communities. This premise is clearly indicated by the variety of interpretations within each religious tradition, and of their local adaptations at various stages of history or in different settings during the same historical period. The realities of competing interpretations and contingency of prevalence of one view over another will be illustrated with a brief review of two contrasting views of Hinduism, its role in politics, and its relationship to the state in India. I will also attempt to make the same point by a similar contrast between Islamic fundamentalism and liberal interpretations of Islam. The experience of liberation theology in Latin American will be presented in the last section of this chapter to illustrate the possibilities of an integrated religious and civil society response to the inequities of economic globalization.

Hinduism between Gandhi and Religious Nationalism

One view of religion that clearly illustrates the thesis of this chapter is the one Gandhi articulated and sought to implement during the struggle for the independence of India. For him religion was a source of possibilities of social, political, and cultural identity and expression that were neither restricted to a set of practices or personal beliefs nor ultimately delimited by scripture (Parekh 1997, 37). The way he understood and applied his conception of religion drew on his reading of Hinduism, but in the sense of "the peculiar mix of classical and folk Hinduism and the unselfconscious Hinduism by which most Indians, Hindus as well as non-Hindus, live" (Nandy 1983, 104). This flexible and unsystematic framework allowed Gandhi to incorporate insights from diverse perspectives to define religion as an expression of social, cultural, and political values.

Gandhi's "thinking was always inherently anti-systematic, and operated as a kind of radical cultural eclecticism. . . . [He] freely borrowed ideas from different religions, particularly Christianity, Buddhism, and more strategically from Islam, [and produced] creative synthesis of different aspects of different religious" (Young 2001, 346–47). His notion of religion offers those to whom religion is an important dimension of their worldview and normative frame of reference the possibility of full membership in, and engagement with, pluralistic civil society at the local, national, and global level. To him, the spiritual was the foundation that orients *all* aspects of life, and religious expression is entwined with cultural, political, and social values, whereby religious identity is neither the sole province of the individual nor the only basis for political or social action. Religion provides the individual an ethic to live by (*swaraj*, or self-rule), a mode and medium of political action and expression, and a basis of political independence (Young 2001, 338).

Gandhi saw tradition, politics, economics, social relations, and autonomy as tightly linked to what is currently referred to as "development," but he was critical and suspicious of modernization (which today would be called economic globalization) because it undermines harmony (Terchek 1998, 119). He believed that the danger of modernization is that it diminishes the sense of duty individuals once carried for one another by enmeshing them in interlocking dependencies as consumers and producers who are strangers to each other and therefore do not care much for one another. Instead, he sought "a society of mutuality among people who know and care about each other and who recognize the many debts they owe one another" (Terchek 1998, 110).

In relation to the thesis of this chapter in particular, Gandhi regarded as problematic the distinction between the public and the private sphere, whereby morality belongs in the private sphere, and economic choice and political freedom in the public sphere. He questioned the notion of autonomy associated with modernization when it constricts and diminishes the lives of any segment of the population. For him, the moral costs of modernization *must be part of the calculation* about any supposed increase in autonomy that modernization delivers. Since institutions alone could not ensure autonomy and freedom, Gandhi sought to hold them accountable to moral autonomy and equality (Terchek 1998, 111). He also insisted that "any new technology must be *primarily judged* by its effects on the present generation, particularly its *most vulnerable members*, and not by some future good (108, emphasis added). Gandhi also "reminds us that people have multiple needs that are affected by the economy, not just economic ones" (109).

As if to confirm Gandhi's apprehensions about modernization and traditional understandings of religion, a drastically different view of religion and politics was advanced by the Hindu fundamentalism of the Bharatiya Janat Party (BJP) in India during the 1990s. For our purposes here in particular, there seems to be a strong association between religious radicalism and economic globalization in the rise of the BJP to national power. The distinct subset of the Indian population that can be identified as the core of the support for the movement were the same groups who have been most threatened by the new economic liberalization initiatives aimed at greater privatization and increased global competitiveness (Freitag 1996, 226–27). There were of course other factors in the rise of Hindu fundamentalism. For example, a major sequence of events in this process was the destruction of the Babri mosque on December 6, 1992, at Ayodhya that led to widespread communal tension and Hindu-Muslim riots. Claiming that this mosque had been built on the site of the destroyed Ram temple (birthplace of the god Ram), Hindu nationalists launched a political protest movement that seeks to erect a Ram temple on the site of the Babri mosque.

Thus, as often happens in a variety of settings, religious symbols and discourse were used by disadvantaged groups at the local and national level to mobilize politically in face of the harsh economic consequences of globalization. In the case of India, religion and fears about the impact of globalization combined in propelling a right-wing party with a strong religious agenda into controlling the national government of one of the most religiously and ethnically diverse countries in the world. In terms of the thesis of this chapter, does this mean the permanent loss of the Gandhian view of religion and politics, or is it a setback that can be reversed under certain favorable conditions?

Islamic Fundamentalism and Liberal Islam

A similar politics of religion can be observed in postcolonial Islamic societies in different parts of the world. For our purposes here, the problem with fundamentalists, whether associated with religious, secular, nationalistic, or other forms of ideology, is the determination to mobilize all the resources of their societies for the realization of their own specific vision of the public good. Each form of fundamentalism will probably have its own characteristic features and particular forms of discourse in relation to its own frame of reference. With this caveat in mind, I am using the term here as a shorthand reference to a complex and controversial ideological and political manifestation of the politics of religion, while focusing on its Islamic expression because of my familiarity with the subject and concern about its implications.

What is commonly known today as Islamic fundamentalism can be found in different stages of history of various societies, always as an exceptional response to severe crisis rather than the normal state of affairs among Islamic societies, or continuously in any one of them. This is true for the first Islamic civil war of the mid–seventh century, the jihad movements of eighteenth- and nineteenth-century West Africa and Sudan, to the current movements in various parts of the Muslim world (Al-Azm 1993–94; Lapidus 2002, 416–28). In other words, Islamic fundamentalism should be understood as an indigenous response to profound social, political, and economic crises and *not* as the inevitable outcome of Islamic religious scripture or history. As both a product and an agent of social change in Islamic societies, emerging as a result of certain configurations of factors in each case, and seeking to influence the course of events in favor of its own social and political objectives, each movement is best understood in its own specific context (An-Na'im 2002a). Whatever one may think of such movements, their declared hostility to other religious communities and repression of internal dissent seriously undermine the prospects of interreligious and intrareligious consensus and solidarity that are needed for GCS to effectively check the excesses of economic globalization.

Islamic fundamentalist movements tend to claim legitimacy and seek political power in the postcolonial context of various Islamic societies in the name of the right of Muslim peoples to self-determination through the strict observance of Sharia (traditional formulations of the normative system of Islam). Accordingly, I suggest, they should be judged by the validity of their claim to represent and exercise genuine national self-determination and by their ability to deliver on that promise. One question that can be raised in this regard is how to verify the claim of Islamic fundamentalists that they represent the totality of national population at home, especially when they suppress all political dissent or opposition as religious heresy. Another question is whether such movements really understand, and operate under, the realities of global relations under which the right to self-determination can be realized today.

On the first count, Islamic fundamentalists must maintain a total and credible commitment to democracy at home so that Muslims can continue to express their support or opposition freely and without fear of violent retaliation. These movements must also respect the equal citizenship of non-Muslim nationals of the state because that is the only possible basis of peace, political stability, and economic development at home, as well as acceptance by and cooperation with the international community abroad. On the second count, fundamentalists must accept the principles of the rule of law in international relations because that is also essential for peace, political stability, and economic development of their own country.

It would therefore seem clear that Islamic fundamentalism is unacceptable as a legitimate expression of the collective right of Muslims to self-determination because of the inherent inconsistency of its ideology with the conditions under which Islamic societies must exercise this right today, both within those societies and in their relations with the non-Muslim world. Regardless of the apparent appeal of fundamentalism to many Muslims today, it is clear that the internal and external context in which Islamic identity and self-determination can be realized is radically different from what it used to be in the precolonial era. A primary underlying cause of this transformation of local context in each case is that all Islamic societies are now constituted into nationstates, which are part of global political, economic, and security systems. They are all members of the United Nations and subject to international law, including universal human rights standards. None of these states is religiously homogeneous, politically insulated, or economically independent from the non-Muslim world.

It is therefore clear that the right to self-determination cannot mean that Muslims are completely free to do as they please in their own country, let alone in relation to other countries, because their right to self-determination is limited by the rights of others. In other words, it is neither legally permissible nor practically viable for fundamentalists to force other citizens of the state (whether Muslim or non-Muslim) to accept and implement their view of Sharia as a matter of state policy. As I have argued elsewhere, the idea of an Islamic state is not only unprecedented in Islamic history but also morally and politically untenable, and practically unviable in the modern context (An-Na'im 1999). That is, in addition to the fact that the idea of an Islamic state, as presently advocated by fundamentalist movements, has no precedent in more than fifteen centuries of Islamic history, recent experience in countries like Iran, Pakistan, and Sudan illustrates that this idea is also practically unviable today. The idea is morally untenable because whatever views of Sharia are enforced by those who control the state will violate the freedom of religion of those Muslims who disagree with those views, as well as the human rights of women and non-Muslims (An-Na'im 1990).

Islamic fundamentalism is problematic for the thesis I am exploring in this chapter because of its violent intolerance of all differences, both within the same tradition and in relation to other religious and ideological perspectives. Movements that subscribe to this view tend to drastically repress internal dissent through intimidation and charges of heresy, which seriously inhibits any possibility of internal contestation of the exclusivity of their interpretation of Islam. The intolerance of Islamic fundamentalists of other religious communities and commitment to an expansive view of jihad not only obstructs the development of interreligious alliances in GCS but also constitutes a serious threat to international peace and security (An-Na'im 1988). As already emphasized, however, it is also part of the thesis of this chapter that religious traditions are open to change and transformation in favor of global solidarity for social justice.

The question is therefore how to achieve the necessary transformation within each religious tradition, Islam in this case, that would enable GCS to organize across religious and cultural divides to mobilize and pressure agents of economic globalization to integrate social justice concerns in their calculations. Such transformation obviously requires a combination of elements, including theological arguments about different interpretations of the religion in question and an appreciation of conditions under which some of them may prevail over others. This process is also affected by factors that facilitate free debate and dissent at home, and the rule of law in international relations abroad. As to be expected, these necessary conditions are neither completely lacking nor sufficiently secured. For instance, while some Islamic countries are better than others in securing the necessary domestic conditions, it is clear that the "space" for free debate and dissent is seriously lacking in many of them. While the idea of GCS raises expectations of collaboration in promoting such conditions for favorable change, a positive role for religion in the democratization of Islamic societies does not appear to be supported by GCS because of the fear that, given the choice, Muslims will choose fundamentalist Islam. Ironically, this lack of support may turn into a self-fulfilling prophecy, whereby Islamic fundamentalism prevails because genuine and sustainable democratization is not given a chance.

Like other societies, moreover, Muslims tend to become defensive and conservative when they perceive themselves to be under attack, especially when they see that their personal safety and national sovereignty are not protected by international law. That is, Islamic fundamentalist notions of jihad are legitimized by the prevalence of similar notions of lawlessness and self-help by major powers. It is from this perspective that I believe that the manner and scale of the military retaliation by the United States against the terrorist attacks of September 11, in its unilateral use of force abroad and denial of due process of law for foreign captives, are tantamount to a fundamental repudiation of the premise of peaceful coexistence (An-Na'im 2002c). The proponents of jihad as aggressive war are more likely to gain legitimacy among the majority of Muslims in a world where military force and self-help prevail over the rule of law in international relations.

In my view, there is an alternative, more liberal, understanding of Islam that is capable of challenging the theological and ideological basis of Islamic fundamentalists and denying them the moral and political force of Islam in many parts of Africa and Asia. To speak of liberal Islam raises the question of whether it has to conform to a particular Western understanding of liberalism and secularism. An underlying tension regarding this question relates to the meaning of secularism and its implications for liberalism—that is, whether a commitment to liberalism would necessarily entail a commitment to a "secular" view of the relationship between religion and the state, and what that means in practice in different contexts. Another pertinent inquiry relates to the conditions that are likely to facilitate and promote the development of liberal Islam. For instance, what is the role of the nation-state and transnational movements in generating or sustaining liberal understandings of Islam in different parts of the world?

It is not possible to examine all these questions here, but a sampling of how they might be addressed may be helpful. For instance, there is a general aversion, at times even hostility, to secularism, which is seen as an antireligious Western ideology. The Indonesian scholar Nurcholish Madjid calls for a revitalization and liberalization of Islamic thought and understanding through what he calls "secularization." He insists, however, that does not mean the application of secularism, because "secularism" is the name for an ideology, a new closed worldview that functions very much like a new religion (Madjid 1998, 286). This common aversion to what is perceived to be a "Western-imposed conception of secularism" is probably due to associating it with colonialism and militant antireligious attitudes. To dispel this apprehension, secularism should be understood as a doctrine of public policy that is necessary for freedom of religion, rather than antagonistic to religion, as well as being indigenous to Islamic history, instead of being imposed by colonialism (An-Na'im 2001).

As a general principle, the separation of religion and the state simply means that the state should not impose one view of Islam that would deny Muslims themselves freedom of choice among competing interpretations of their religion that are all equally valid and legitimate (An-Na'im 1999). Keeping the state neutral regarding the wide variety of views about the position of Sharia on issues of public policy and law would enable Muslims to freely debate which view should prevail at any given point in time. Instead, state law of general application should be based on "public reason," that is, justifications that all citizens can share, reject, or accept without fear of charges of heresy or intercommunal hostility. In contrast, claiming that any proposed legislation becomes law *because* it is Sharia (the will of God) as such means that it is beyond criticism or amendment. Whatever the source, moreover, the policy and law enforced by the state must always respect the equal fundamental constitutional and human rights of the totality of the population, Muslims and non-Muslims, men and women.

This rehabilitation of secularism in modern contexts of Islamic societies is integral to conceptualizations of liberal Islam as an interpretive approach that contrasts the historical context of the original formulation of religious doctrine by early Muslim scholars with the modern context in which Islam is to be understood and applied today. In general, the proponents of this approach tend to distinguish between one aspect of Islam as a religion with its sacred, unchanging, eternally determined body of rules for believers, and another aspect that is capable of development and transformation through time. The need for reinterpretation requires the use of fresh and creative *ijtihad* (independent reasoning and interpretation of the scripture). The proponents of a liberal interpretation of Islam also hold that since the law must have the purpose of serving humankind, it must be adaptable to its needs (Dalacoura 1998, 63–64).

Although the terms in which the debate and discussion of Islamic liberal thought must be framed, as well as the content and tensions of that discussion, may be different from those of debates about liberalism in other parts of the world, such differences should not be exaggerated either. For example, Islamic liberal thought cannot assume or presuppose Western conceptions of secularism, the nation-state, or a well-organized and active civil society. But such conceptions and institutions are evolving in different parts of the Muslim world, though necessarily in local terms, as should be expected. Moreover, since liberal Islam has to tackle these issues in the specific history and context of each Islamic society, one should expect of a wide diversity of perspectives on Islamic liberalism, reflecting such factors as the nature of the nation-state and the dynamics of its relationship with civil society (Hermassi 1995).

The tentative conclusion of this section is that religious traditions are constantly being contested by competing interpretations of the scripture in the specific context of each community of believers, which is more conducive for religious pluralism and interreligious consensus in some setting than in others. This raises the possibility of more inclusive conceptions of religion that can facilitate solidarity around shared concerns of different religious communities, as discussed in the final section of this chapter. I will now turn to a brief elaboration on the moral deficit of economic globalization that I am proposing can be redressed through an overlapping consensus among different religious traditions, as mediated by an emerging global civil society.

Morality of Globalization

The antecedents of what is presently known as globalization as a conduit of trade, culture, travel, economics, knowledge, science, and technology go back thousands of years in human history (Sen 2002, A2). What is new is a fundamental change in the scale, intensity, and speed of these processes due to enormous advances in the technology of travel and communication that have also had far-reaching social and political consequences. As indicated earlier, the problem with the economic dimensions of globalization is their indifference to the social consequences of this unrelenting drive for rapid growth and profits, at the cost of making the poor poorer, or at least denying them their fair share of the global economic pie (Sen 2002, A5). For example, in the midst of rising wealth generated through globalization, nearly a billion people struggle to live on less than one U.S. dollar a day, the same as in the mid-1980s (Oxfam 2002, 5). There is also a gross widening of the gap between the wealthy and the poor, even within the rich developed countries. For instance, the chief executive officers of American corporations were paid on average 458 times more than production workers in 2000, up from 104 times in 1991 (IFG 2002, 30).

These negative consequences of economic globalization are neither inevitable nor irreversible because the same processes have resulted in the rapid intensification of the integration of ideas, knowledge, norms, values, and consciousness that can be conducive to the promotion of social justice and universal human rights on a global scale. The possibility of using the same processes and dynamics of globalization to redress economic, social, and political problems is critical for what I am referring to here as the "morality of globalization." Relevant questions in this regard include whether it is possible to transform the values underlying economic globalization to facilitate its becoming more morally responsible and responsiveness to human suffering everywhere. This in turn requires appreciation and engagement of ways to influence primary actors in the sphere of economic globalization.

The main entrepreneurs of economic globalization are major transnational corporations whose primary motivation is maximizing profits through free trade and corporate deregulation (IFG 2002, 20). As corporations become less regulated, it becomes very difficult for national governments to protect local jobs and resources or to influence how the market works. The same developments tend to favor a global monoculture to maximize potential markets and facilitate better production, more cost-effectiveness, and greater profit. But these features of economic globalization are challenged on the ground by competing ideas and values within and among different segments of society, as well as at the transnational and global level. Mediation among these competing values and interests requires a combination of the political dynamism of democratic governance and normative guidance of international human rights standards within the framework of a credible and legitimate international legal order. While democracy can facilitate the functioning of the market, it should also serve to correct the market's negative effect on social justice. However, democratic structures are unlikely to effectively regulate economic globalization without the support of agreed standards that are accepted as binding on the actors through appropriate institutions.

In principle, governments should be allowed to set policies on the development and welfare of their people, provided that they are politically and legally accountable to local and national constituencies. Both aspects of this proposition are integral to the international law principle and collective human right to self-determination, including the right to determine the terms under which governments enter into trade with others or invite others to invest in their economies (IFG 2002, 78). However, this principle and right will be totally subverted without effective transparency and accountability of governments to civil society. In other words, the legitimacy of economic globalization depends on the transparency of economic institutions and processes and their accessibility to civil society actors who can ensure their accountability to generally agreed objectives of social policy.

Economic globalization is also pushing toward privatization of elements that have always been out of the reach of the trading system. For instance, aspects of life that have been accepted as the collective and inalienable property of all peoples, the common heritage of humankind, are now being marketed as commodities in the global markets (IFG 2002, 22, 81). It is now possible to gain property rights to genetic structures of human life through rules on intellectual property. Lifesaving medication, healing herbs that have been known and used by local communities since time immemorial, even lakes and streams, are being monopolized by corporations through patent laws, to be sold at prohibitively high prices. Patent holders have the right to exclude the whole world from making, duplicating, or selling what is deemed to be patented property, without regard to collective human investment in the development of these resources in the first place.

As new markets tend to reward existing markets that already have productive resources, such as land, financial and physical assets, and human capital, economic globalization offers a high return to countries that have stable political systems, secure property rights, and adequate human services because they are better able to cope with market changes. Conversely, countries stricken with poverty, unstable political systems, and insufficient human services are disadvantaged by increased globalization because they are unlikely to have the resources to protect themselves in ruthlessly "free markets." Global entrepreneurs are thereby enabled to withdraw their investment and transfer it elsewhere when an enterprise fails to maximize the return, even if it functions well in social terms.

The inability of poor countries to participate in economic globalization and all its devices—ironically because they lack the freedom to do so—has become the sure means of keeping most of the population of the world in bondage and captivity (Sen 1999, 7). The market values that are the driving force behind globalization should include mechanisms and processes for combating corruption and promoting trust in economic, social, or political relationships that enable all aspects of global society to flourish (Sen 1999, 9). Globalization must therefore be conceived to mandate the removal of major sources of restriction and limitation of freedom, such as poor economic opportunities, poverty, systematic social deprivation, and neglect of public facilities.

A possible and viable framework for this conception, I believe, is the universality of international standards of human rights, provided this paradigm is taken to include affirmative obligations of the state to promote social and economic rights, like the human rights to education and healthcare, as well as political and civil rights, such as the liberty to participate in public discussion and scrutiny (Sen 1999, 3). Article 22 of the Universal Declaration of Human Rights of 1948 (UDHR) refers to the economic, social, and cultural rights as "indispensable for [one's] dignity and free development of [one's] personality" and to "the right to social security," which entitles everyone to access to welfare provisions (Eide 2003, 9). At the core of social rights is the enjoyment of an adequate standard of living, which requires, at a minimum, that everyone shall enjoy the necessary subsistence rights—adequate food and nutrition, clothing, housing, and the necessary conditions of care and health services. Closely related to these rights is the right of families (mothers and children) to special assistance.

The enjoyment of these social rights also requires certain *economic* rights, like the right to property, the right to work and other work-related rights, and the right to social security. Most of the people of the world ensure the livelihood of their families through work outside the formal sector (IFG 2002, 73). The majority of indigenous people work in areas that are not often integrated into the national or global market. Small-scale entrepreneurial activities and subsistence agriculture can be found in rural areas; these activities, however, often do not offer regular income. People living in the urban areas of poor countries sometimes have to survive without regular jobs or incomes. In most countries around the world, economic globalization is depriving greater numbers of people of the essential means of human dignity. The right to social security is essential when a person does not own sufficient property or is not able to secure an adequate standard of living through work, due to unemployment, old age, or disability (Eide 2003, 10).

Education is both a social and a cultural right. The right to education obligates states to develop and maintain a system of schools and other educational institutions to provide education to everybody—free of charge, if possible. The obligations of states to promote equality of opportunity and treatment in education are laid down in greater detail in the UNESCO Convention against Discrimination in Education of 1960 (Eide 2003, 10). Since it enhances the human capital of society at large, education is one of the few human rights where the individual has a corresponding duty to exercise the right.

Moreover, there is clear interdependence between such economic and social rights, on the one hand, and what is commonly known as civil and political rights, on the other, such as freedom of opinion, expression, and association; protection against arbitrary arrest or detention; equality before the law; and the right to effective remedy for any violation of one's rights. For example, freedom of association is an enabling right that facilitates the development and realignment of power and the space for other elements of civil society. This includes the right to form and participate in trade unions without state interference. Freedom of association allows local communities to be empowered through bargaining and choice, to participate in economic activities that enhance their political power and ability to pursue effective remedies for the violation of their rights (Eide 2003, 10). This human right enables workers to challenge unjust and discriminatory practices such as the failure of employers to provide equal pay for equal work, as happens routinely to women around the world.

For our purposes here, civil and political rights are particularly important for enabling one to effectively participate in the political process of electing government and holding it accountable for its policies. This would enable disadvantaged segments of the population to have a voice in the direction of their country's social and economic development, including such matters as increasing the minimum wage, protecting union activists from retaliation, enforcing prohibitions on discrimination, regulating industries, or ensuring that investments are made with social values in mind. But the practical utility of such civil and political rights can be seriously diminished by the policies of liberalization and withdrawal of subsidies, which are the conditions imposed by the International Monetary Fund (IMF) and the World Bank. In curtailing the ability of the state to determine its own economic and social policies in this way, these global actors tend to undermine the relevance and efficacy of democratic and constitutional governance in developing countries. Thus, the populations of developing countries are struggling for constitutionalism and democratic governance at a time when the state they seek to control and hold accountable is losing control over its own economic and social policies.

This is particularly serious because, as noted earlier, when religious communities feel threatened by external forces, like economic globalization, they are likely to drift into fundamentalism as an apparently easy and categorical answer to all their problems. As is to be expected, fundamentalists take advantage of the situation to dominate public discourse and eventually control the state. A frequent response from those threatened by the rise of religious fundamentalism, whether ruling elites or liberal intellectuals, is to insist that religion must be relegated to the purely private domain, thereby denying it a role in promoting the social responsibility of economic actors.

The tentative conclusion of this section is that the human rights paradigm seems to offer the possibility of a comprehensive and systematic response to the challenges of economic globalization. In terms of the thesis of this chapter, this paradigm is a good candidate for being the basis of the sort of interreligious solidarity and consensus that is needed for infusing moral values into the processes of economic globalization in the interest of social justice. Although there are good reasons for viewing the process of globalization with apprehension, it clearly has many potentially positive aspects if it is pursued for the common good, not just for the benefit of a few. Globalization has opened up profound possibilities for human development and enhanced the quality of life for many people around the world. Information technology has collapsed time and space for far-off events, making them easily accessible to people everywhere and promoting the exchange of ideas and customs between peoples of different countries. Live communications enable people to instantaneously participate in the historical development of different societies and to create and promote global concern over social concerns, human security, and environmental issues. Ways of thinking and behaving are now challenged beyond accepted traditional patterns, thereby enhancing possibilities of solidarity across political, social, cultural, and religious boundaries. These aspects of globalization can be particularly helpful in creating and sustaining interreligious understanding, solidarity, and consensus-building. They can also facilitate the development of a global civil society and enable it to more effectively mediate the excesses of economic globalization.

Global Civil Society and Human Rights

The question here is whether there is, or can be, a GCS with such a degree of consensus and solidarity among groups with similar or shared concerns that enables it to act collectively in moderating the exclusivity of religion and excesses of economic globalization. Relevant questions include whether local civil society, *as it exists on the ground* in different parts of the world, is organized and motivated in ways that facilitate or hinder the sort of consensus and solidarity that promote and sustain GSC as envisioned here. Assuming or to the extent that is the case, how do differentials in power relations among various actors in GCS affect the agenda, strategies, and outcomes of their solidarity? In relation to the subject of this chapter in particular, for millions of people around the world, social, political, and cultural issues are inextricably tied to perceptions of religious identity in local context, as well as religious rationale of social institutions and behavior. Questions raised by this focus include how to account for that dimension of religion in the lives of individuals and communities in theorizing about economics, development, nationalism, and the nature and dynamics of the public sphere where GCS is supposed to operate. Indeed, are different religious conceptions or formations of local civil society compatible with any uniform understanding of a global civil society?

The term "civil society" can be understood as signifying particular types of social processes that relate to an intermediary participatory realm between the private and the public sphere, a network of institutions mediating between an administrative source of power and the political-social actions and practices of peoples. *"Civil Society is not a thing*, but a set of conditions within which individuals interact collectively with the state" (Gupta 2000, 159, emphasis in original). As such, civil society can be found to *exist, in and of itself*, throughout the world, and not only in Western or developed, stable countries. Thus, we are concerned here with the nature and dynamics of the social processes and intermediary participatory realm that signify "civil society," whatever that may be in each setting. In other words, it is a matter of whether one is looking for the concept in one place as it has been conceived in another, or in terms of the place where one is looking. That is, civil society needs to draw "upon available and still surviving traditions of togetherness, mutuality and resolution of differences and conflict—in short, traditions of a democratic collective that are our own and what we need to build in a changed historical context" (Kothari 1989, 29).

But how does this view of civil society deal with the question of which normative content the concept should have for it to be a useful medium of analysis or comparison? That is, does opening the concept to different possibilities of meaning than what it has in its so-called countries of origin raise the risk of rendering it meaningless? If whatever "intermediary participatory realm between the private and the public sphere" happens to be on the ground would qualify as "civil society," the term would be meaningless. But if some social processes qualify as civil society and others do not, the question becomes, what is the difference between the two types of intermediary realm? In other words, how do the descriptive and prescriptive aspects of any definition of civil society operate in relation to each other? How can the realities of civil society on the ground be reconciled with what they ought to be for the institution to serve its purposes?

Some scholars define civil society in terms of civility, associability, and citizenship, understood as follows. Civility is tolerance of the other so that groups and individuals with very different ideas can live together in peace, working within a representative and participant system for their individual goals. Associability is a spirit of cooperation for citizens to peacefully and openly organize around political issues, professions, or any common interest. Citizenship is a crucial component that underpins civil society (Schwedler 1995, 10–11). While these ideas are certainly critical, I believe that each of these terms can take on a range of meanings that cannot be separated and distilled from the contexts in which they are lived and practiced. For instance, instead of limiting the definition of "civility" to what has been elucidated in the tradition of Western liberal political thought, the term should also include other notions about civic association that exist in other cultural traditions.

For the purposes of this chapter in particular, a central question is, how can religion provide a basis for these normative components in many regions and cultures of the world? In response, I would first question the underlying dichotomy between religious and secular conceptions of the self in discourse on civil society in this context. The issue is not whether there can be a "religious civil society" as opposed to a "secular civil society," for that merely reproduces the dichotomy. Rather, it is how to develop a normative definition of civil society with due regard to an understanding of religion, without forfeiting the normative premise of civil society. Since religion is a necessary form of associational life for most people around the world, it is imperative to include it in any understanding of the normative elements of civil society.

Indeed, where it provides the basis for a powerful critique of those aspects of the state that are inimical to civil society, religion may provide the impetus that civil society needs. Thus, for instance, Islam was the most feasible and practical ideology and language available to Iranians in the 1970s. It was a rallying point for the political aim of ridding themselves of the Shah and American hegemony, since "In uniting under the leadership of Ayatollah Khomaini and the progressive ideology of Ali Shariati, Iranians were taking self-assertive, constructive steps forward to deal with the political realities of today's world. . . . [Islam] was the more effective as a revolutionary ideology and ethos because it does not recognize a distinction between political and religious effort, nor does it regard politics as outside the realm of religious concern" (Hegland 1987, 194). For Iran itself and other situations like those in Pakistan and Sudan, however, carrying that motivating link between religion and politics into a formal and institutional unification of religion and the state has been profoundly problematic for any coherent sense of civil society.

Thus, assuming that one accepts the need to incorporate the role of religion in different societies into conceptions of GCS, the next question is, how can that be done in ways that are consistent with the nature and dynamics of both sides of this process? That is, how can religion be included without comprising the authenticity of religious experience, on the one hand, or undermining the core meaning and function of global civil society, on the other? While each society must struggle with these issues on its own terms and in its specific context, as suggested earlier, there is need for an overarching framework that can facilitate the necessary process of internal transformation within each religious tradition, as well as the sort of transreligious consensus and solidarity that are necessary for GCS to emerge and operate effectively.

In my view, the human rights paradigm, as explained briefly earlier, provides the means for such consensus and solidarity to materialize, as well as the normative content of social justice and individual freedom that GCS should strive for. But the human rights paradigm itself is constantly being challenged as a form of "cultural imperialism" that is seeking to impose Western values on other societies and undermined by charges of practical inefficacy and irrelevance. The first issue relates to the universality of the human rights, while the second refers to their realistic efficacy on the ground.

As I have argued elsewhere (An-Na'im 1992), the universality of human rights has to be constructed through an internal discourse within and among different cultural and religious traditions, rather than simply proclaimed through international declarations and treaties. The objective of internal discourse is to transform people's attitudes in favor of acceptance of diversity of perspectives within and among traditions, and the deliberate promotion of cross-cultural consensus and solidarity on universal values. The fact that this process is taking place in one setting can be cited by the proponents of the universality of human rights in another setting to enhance the legitimacy and efficacy of the process in their own situation. Thus, it would enhance the credibility and efficacy of Muslim advocates of the universality of human rights to be able point to such efforts taking place in European and North American settings. Conversely, Muslim advocates may be dismissed are romantic fools, if not agents of hostile foreign powers, if they are unable to point to similar efforts by other advocates in their respective situations.

Moreover, there is synergy between the theoretical legitimacy and practical efficacy of human rights standards, whereby each side of this formula influences the other, whether positively or negatively. Thus, successful internal discourse and cross-cultural dialogue in favor of the universality of human rights would lead to greater commitment to the practical im-plementation of these rights, which will in turn promote the local legitimacy of human rights. That is, as human rights norms become better observed in practice as a product of the indigenous values and policy objectives of each society, the practical relevance and efficacy of these norms will be enhanced, thereby leading to more observance, and so forth. The reverse is also probably true: the lack or failure of internal discourse and cross-cultural dialogue means less commitment to the practical implementation of human rights norms, which will then be taken as evidence of their inefficacy and irrele-vance. That perception may then reinforce earlier negative attitudes about the whole paradigm and therefore diminish political commitment to their im-plementation (An-Na'im 1997a).

In this light, human rights norms can be an effective framework for challenging the negative consequences of economic globalization to the extent that they are accepted by different societies as culturally legitimate, as well as practically effective in achieving that objective. Yet these norms are unlikely to be accepted and implemented unless they do deliver on their promise. The way out of this apparent paradox, I suggest, is to see the process as an in-cremental synergy of cultural legitimacy and practical efficacy in the following logical sequence: the negative social and human consequences of economic globalization can lead to calls for a global framework and strategy to mobilize the political will to redress those problems. Taking the human rights para-digm as a possible candidate for that role, local actors can then seek to pro-mote the legitimacy of these rights. As they are able to point to the ways in which this paradigm can in effect redress the problems of economic global-ization, its practical implementation will begin to increase, thereby initiating the synergy between theory and practice envisaged here.

Since this process has to be undertaken by human actors, as indicated by my emphasis on the role of human agency at the beginning of this chapter, the question becomes how to motivate people to act in this way and encourage their communities to give this approach a chance. Thus, in accordance with the thesis of this chapter, GCS can be the medium for this process, and religion can play a critical role in motivating and mobilizing people in this direction. At the same time, the technical and material benefits of glob-alization can facilitate the development of interreligious and transcultural consensus and solidarity in support of human rights as a framework for redressing the negative consequences of economic globalization.

Possibilities of Mediation

To illustrate the proposition that religion can enable GCS actors to bring moral constraints to bear on purely economic globalization in the interest of social justice, I will review in this final section the experience of liberation theology in Latin America as an example of efforts to infuse moral values into economic globalization.

Liberation theology is best known for its Latin American experience, where it emerged around 1968–71 as a radical religiously motivated challenge to oppressive structures in various parts of the continent (MacLean 1999, 123; Turner 1994, 3, 9). To its founders, the fundamental tenets of liberation theology combined the love of God with the urgency of solidarity with the poor (Gutiérrez 1999, 27) and emphasized human agency in taking direct action to help the poor. The movement used Marxist ideology in pursuit of a socialist system for sharing wealth (Fitzgerald 1999, 229; Turner 1999, 4). Its ideology is based on the assumption that oppressed peoples and classes are fundamentally in conflict with the wealthy nations and oppressive classes (Gutiérrez 1973, 36). Subsequent developments sought to expand the scope of the movement in the 1980s and 1990s to include race, gender, culture, and ecological issues (Turner 1994, 5; Tombs 2001, 46–48), though it remained primarily an ecclesiastic movement with a focus on the liberation of the poor (Berryman 1987, 157; Duque 1995, 54).

While the movement was by no means uniform, its various currents shared the same three assumptions: that the majority of individuals live in a state of underdevelopment and unjust dependence, that this state is sinful as viewed by Christian terms, and that it is the responsibility of the members of the church to work to overcome this sinful state (Galilea 1979, 167). The same fundamental theme was defined by Gutiérrez (1999, 27) in terms of "solidarity with the poor and rejection of poverty as something contrary to the will of God." This fundamental underlying theme of the whole movement was linked to the work of grassroots Christian communities and the evangelical mission of the church (Gutiérrez 1999, 19).

In a paradigm shift from classical doctrine, liberation theology focused on putting God's will into practice in solidarity with the poor, in contrast to the "detachment and reflection" of traditional theology (Gutiérrez 1999, 28–29; Rowland 1999, 4). The movement also preferred social science analysis over the philosophical reflection of classical theology in its effort to link action with thinking (Richard 1991, 2; Williams 1998, 199). Leading theologians of the movement also stressed the importance of the communitarian experience as essential to liberation practice and saw that methodology as manifest in spirituality and in one's life as a Christian. Liberation theologians distinguished between material poverty, as "the lack of economic goods necessary for a human life worthy of the name," and spiritual poverty, as "an interior attitude of unattachment to the goods of this world" (Gutiérrez 1973, 204). They also maintained that, from a Christian perspective, poverty is contrary to human dignity and against the will of God (Gutiérrez 1973, 291).

Applying its social science approach, liberation theology viewed the cause of poverty in Latin America as inequality in the system of power and ownership that inhibits access of the masses to participation in society (Boff 1979, 129). Instead of the prevalent view that third world countries only need to "catch up" with developed industrialized countries, liberation theologians argue that massive poverty is "the result of *structures of exploitation and domination*; it derives from centuries of *colonial domination* and is reinforced by the present international *economic system*" (Dussel 1984, 89, emphasis in original).

However, the movement always had an ambivalent relationship with the Vatican. The Vatican's response has been consistently wary of the political role of liberation theology, especially its use of Marxism as a tool of social analysis, while at the same time apparently supporting the movement's agenda of social justice. To the Vatican, liberation theology's advocacy of an alternative church (the *iglesia popular*) was an affront to the official church (Gibelleni 1988, 46). Leading liberation theologians like Gutiérrez and Boff continued to insist that Marxism is used only as a conduit to understanding societal forms of oppression. But the Vatican and other critics held that Marxism cannot be used for empirical analysis without regard for its critique of religion itself (Turner 1999, 203).

Liberation theology continues to be practiced at the grassroots level, and those who spearheaded efforts to further the movement during its inception continue to be prolific in their writings. However, new strains have emerged, and although the underlying theme remains liberation from oppression, diverse perspectives within the movement have their own strong new agendas. Liberation theology has also lost large numbers of supporters due to changes in political, social, and religious circumstances throughout Latin America. Commentators mention several factors as contributing to the decline of liberation theology in recent years, such as the failure of Marxism, conflict with the Vatican, and the rise of Pentecostalism. Adding issues of race, gender, culture, and sexuality, as well indigenous people's and ecological concerns, to its agenda is necessary for the movement's relevance but also diminishes the clarity of its original focus (Tombs 2001, 53–56). Another factor in the decline of the movement is the rise of Pentecostal churches that are posing a serious challenge to Catholicism as the underlying doctrine of liberation theology (Tombs 2001, 55). The focus of liberation theology on a purely socioeconomic analysis of conflict without addressing the dynamics of culture and religion may have contributed to Latin Americans turning to other religious movements (Moltman 1998, 74). Recent more sustainable and thoroughgoing democratization in the main Latin American countries where liberation theology had its strongest following may have also diminished the need for this particular avenue of political resistance and economic protest.

On the other hand, the strong focus on poverty and development linked liberation theology to other intellectual and political currents in the region, as well as to global trends. For example, Paulo Freire criticized the churches for failing to exercise the true prophetic function and called on them to take sides in struggles for political liberation, or they will end up supporting repressive regimes. Freire also sees a relationship between black theology and Latin American liberation theology in that both have a political nature, aligned with the struggle of the oppressed, and emphasize revolutionary praxis (Elias 1994, 145). Black North American liberation theology parallels liberation theology in that its leaders also deviated from the traditional theological paradigm.

Other parallel Christian theological trends in Africa, in Asia, and among feminists have also emerged as reactions against the European and North American theological establishment that tended to assume that its theology was the only model of "Christian" theology. Each of these emerging theologies has its own focus and priorities, which do not necessarily coincide with those of Latin American liberation theology. African theology, for instance, tends to focus on the problem of "indigenisation and the role of native African religions" (Ferm 1992, 3). While each strain of theology is uniquely suited for its context, they are all linked by the preferential option for the poor. Dialogue between Latin American liberation theologians and feminist theologians has taken place mostly in the context of international ecumenical conferences, but that has been rare, superficial, and cautious (Vuola 1997).

I am not in a position to assess the scale and scope of the success and failures of liberation theology or to predict its future prospects in Latin America or elsewhere. All I am suggesting here is that it seems to have been (and may continue to be) a good example of a religious challenge to the negative consequences of economic globalization, especially in its local and national manifestations. However, the main question for the thesis of this chapter is whether the highly contextual nature of this Christian liberation theology and similar trends in other religious traditions, like liberal Islam or Gandhian Hinduism, would permit the forging of transreligious consensus and solidarity of GCS. The main challenge here, as explained earlier, is how to transcend the exclusivity of religious traditions to subscribe to a shared normative content and collaborative strategies in infusing moral constraints on economic globalization. In particular, are such diverse religious movements likely to agree on the universality of human rights as an overarching framework for infusing moral values into the institutions and processes of economic globalization in the interest of social justice?

I believe that this is possible through the processes of internal discourse and cross-cultural dialogue, as explained earlier. The idea of overlapping consensus requires unity of purpose and mutual respect for difference, not ideological and associational uniformity. But this consensus-building must also take account of the unevenness of political and institutional power relations between different regions of the world. The process of inclusion and incorporation of local or regional participants, like liberal Islam and liberation theology, should also be sensitive to the risks of serious cross-cultural misunderstandings, which can be compounded by religious and cultural normative differences among all participants in GCS.

BIBLIOGRAPHY

Al-Azm, S. J. 1993–94. "Islamic Fundamentalism Reconsidered: A Critical Outline of Problems, Ideas and Approaches." Pts. 1 and 2. *South Asia Bulletin* 13: 93–121; 14: 73–98.

Anheier, H., M. Glasius, and M. Kaldor. 2001. "Introducing Global Civil Society." In *Global Civil Society 2001*, edited by H. Anheier, M. Glasius, and M. Kaldor, 3–22. Oxford: Oxford University Press.

An-Na'im, A. A. 1988. "Islamic Ambivalence to Political Violence: Islamic Law and International Terrorism." *German Yearbook of International Law* 31: 307–36.

———. 1990. *Toward an Islamic Reformation: Civil Liberties, Human Rights and International Law*. Syracuse, NY: Syracuse University Press.

———. 1992. "Introduction." In *Human Rights in Cross-Cultural Perspectives: Quest for Consensus*, edited by A. A. An-Na'im, 1–18. Philadelphia: University of Pennsylvania Press.

———. 1997a. "The Contingent Universality of Human Rights: The Case of Freedom of Expression in African and Islamic Contexts." *Emory International Law Review* 10 (3): 29–66.

———. 1997b. "Islam and Human Rights in Sahilian Africa." In *African Islam and Islam in Africa*, edited by Eva Evers Rosander and David Westerlund, 79–94. Uppsala, Sweden: Nordic Africa Institute and Uppsala University.

———. 1999. "*Shariᶜa* and Positive Legislation: Is an Islamic State Possible or Viable?" In *Yearbook of Islamic and Middle Eastern Law*, vol. 5, edited by Eugene Cotran and Chibli Mallat, 29–42. The Hague: Kluwer Law International, 2000.

———. "Synergy and Interdependence of Religion, Human Rights and Secularism." *Polylog: Forum for Intercultural Philosophizing*. http://www.polylog.org/them/2/fcs7-en.htm.

———. 2002a. "Muslim Fundamentalism and Social Change." In *The Freedom to Do God's Will: Religious Fundamentalism and Social Change*, edited by Gerrie ter Haar and James J. Busuttil, 25–48. London: Routledge.

———. 2002b. "Religion and Global Civil Society: Tactical Co-operation or Reluctant Partnership?" In *Global Civil Society 2002*, edited by H. Anheier, M. Glasius, and M. Kaldor, 55–76. Oxford: Oxford University Press.

———. 2002c. "Upholding International Legality against Islamic and American Jihad." In *Worlds in Collision: The Great Terror and Global Order*, edited by K. Booth and T. Dunne, 162–171. London: Palgrave.

Berryman, P. 1987. *Liberation Theology: The Essential Facts about the Revolutionary Movement in Latin American and Beyond*. New York: Pantheon.

Boff, L. 1979. "Christ's Liberation via Oppression: An Attempt at Theological Construction from the Standpoint of Latin America." In *Frontiers of Theology in Latin America*, edited by R. Gibelleni. Maryknoll, NY: Orbis Books, 100–132.

Dalacoura, K. 1998. *Islam, Liberalism and Human Rights*. London: I. B. Tauris.

Duque, J., ed. 1995. *Por una sociedad donde quedan todos*. San José, Costa Rica: Editorial Departamento Ecuménico de investigaciones.

Dussel, E. 1984. "Theologies of the 'Periphery' and the 'Centre': Encounter or Confrontation?" In *Different Theologies, Common Responsibility: Babel or Pentecost?* edited by Claude Geffró, Gustaro Guttieréz and Virgil Elizondo, 87–97. Edinburgh: T & T Clark.

Eide, A. 2003. "Making Human Rights Universal in an Age of Economic Globalisation." In *Praxis-Handbuch UNO: Die Vereinten Nationen im Lichte globaler Herausforderungen*, edited by S. Von Schlorlemer 241-62, Berlin: Springer.

Elias, J. 1994. *Paulo Freire: Pedagogue of Liberation*. Malabar, FL: Krieger.

Ferm, D. W. 1992."Third-World Liberation Theology." In *World Religions and Human Liberation*, edited by D. Cohn-Sherbok, 1–20. Maryknoll, NY: Orbis Books.

Fitzgerald, V. 1999. "The Economics of Liberation Theology." In *The Cambridge Companion to Liberation Theology*, edited by C. Rowland, 218–234. Cambridge: Cambridge University Press.

Freitag, Sandria. 1996. "Contesting in Public: Colonial Legacies and Contemporary Communalism." In *Contesting the Nation: Religion, Community, and the Politics of Democracy in India*, edited by D. Ludden, 211–35. Philadelphia: University of Pennsylvania Press.

Galilea, S. 1979. "Liberation Theology and New Tasks Facing Christians." In *Frontiers of Theology in Latin America*, edited by R. Gibelleni, 163–183. Maryknoll, NY: Orbis Books.

Gibelleni, R. 1988. *The Liberation Theology Debate*. Maryknoll, NY: Orbis Books.

Gupta, D. 2000. *Culture, Space and the Nation-State: from Sentiment to Structure*. New Delhi: Sage Publications.

Gutiérrez, G. 1973. *A Theology of Liberation*. Maryknoll, NY: Orbis Books.

———. 1979. "Liberation Praxis and Christian Faith." In *Frontiers of Theology in Latin America*, edited by R. Gibelleni, 1–16. Maryknoll, NY: Orbis Books.

———. 1984. *The Poor and the Church in Latin America*. Sydney: Catholic Institute for International Relations.

———. 1999. "The Task and Content of Liberation Theology." In *The Cambridge Companion to Liberation Theology*, edited by C. Rowland, 1–16. Cambridge: Cambridge University Press.

Hegland, M.E., 1987. "Islamic Revival or Political and Cultural Revolution? An Iranian Case Study." In *Religious Resurgence: Contemporary Case Studies in Islam, Christianity and Judaism*, edited by R. T. Antoun and M. E. Hegland, 194–219. Syracuse, NY: Syracuse University Press.

Hermassi, A. 1995. "Notes on Civil Society in Tunisia." In *Toward Civil Society in the Middle East? A Primer*, edited by J. Schwedler, 77–78. Boulder, CO: Lynne Rienner.

International Forum on Globalization. 2002. *Alternatives to Economic Globalization*. San Francisco: Berrett-Koehler.

Juergensmeyer, M. 2000. *Terror in the Mind of God: The Global Rise of Religious Violence*. Berkeley: University of California Press.

Kothari, R. 1989. "Human Rights: A Movement in Search of a Theory." In *Rethinking Human Rights: Challenges for Theory and Action,"* edited by S. Kothari and H. Sethi. New York: New Horizon Press.

Lapidus, Ira M. 2002. *A History of Islamic Societies*, 2nd Edit. New York: Cambridge University Press.

MacLean, I. S. 1999. *Opting for Democracy: Liberation Theology and the Struggle for Democracy in Brazil.* New York: Peter Lang.

Madjid, N. 1998. "The Necessity of Renewing Islamic Thought *and* Reinvigorating Religious Understanding." In *Liberal Islam*, edited by C. Kurzman, 284–94. New York: Oxford University Press.

Mandaville, P. 2001. *Transnational Muslim Politics: Reimagining the Umma.* London: Routledge.

Moltman, J. 1998. "Political Theology and Theology of Liberation." In *Liberating the Future: God, Mammon and Theology*, edited by J. Reiger, 61–80. Minneapolis, MN: Augsburg Fortress.

Nandy, A. 1983. *The Intimate Enemy: Loss and Recovery of Self under Colonialism.* Delhi: Oxford University Press.

Neier, A. 2001. "The Military Tribunals on Trial." *New York Review of Books* 49 (2): 11–15.

Parekh, B. 1997. *Gandhi.* Oxford: Oxford University Press.

Richard, P. 1991. "La Teología de la Liberación en la nueva coyuntura." *Pasos* 34 (March–April): 1–8, Segundo Epoca.

Rowland, C., ed. 1999. *The Cambridge Companion to Liberation Theology.* Cambridge: Cambridge University Press.

Sen, A. 1999. *Development as Freedom.* New York: Knopf.

———. 2002. "How to Judge Globalism." *The American Prospect: Globalism and Poverty* 13 (1): A2–A6.

Schwedler, J. 1995. "Introduction: Society and the Study of Middle East Politics Civil" in *Toward Civil Society in Middle East the A Primer*, edited by J. Schwedler, 1–30. Boulder, Co: Lynne Renner Publications.

Shah, G. 1991. "Tenth Lok Sabha Elections: BJP's Victory in Gujarat." *Economic and Political Weekly*, December 21, 2921–24.

Terchek, R. J. 1998. *Gandhi.* New York: Rowman and Littlefield.

Tombs, D. 2001. "Latin American Liberation Theology Faces the Future." In *Faith in the New Millennium*, edited by S. E. Porter, M. Hayes, and D. Tombs, 32–58. Sheffield, England: Sheffield Academic Press.

Toprak, B. 1995. "Islam and the Secular State in Turkey." In *Turkey: Political, Social and Economic Challenges in the 1990s*, edited by C. Balim, E. Kalayciouglu, C. Karatas, G. Winrow, and F. Yasamee, 90–96. London: Brill.

Turner, D. 1999. "Marxism and Liberation Theology." In *The Cambridge Companion to Liberation Theology*, edited by C. Rowland, 199–217. Cambridge: Cambridge University Press.

Turner, J. D. 1994. *An Introduction to Liberation Theology.* Lanham, MD: University Press of America.

Vuola, E. 1997. *Limits of Liberation.* Helsinki: Suomalainen Tiedeakatemia.

Watkins, Hevin, and Penny Fowler. 2002. *Rigged Rules and Double Standards: Trade, Globalization and the Fight against Poverty.* Oxfam: Oxfam Publications.

Williams, D. T. 1998. *Capitalism, Socialism, Christianity and Poverty*. Hatfield, Pretoria: J. L. Van Schaik.

Young, R. J. C. 2001. *Postcolonialisms: An Historical Introduction*. Malden, MA: Blackwell.

Zaman, H. 1999. "The Taslima Nasrin Controversy and Feminism in Bangladesh: A Geo-political and Transnational Perspective." *Atlantis* 23 (2). Twenty-fifth anniversary download promotion, http://www.msvu.ca/atlantis/issues/V23_2/5.pdf.

3

Globalizing Civil Religion and Public Theology

Steven M. Tipton

To deepen and thicken conceptions of a global civil society, to make them more nuanced in their analysis of cultural complexity, more interactive in their institutional dynamics, and more attuned to the mixed modes of their moral contestation in social-historical context, we need to look more closely at the role of religion not only *in* global civil society but also underlying and surrounding it. There religion takes part in a multivocal cultural conversation and moral argument of public life, more or less diversified within each national society and more or less distinctive from one society to the next. There religion inspires and enacts a part that is at once dramatic and constitutive when it comes to shaping the moral order and practical arrangement of the whole of a world polity in the making.

Even if we recognize the red-white-and-blue exceptionalism of the peculiarly Low Church Protestant heritage of civil society in the United States, and especially if we do not, one valuable way to begin to deepen and diversify our view of religion in global civil society is to start with the religious conversation and argument that ground our own public institutions and revise them by continuing to judge and justify their practice through the interplay of public theology and civil religion in America. Public theology, civil religion, and political ideology interact in American political culture through the shifting social arrangement of American public institutions. This interplay of ideals and institutional structures unfolds in an increasingly global context that invites reinterpretation of its own development, and it promises in turn to shed more light on the complicated and contested meaning of global civil society.

Reading Rousseau and Émile Durkheim through Talcott Parsons, the sociologist Robert Bellah (1970, 175) identified "civil religion in America" as a "collection of beliefs, symbols, and ritual with respect to sacred things and institutionalized in a collectivity." Existing alongside yet distinct from churches, synagogues, and temples, as well as political ideologies, this concept of civil religion defines a religion-like dimension of culturally constitutive depth in the public realm of every modern society, no matter how secular it seems. Conversely, it suggests that the United States, no matter how peculiarly uplifting or troubling it seems as "a nation with the soul of a church," in the memorable phrase of G. K. Chesterton invoked by Sidney Mead (1975, 45), is not so exceptional after all.

Indeed, Durkheim ([1912] 1995, 44) similarly defines religion as "a unified system of beliefs and practices relative to sacred things, that is to say, things set apart and forbidden—beliefs and practices which unite into one single moral community called a Church, all those who adhere to them." Thus religion forms the womb of all civilization and gives birth to the moral order and unity of every society. Reading Rousseau through Tocqueville and reflecting on the French Revolution's cult of reason amid the strife of Europe on the brink of World War I, Durkheim grounds his hopes for the moral reintegration of modern society in a state-centered civil religion to celebrate "the cult of the sacred individual." He combines it with a national program of moral education in the public schools and the corporate morality of syndicalist guilds to tie the specialized activity and relationships of workers within the modern division of labor to their moral responsibility as democratic citizens for the society as a whole.

Whether construed narrowly to refer to denominational statements on public policy or broadly to take in the social teaching of the Christian churches and their counterparts among the world religions, the idea of public theology offers an instructive counterpoint to conceiving religion and politics in terms of a unitary civil religion or public philosophy. In either sense it develops insights long shared by the social study of religion and the cultural history of theology into the dialectical process by which religion enters into the cultural constitution of all social institutions, particularly the polity, even as social differences imprint the structures of religious community and belief. History and theology grow out of each other, as Ernst Troeltsch ([1911] 1992) and H. Richard Niebuhr (1929) argue. This diversifies publics in both politics and religion yet makes for coherence of conversation among them.

Public theology is "an effort to interpret the life of a people in the light of a transcendent reference," writes the historian Martin Marty (1981, 16) in terms drawn from Benjamin Franklin on education instead of Jean-Jacques Rousseau on civil religion. American Christianity counterposes diverse forms of public theology by this account, beginning with the Constantinian ethos of Catholic colonies and the Calvinist covenant of Puritan New England. It includes the antitheocratic, critical theology of the dissenting Roger Williams; the transcendent backdrop to civil affairs lit by religious affections in Jonathan Edwards; and the immanence of the holy republic arising from redemption and liberal legislation, as envisioned by Horace Bushnell and revised by the Social Gospel. Varieties of public theology have multiplied in twentieth-century America with the cultural disestablishment of Anglo-Protestantism amid broader recognition of Roman Catholic and Jewish social teaching, exemplified by the American bishops' pastoral letters on peace in 1983 and the economy in 1986, and the development of "Jewish social ethics" (Novak 1992). The distinctive social witness of the African American churches has emerged nationally. Religious pluralism has grown to include communities of Muslims, Buddhists, Hindus, and members of other faiths. Academic communities have nurtured liberationist, feminist, black womanist, ecological, and related theologies among religious leaders and encouraged them to tackle the task of constructing a public theology.

From the beginning, public theologies have coexisted with various forms of public philosophy in America, predicated on traditions of civic republicanism, Lockean democracy, natural law, and constitutionalism. These philosophies extend from the Enlightenment faith in "the laws of Nature" held by such deist founders as Jefferson and Franklin, through ideals advanced by Walter Lippmann and John Courtney Murray of a consensus juris capable of sustaining civil debate over public goods, to current controversies around the world over religion in the public sphere, multiculturalism, and the politics of recognition (Casanova 1994; Fraser 1992; Taylor 1992).

Public Theology and Civil Religion

In its diversity, public theology lends conceptual leverage to Marty's (1987) attempt to discern "two kinds of civil religion," featuring priestly and prophetic versions of alternative national visions, one of the nation under God and the other of national self-transcendence, with liberty and justice for all. It likewise figures in his rehearsal of a rich repertory of diverse national narratives and rites, conversationally commingled across group boundaries to "re-story" and restore the bodies politic of the American republic into an "association of associations" through cohesive sentiments and symbols (Marty 1997). These stem less from veneration of the Constitution than from family reunions, civic volunteering, and Labor Day weekend baseball games. Their mutuality of affection owes more to Jonathan Edwards and the Scottish Enlightenment than to the solitary sentiments of Rousseau or Durkheim.

Conversely, in "Religion and the Legitimation of the American Republic," Robert Bellah (1980a) elaborates the idea of civil religion in terms that clarify the meaning of public theology. Lacking both an established church and a classic civil religion on the model of Plato's laws or Rousseau's social contract, the American republic has institutionalized the free exercise of religion in ways that mediate tensions in its ambiguous political identity. It is a religiously resonant republic that depends on the participation of public-spirited citizens for its shared self-government, and a liberal constitutional democracy that pledges to secure the individual rights of self-interested citizens who pursue wealth and wisdom through free markets for economic and intellectual exchange.

Religion mediates this tension, first, by fixing a "superstructural" locus of moral sovereignty above the sovereignty of the state and the people. Thus the Declaration of Independence begins by reference to "the laws of Nature and of Nature's God," which stand above the laws of humankind and judge them. Solemn reference to a distinctly though not entirely biblical God who stands above the nation and ordains moral standards to judge its conduct becomes a permanent feature of American public life. But civil-religious ideals are thinly if securely institutionalized within American government, without explicit legal sanction or support in the Constitution or the liberal side of the American cultural heritage it expresses. It follows, argues Bellah, that the religious needs of a genuine republic would hardly be met by the formal and marginal civil religion that has been institutionalized in the American republic. "The religious superstructure of the American republic has been provided only partially by the civil religion" (Bellah 1980a, 13). It has been provided mainly by the religious community entirely outside any formal political structures.

To refer to this symbolization of the ultimate order of the national moral community that frames the civic virtues and values of a republic, states Bellah (1980a, 14), "we can speak of public theology, as Martin Marty has called it, in distinction to civil religion. The civil millennialism of the revolutionary period was such a public theology and we have never lacked one since." From the beginnings of the American nation, the diversity and range of its public theology are significant morally as well as analytically, Bellah reflects, since "most of what is good and most of what is bad in our history is rooted in our public theology" (15). Every movement to make America more fully realize its professed values has "grown out of some form of public theology, from the abolitionists to the Social Gospel and the early socialist party to the civil rights movement under Martin Luther King and the farm workers' movement under Caesar Chavez." But so has "every expansionist war and every form of oppression of racial minorities and immigrant groups."

Public theology, in sum, has always unfolded as an argument and a conversation within communities of faith as well as among them, and in their relations to public dialogue in the polity. Compare the Social Gospel and the Gospel of Wealth, for example, or the movements to abolish slavery and alcohol or to outlaw abortion and nuclear arms. Specific social issues and religious traditions describe dimensions of diversity and change in the history of public theology in America, marking shifts in its relationship to political ideology on one side and church religion on the other. So, too, do the institutional forms and settings of public theology, particularly those situated in between communities of faith and the national community.

Public Theology and Political Ideology

Since 1960 the number of nondenominational religious organizations specifically devoted to governmental and public affairs on the U.S. national scene has multiplied, with some 300 new groups springing up by the mid-1980s, followed by hundreds more over the past generation. They include the Christian Coalition, for example, and People for the American Way, Focus on the Family and The Interfaith Alliance. The exponential growth of these politically oriented parachurch groups has far outpaced the growth of denominational churches themselves (Wuthnow, 1988, 107–117). But its yield is dwarfed in turn by the concurrent mushrooming of some 1500 new nonreligious national political associations, from Common Cause to the American Enterprise Institute, between 1960 and 1985, and of thousands more since then, from MoveOn.org to American Progress. They stand formally free of political parties yet often couple public-interest advocacy, policy research and civic education with political lobbying and campaign advertising backed by direct electoral mobilization and organizing.

The recent rise of such freestanding political associations, religious and nonreligious alike, constitutes one element in a system of increased interpenetration between an expanded state and other sectors of society. This changes how other institutions work and how they think and communicate. Not only commerce, defense contracting, and agribusiness but also churches, schools, and families grow more legalized and politicized. The polity itself grows more crowded and densely organized. It builds up a more nationally integrated yet more contested and multivocal argument about how we ought to live together (Bellah et al. 1991).

A decade's sociological evidence indicates that the members of politically oriented parachurch groups tend to divide into two contrasting social clusters (Wuthnow 1988, 173–240). Typically older, less educated cultural conservatives fill the ranks of groups that fight abortion and pornography, and champion creationism, school prayer, and family values. Typically younger, more educated cultural liberals belong to groups dedicated to nuclear disarmament, racial and gender quality, environmental protection, and economic justice. Armed with such evidence, some observers warn against the social class divisions and "culture wars" they see parachurch groups declaring (Hunter 1991). Little evidence has emerged of more polarized or ideologized social opinions among Americans generally, or among religious liberals and conservatives in particular, with the exception of attitudes on abortion and differences between Republican and Democratic party identifiers (DiMaggio, Evans, and Bryson 1996). Within religious institutions, however, major denominations and some congregations show "caucus-church" signs of growing more politicized if not polarized along the lines of identity politics (Bellah et al. 1991, 184–216). In media wars waged by direct-mail and e-mail campaigns, fax blitzes and televised sound bites, religious lobbies turn public theology in the direction of political ideology insofar as they bypass the unified demands of congregational religious practice and teaching in strategic efforts to manage public opinion, mobilize partisan constituencies, and play group-interest politics with public officials.

To balance the view that Americans now face a dangerous dichotomizing of civil religion into "separate and competing moral galax(ies)" or an uncivil war of orthodox and progressive believers with worldviews that are "worlds apart," it is also worth weighing the notion that we are in the midst of a fertile if painful broadening of public theology's contested ambit among a larger, more educated and urbanized middle class (Hunter 1991, 128). Into this nonetheless coherent argument over how we ought to order our lives together have come culturally conservative Protestants, Catholics, Jews, and religious "others" in sufficient numbers and with sufficient eloquence and clout to make their voices heard.

If Americans are willing to keep listening to one another and trying to persuade one another by example and critical, conciliar dialogue alike, then this broadening of public theology promises to deepen and enrich the moral argument of our public life as a whole. In a sense it has already done so, particularly for those problems such as abortion, gender and the family, peace, and the poor, which have no neat solutions within the one-dimensional moral universe of individual interests, rights, and entitlements crowned by the national interest. For the counterposed ideologies of free-market capitalism and welfare-state liberalism at the core of American party politics today are equally mortgaged to individualist axioms that leave citizens blinded to their interdependence and unmoved by their need to share responsibility for the commonweal, which public theologies persist in proclaiming (Walzer 1980; Bellah et al. 1991).

Public theologies proclaim these themes of interdependence and shared responsibility within an ongoing cultural conversation that embraces multiple moral traditions and languages inseparable from the social practices and institutional settings that embody them. So we often disagree, and understand one another when we do. Even as philosophical liberals and their communitarian critics debate the role of religion in forging or fragmenting political consensus, the moral argument of public life continues comprehensibly within each one of us and among us all (Rawls 1993; Sandel 1996). We are held together by the coherence of our disagreement, not by some comprehensive cultural agreement conceived as a value consensus or a value-neutral set of procedural rules and individual rights, because all of us share a common culture woven of traditions that themselves embody continuities of conflict over how we ought to live. And all of us lead lives that span the different social institutions and practices to which moral traditions and public theologies ring true—more or less arguably true—including a polity that is at once a religiously resonant republic and a liberal constitutional democracy.

Global Prospects, Problems, and Projections

An increasingly international kind of social life, gradually developing through the global expansion of the division of labor in the world's economy and its political-legal regulation, would universalize forms of religious belief, Durkheim judged ([1912] 1995, 428–29). If a genuinely transnational sovereignty emerged with the attainment of some kind of coherent world order, Bellah (1970, 185–86) likewise anticipated, it would precipitate new symbolic forms of civil religion, whether they were to grow from the flickering flame of the United Nations or, we might add, from the latter-day spread of transnational NGOs such as the civil rights, nuclear disarmament, and environmentalist movements. "We have at last for many purposes a world civitas," Bellah (1980b, xiv) later concluded, but its lack of civility and justice pointed toward the need for a world civil religion that would transcend American civil religion yet make the most of its traditions of openness, tolerance, and ethical commitment.

Over the past half century the globalized division of labor in the world's economy has grown into an unarguable fact of social life, from the export of American films and arms around the world to the import of OPEC oil, consumer goods from Asia and NAFTA, and software from Bangalore. The shifting forms of its political-legal regulation, however, remain open to instructive argument as matters of historical reason, comparative jurisprudence, social theory, and moral judgment. So, too, do the religious roots and moral implications of such regulation with respect to conceptions of both civil religion and public theology, seen not simply as creeds and codes but as dimensions of depth in public institutions understood as practical moral dramas born from the womb of religious rites and myths.

In 2005 it is open to debate whether a genuinely transnational sovereignty is emerging within a coherent world order that promises new symbolic forms of civil religion, for example, those that consecrate the dignity and equality of all persons at the heart of their human rights as individuals and their civil rights as members of peoples who deserve to govern themselves. It is likewise open to debate whether such ideals and social movements, among diverse others around the world, more accurately count as public theologies by

virtue of their diversity and their contestation over both political predomi-
nance and regnant cultural construal of the moral ends and goods that justify
social authority, including the practical meaning and institutional embodi-
ment of justice, freedom, and progress.

To pursue this debate the following sections of this chapter explore two
key angles of vision for globalizing the concepts of civil religion and public
theology, one defined by an institutionalist theory of the "world polity"
originated by the sociologist John Meyer and his associates, which favors an
emphasis on civil religion, and the other an account of popular nationalism by
the historian Robert Wiebe, which favors an emphasis on public theologies.
Taken in tandem, both angles of vision are noteworthy, I conclude, for the
joint witness they bear to the ways that civil religion and public theologies,
broadly understood, continue to interact and thereby contribute to shaping the
modern world, especially in light of the predicament America now faces, as
Michael Ignatieff (2003) puts it, between bearing the burdens of empire and
carrying out the responsibilities of a republic in seeking to build a more
peaceful, stable, and democratic social order around the world without be-
traying it at home.

The World Polity as Global Cathedral

Institutionalist theories of an emerging world polity conceive it as a broad
cultural order with explicit origins in Western society and religion, closely
linked to the rise of a world commodity economy but not reducible to a reflex
of it. As such, argue John Meyer John Boli and George Thomas and his
coauthors, the world polity both creates and embodies the individual and the
nation-state itself as the two great primordial social units of the modern world.
It endows both units with global legitimacy exogenous to individual societies.
It confers authority on states to order and organize societies politically, in
behalf of all their individual members, according to modern moral ideals of
rationality, progress, and justice seen not only as social goods but as institutional virtues (Meyer, Boli, and Thomas 1987; Meyer, 1987).

Indeed, the world polity defines Western, and now worldwide, society,
particularly the modern state, as "a rational project of creating progress and
justice—in the traditional West, the millennium," write John Meyer, John
Boli, and George Thomas (1987, 25). It institutionalizes a purposive cultural
and moral undertaking aimed at this-worldly yet practically soteriological
ends, in Max Weber's sense (Weber [1915] 1946), to represent a definitive
world image and take a decisive stand in the face of the world, worked out as
a redemptive way of life in answer to the question, what must we do to be
saved? This Weberian sort of rationalization involves reordering social action
by means of technical development and expanded economic exchange to serve

the moral ends of progress and justice. The rational project of the world polity thereby specifies these ends as cultural categories and interrelates them with particular social practices and entities, for example, justice in terms of human rights accorded individual personalities, and progress in terms of greater production and more equal distribution of social goods and opportunities such as schooling, income, and consumer items.

Both the individual and the nation-state are "institutional myths" in this Weberian account, evolving out of the rationalized theories of economic, political, and cultural action. By contrast to traditional societies in which persons are immersed in corporate identities classified by age, gender, kinship, or communal or occupational statuses, write Meyer, Boli, and Thomas (1987, 26), "Modern 'individuals' give expression to the institutionalized description of the individual as having authorized political rights, efficacy, and competence; they consider themselves effective choosers of their occupations, investments, and consumption goods; and they willingly give vent to an extraordinary range of cultural judgments" in accord with this myth, however at odds their judgments may be with the internal inconsistencies and self-contradictions of their actual behavior. Rationalizing the goal of progress likewise defines the social entity of the nation-state, specified to set the boundaries within which progress is to occur, for example, in measurable units of GNP, life expectancy, literacy, or book production; and the productive means by which progress is to be achieved via expanded technique and exchange in measurable units of labor, capital, professional knowledge, and corporate output and earnings.

The high generality of modern institutional definitions and rules, argue Meyer, Boli, and Thomas stems from the fact that they represent universalized claims linked to rules of nature and moral purpose—of justice in terms of human rights, for example, and progress in terms of increased economic production and exchange—which together legitimate economic, educational, or political action across national societies. In practice, accordingly, specific institutional claims and definitions tend to be very similar everywhere. Socialist notions of justice, progress, and technical efficiency, for example, actually resemble their capitalist counterparts, albeit favoring equality somewhat more than liberty and taking organizational form within the administrative framework of a bureaucratic state rather than a bureaucratic business corporation. It follows, reason Meyer, Boli, and Thomas that one "must see these institutions in all of the[ir] diversity not only as built up out of human experience in particular local settings, but as devolving from a dominant universalistic historical culture. The diverse versions of these general themes are interpretable by the differential penetration and historical syntheses of distinct (sometimes contradictory) elements of this culture" (Meyer, Boli, and Thomas 1987, 27).

The globalized institutions of the world polity originate in Western culture, Meyer, Boli, and Thomas holds, and in particular they devolve from

Western religion and the global Christian church, circa 1500, representing on earth the heavenly kingdom of God (Meyer, Boli, and Thomas 1987, 28). Transnational in its pre-Reformation structure, this Christian church created a unified system of symbols and language that spanned diverse cultures and peoples in the older sense of "nations," embracing them within a universal salvific mission to bring "the way, the truth, and the life" to all humankind across every mundane boundary. By the proselytizing "power of the Word," this Christian church originated the sweeping, all-encompassing scope of universalist ideology per se. It provided the fundamental ontological structure of the Western cultural account, argue Meyer, Boli, and Thomas which carried over into the world polity via its institutional definition of "transcendental reality (God, Christ, Spirit), humanity (God's creation/children) and human nature (sinful yet creative). That which is was an issue that could be addressed only within the context of the church's symbolic structure" (Meyer, Boli, and Thomas 1987, 28).

These definitions constitute the ultimate source of modern social authority, which penetrates every limb of the larger social body and guides all social action. In sum, write Meyer, Boli, and Thomas:

> This, then, was the overarching cathedral within which the modern cultural system developed: a common, highly legitimated, boundaryless polity where ultimate authority was located at the peak of the vaulted dome (God) and devolved on human entities (popes and priest, kings and nobles) as subordinate beings, with much to say about social ontology, actors, and the relationships among action, nature, and the ultimate.... The content of the overarching framework has changed with the transition of the West from feudal agrarianism to state-directed technical/economic progressivism, but the location of authority and definitions of reality have remained at the highest level, transcending all of the social entities (including the nation-state) that it encompasses. (1987, 28)

As modern social organizations evolve with the rise of nation-states and their shift from absolutist to parliamentary forms, they continue to embody moral purposes and ontological categories inherent in this Western cultural account, according to Meyer, Boli, and Thomas even as they amplify and alter them. Development of the state as a rational project in tandem with the expansion of technologized economic production and exchange has apparently secularized human destiny in terms of material progress. At the same time, however, it has elaborated GNP into increasingly symbolic, sacramentalized forms of social activity, expression, and experience, which range from television advertising to scholarly research. It has extended notions of justice to cover a much broader spectrum of human rights, multiplied and diversified from traditional negative legal-civil rights to positive political and social rights taking in more comprehensive entitlements and claims to social and cultural participation as well as material consumption.

The rise of the world polity as a transnational system of nation-states not only regulates and subordinates the world's system of economic exchange, argues Meyer, but also subordinates the status of the individual, especially the autonomous authority of the individual as a free-market actor serving as a legitimate agent of his own interests in economic exchanges and contractual agreements on an essentially early-modern model. As a modern citizen, meanwhile, the individual retains or extends moral value in the form of individual rights, entitlements, and protections derived from individual membership in the state. In legal and moral principle, the individual retains "a shadow primordiality" expressed in wider cultural "myths of ultimate individual progress and welfare," writes Meyer (1987, 66–67), which justify modern nation-states. In practice, however, the modern state increasingly accounts for individuals as human capital or human resources used as means to the ends of societal administration, education, employment, and related purposes through which the state itself achieves greater primordiality as the ultimate social agent and consumer.

As the world polity eclipses the world exchange economy in legitimacy in the modern era, Meyer contends, cultural depictions of the natural world around human society shift away from an impersonal, lawful, and effectively infinite system open to indefinite expansion by entrepreneurial economic production and exchanges. They shift toward a natural environment infused with scientific, technical, and naturally lawful moral ordering that requires new forms of limitation or regulation of social-economic activity to control air pollution or global warming, for example, which strengthen the world polity and its regulatory authority. Cultural doctrines about the natural and moral universe humans collectively confront undergo elaboration in terms of scientific and social scientific ideas about the structure, origins, and future of the natural and social worlds. Agreement that "humans face a common transcendental other" also rises and converges, says Meyer (1987, 68–69), as various world religions intermingle beliefs and practices across societies. The world polity gains ascendancy over economic activity as it depicts the natural environment posing collective problems for human society that stem from self-interest and competition no longer seen as unproblematic sparkplugs for the economic engine of social progress. Justification for strengthening the authority of the world polity and the nation-state system it supports also stems, ironically or not, from growing concern to regulate human competition in the form of military conflict among nations, particularly the need to control nuclear arms and other weapons of mass destruction, and to delegitimate war as an instrument of national policy. The world polity develops an increasingly integrated conception of the world economy as a system of highly unequal distribution among nations, which poses problems of equity that require further mobilization of worldwide rules of commutative and distributive justice, not simply redoubled efforts to expand production.

Nationalism and Narcissism

Theories of an emerging world polity, in sum, posit the global spread of cultural and moral categories of freedom institutionalized in terms of legal-civil, political, and social rights; and justice in terms of due process of law, representative self-government, and fair distribution of the fruits of progress measured in terms of economic production and public provision of such social goods as education, health care, housing, and social security to all citizens. Such ideals of social goods and the virtues of institutions are grounded in conceptions of the dignity of all persons and their equally inalienable rights that echo Durkheim's notion of a civic cult of the sacred individual to reintegrate the moral order of modern societies. At the same time, conceptions of a world polity can be fleshed out and colored in to distinguish the varieties of civil religion along lines drawn by Robert Bellah and Phillip Hammond (1980) and implied by distinctions among individualist, corporatist, statist, and segmental forms of polity among national societies around the world, traced by Ronald Jepperson and John Meyer (1991, 214–28).

Conceptions of a world polity are also noteworthy for acknowledging the moral conflicts and contradictions framed by such putatively universal human rights and ideals of justice and progress, for example, in Meyer's analysis (1987, 57–63) of less developed "peripheral societies" in relation to more developed "core societies." Although these rights and ideals are featured in the legal constitutions of most nation-states in the world today, as well as the charters of the United Nations and other transnational agencies and INGOs, they are inverted even as they are invoked. They are violated more or less systematically by many nation-states acting against their own citizens, and by some nation-states acting against others, with only spotty moral judgment and political intervention exercised to check such violations by the UN or other agencies claiming to represent a genuinely transnational sovereignty.

"Multilateral solutions to the world's problems are all very well," as Michael Ignatieff (2003, 24) has recently observed in a related analysis of global moral conflicts and contradictions, "but they have no teeth unless America bares its fangs." In doing so, he says, it reveals a peculiarly twenty-first-century kind of imperium, one without consciousness of itself as such. It is "an empire lite, a global hegemony whose grace notes are free markets, human rights and democracy, enforced by the most awesome military power the world has ever known," and supported by "a people who remember that their country secured its independence by revolt against an empire, who like to think of themselves as the friend of freedom everywhere." Thus, "America has no empire to extend or utopia to establish," as President George W. Bush (2002, 2) declared at West Point in June 2002, while the President's National Security Strategy (United States White House 2002, iii), set out in September 2002, committed America to lead other nations toward "a single sustainable model for national success: freedom, democracy, and free enterprise."

This bifocal vision poses practical moral conflicts between bearing the burdens of empire and meeting the responsibilities of a republic, Ignatieff (2003, 24) points out. "What empires lavish abroad, they cannot spend on good republican government at home: on hospitals or roads or schools. A distended military budget only aggravates America's continuing failure to keep its egalitarian promise to itself." It also reflects a growing gap between America and its international allies, and between ideals of the transnational world order they espouse and the geopolitical arrangements they enact. In the twenty-first century, Ignatieff (2003, 50) observes, the United States has become the West's last remaining military nation-state, as its European allies (with the partial exception of Britain) have turned more and more postmilitary and postnationalist. They have played down martial honor and patriotic sacrifice since World War II in favor of economic rebuilding, while leaving much of the cost of their military defense to the United States, whose military budget has grown to exceed the next dozen nations, most of them its allies.

As the steady drumbeat of the American buildup to war with Iraq dramatized so resoundingly by its measured march through the winter of 2002–3—while America's traditional allies hedged or dissented, and the UN Security Council refused to authorize military force—the United States is multilateral only when it wants to be, and unilateral whenever it chooses to be. It enforces a new division of geopolitical labor: Americans do the fighting; the British, French, and Germans do the policing; and the Dutch, Swiss, and Scandinavians provide the humanitarian aid. This arrangement differs markedly from the integration of American power within a transnational legal-political, economic, and environmental order anchored by the UN and including the World Trade Organization, the International Criminal Court, and the Kyoto Protocol, all of which American administrations approve and agree to abide by, Ignatieff (2003, 50) notes, only when it suits their own purposes to do so.

Both nationalism and narcissism stand in the way of a new world order shaped by American power, Ignatieff (2003, 53) concludes, since the unfinished road of self-determination that leads from European empires to competent, rule-abiding, representative nation-states, including the Muslim countries of the Middle East, does not necessarily run through the U.S. model of individualist liberal democracy and global capitalism. "Our greatest need, in our hour of imperial eminence, is moderation," accordingly counsels Robert Bellah (2003, 24–25), writing on the threshold of war with Iraq. "Our greatest danger, in our present moralistic and belligerent mood, is taking on responsibilities we cannot and will not fulfill. Though we are the greatest military power the world has ever seen, we cannot rule the world alone." Instead, he urges, "We need to build a society—and a world—in which it will be clear that we need one another, that we will bear one another's burdens."

Faith in Diversity versus the Nation-State

The growing dominance of strong nation-states during the cold war and the subsequent preeminence of the United States as the world's sole superpower, likewise argues Robert Wiebe (2002) in his history of popular nationalism, *Who We Are*, have led to a coalescence of liberal-democratic ideals with individual legal rights and global capitalism to obscure the actual social and cultural diversity we need to recognize to make sense of the varied religious and nationalistic movements at work in the world today.

Americans have stayed true to their two-sided heritage, Wiebe (2002, 214) observes, by backing the end of European empires in behalf of home rule and national independence for their former colonies. At the same time, however, the American government has made every effort to "hurry the former colonies into conservative, law-and-order states" built around rule at home in the form of local subjugation by elites willing to make their own people suffer in return for the rewards granted by industrialized great powers for extracting the wealth of weak countries in the form of cheap labor and raw materials. The anticolonial promise of home rule coexists with the neocolonial practice of exploitative elites ruling at home. Where democratic free elections combine with laissez-faire capitalism to increase the political power of an impoverished majority, while concentrating wealth in the hands of a market-dominant majority, often marked off by ethnicity as well as social class (e.g., the Chinese in Indonesia, whites in Zimbabwe, Indians in Kenya; and Europeanized, educated, English-speaking, white *mantuanos* in Venezuela by contrast to the brown-skinned *pardo* of Amerindian or African ancestry), adds Amy Chua (2003), then the pursuit of free-market democracy breeds ethnic hatred as well as global instability.

Around the middle of the twentieth century, argues Wiebe (2002, 215), the rising importance of individualism in American democracy coincided with its powerful appeal as an export, featuring the individualized consumerism of the free world against the collectivism and constraint of Communist China and the Soviet empire:

> As a universe of limitless consumer choices, individualism mocks
> people in poverty everywhere. In these settings it completes the
> trinity: democracy, capitalism, individualism, three aspects of a single
> burden. As a scheme of mandated rights, individualism pits the
> privileges of people one by one against the group values by which a

large majority of the world's population lives—the very majority Westerners have had the greatest difficulty reaching or even understanding. Adding insult to ignorance, educated Westerners have treat[ed] the most popular confrontations with individualism as evidences of a collective insanity."

Strategies that rely on fixed nation-states, global capitalism, and individual rights offer scant promise, judges Wiebe, of giving coherence to a world of splintered loyalties and fragmented conflicts, particularly when they accentuate worldwide differences in economic privilege and military-political power. Since capitalism knows no authority higher than its market transactions, Wiebe contends, it sees no problem in the fact that only a tiny global minority is situated to benefit from its results, while whole nations are robbed of their resources in the name of free markets and free trade. "Individualism as a mandated right simply restates the issue of atomization: from each individual alone to all individuals together," Wiebe (2002, 217) sums up. "What has placed strains on social cooperation in every rich state in the West would shatter community life elsewhere. . . . Uni-Universally mandated rights may link an individual to another individual, but they set culture against culture in a battle of survival."

By contrast, urges Wiebe, we need to recognize and encourage the world's actual diversity of cultures, religions, nationalist ideologies, economies, and moral aspirations. We need to make the most of this diversity to check well-armed true believers in their bloody efforts to impose global monopolies of every kind: socialist or democratic, capitalist or communist, nationalist or theocratic. Diversity by Wiebe's account (2002, 218) takes in democratic dimensions that are at once voluntarist and corporatist, starting with "the proposition that people make decisions for themselves and that initially all of those decisions have equal standing. Economic motivations are not inherently rational and village identities are not inherently backward. . . . Voluntary organizations are a diverse world's lifeblood. Whatever people want, including individualism, they must organize to get." Diversity in a genuinely democratic world demands mutual respect and denounces violence. But it takes moral indignation, outrage, and clashing values as matters of course, and it prizes dissenting moral witness and protest.

Diversity does not mean anything goes. "Groups of people forming a common polity require rules in common, and quite naturally, polities give priority to their perpetuation," emphasizes Wiebe (2002, 218). A polity relying on democratic procedures, for example, has good reason to protect those procedures against groups intent on destroying them. Polities likewise control entry and membership, and they set something like rules of moral grammar and syntax for the civic languages through which politics, governance, and education come to be formulated, debated, and decided. "Not only do polities have the right to defend themselves," grants Wiebe (2002, 218); "their members have every right to protest to the high heavens against actions anywhere that they consider fundamentally unjust and to mobilize as widely as possible in behalf of their outrage."

Privileging loyalty to the state over other social loyalties poses a great danger, warns Wiebe (2002, 219), since "multiple criss-crossing attachments that sometimes stop short of the state and sometimes transcend it, express what people actually feel and how they actually live." Despite its internal contradictions and conundrums, indeed because of them, such a commitment to diversity helps us understand that no monopoly or single social model, including no single principle of diversity itself, can serve as a panacea for the violence, injustice, and inhumanity that beset the world today. We must guard against uncritical celebration of regionalism and nationalism writ small as a "utopianism of the underdog," cautions Wiebe, even as we face up to the massive facts of global realpolitik today that representative self-government cannot spread around the world if the United States supports it only in the individualist image of its own liberal democracy, and that global markets cannot be sustained if their benefits extend only to small local elites and their investor partners concentrated in the world's wealthiest and most powerful nations.

Small-scale diversity holds out the world's best hope today in the form of "a messy order," as Wiebe (2002, 219) puts it, which can nurture the prospects of healthy, adaptive societies against their primary enemy, the nation-state itself, along with the religious and military legions that covet the state's authority. We cannot do without the entire system of nation-states, but we should not trust a one of them, advises Wiebe, nor allow modern religious nationalists to suppress the rich diversity of every world-religious tradition— Islamic, Hindu, Buddhist, Jewish, and Christian—by seizing state power in the name of God. Beyond and beneath the state, through transnational NGOs and small-group initiatives, a variety of humanitarian agencies today help people around the world tackle issues of health, poverty, and empowerment, Wiebe (2002, 220) concludes, and they enable us to imagine "a world freed from the tyranny of guns and gods where diversity wrestles with diversity in a match of wits and dreams, not life and death."

Conclusion

The vision of diversity offered by Wiebe's account of popular nationalism around the world ties into the interplay of civil religion and public theologies, as outlined earlier in the American case. Both share an emphasis on self-government through ongoing moral argument, civic debate, and social reform within representative polities requiring rules worked out in common by diverse constituencies thinking and acting persuasively within cultures conceived as dramatic conversations made up of many voices contesting the construal of multiple moral traditions and remaking them together by the voluntary force of enacting good examples as well as giving good reasons. This contrasts with state-centered views of civil religion celebrating an ostensibly universal moral consensus in support of the state's legal authority. This view of diversity also resonates with Bellah's (1970, 183–86) original stress on the appeal of civil religion to a higher moral authority, which transcends the state and thereby enables free citizens to judge, criticize, and reform the state and its policies instead of simply justifying and celebrating them. This process comes to a head in "times of trial" such as the Civil War or the Vietnam era, when public theologies vie directly over decisive issues such as slavery a century ago or the challenge of responsible American action in a revolutionary world today.

Here we have reached a point, well short of resolving or synthesizing these different views, at which we can nonetheless discern the intersection of Wiebe's conclusions with Bellah's stance, especially since *Habits of the Heart* (Bellah et al. 1985). Recognize the social-cultural diversity of religions and ideologies, along with the trio of socialism, nationalism, and democracy itself, Wiebe urges, as they contend with the current system of nation-states and channel the human aspirations these states have frustrated. Join in the multivocal moral argument of public life, *Habits of the Heart* and *The Good Society* advise (Bellah et al. 1985, 1991). Heed its diverse public theologies vying to reconstrue and critically revise civil religion, not merely to complement or apply it, through modes of moral discourse and logics of argument civil religion frames and sustains in turn.

The nationalist aspirations and religious convictions of other peoples who want to rule themselves and worship as they please, and as they must, require our respect. They also require our recognition of the social and cultural diversity of these peoples and of our interdependence with them. For such recognition is essential to justify our respect by grounding it in our complicated common visions of the dignity and equality of all human beings and their rights to self-rule and religious free exercise. Such recognition is no less essential to guide our aim to realize these rights in a just world of independent, equal, and self-governing states, and of interdependent peoples who need one another to bear the burdens of humankind. That world still struggling to be born embodies ideals at the center of distinctive yet overlapping forms of civil religion emerging around the globe, and it marks the contested core of an ongoing argument among diverse public theologies faithfully seeking to shape the world to come.

BIBLIOGRAPHY

Bellah, Robert N. 1970. "Civil Religion in America." In *Beyond Belief,* edited by Robert N. Bellah, 168–89. New York: Harper and Row.

————. 1980a. "Religion and the Legitimation of the American Republic." In *Varieties of Civil Religion*, edited by Robert N. Bellah and Phillip E. Hammond, 3–23. San Francisco: Harper and Row.

————. 1980b. "Introduction", In *Varieties of Civil Religion*, edited by Robert N. Bellah and Phillip E. Hammond, vii–xv. San Francisco: Harper and Row.

————. "Righteous Empire." 2003. *Christian Century*, March 8, 24–25.

Bellah, Robert N., and Phillip E. Hamond (eds.). 1980. *Varieties of Civil Religion*. San Francisco: Harper and Row.

Bellah, Robert N., Richard Madsen, William M. Sullivan, Ann Swidler, Steven M. Tipton. 1985. *Habits of the Heart*. Berkeley: University of California Press.

————. 1991. *The Good Society*. New York: Knopf.

Bush, George W. 2002 "West Point Graduation Speech." June 1.

Casanova, Jose. 1994. *Public Religions in the Modern World*. Chicago: University of Chicago Press.

Chua, Amy. 2003. "Power to the Privileged." *New York Times*, January 7, 23.

DiMaggio, Paul, John Evans, and Pethany Bryson. 1996. "Have Americans' Social Attitudes Become More Polarized?" *American Journal of Sociology* 102:690–755.

Durkheim, Émile. [1912] 1995. *The Elementary Forms of Religious Life*. Translated by Karen E. Fields. New York: Free Press.

Franklin, Benjamin. [1749] 1987. "Proposals Relating to the Education of Youth in Pennsylvania." In *Benjamin Franklin: Writings*, 323–44. New York: Library of America.

Fraser, Nancy. 1992. "Rethinking the Public Sphere." In *Habermas and the Public Sphere*, edited by Craig Calhoun, 109–42. Cambridge, MA: MIT Press.

Hunter, James Davison. 1991. *Culture Wars*. New York: Basic Books.

Ignatieff, Michael. 2003. "The Burden." *New York Times Magazine*, January 5, 22–27, 50, 53–54.

Jepperson, Ronald L., and John W. Meyer. 1991. "The Public Order and the Construction of Formal Organizations." In *The New Institutionalism in Organizational Analysis*, edited by Walter W. Powell and Paul J. DiMaggio, 214–28. Chicago: University of Chicago Press.

Marty, Martin E. 1981. *The Public Church*. New York: Crossroad.

————. 1987. "Two Kinds of Civil Religion." In *Religion and Republic: the American Circumstance*. Boston: Beacon Press.

————. 1997. *The One and the Many*. Cambridge, MA: Harvard University Press.

Mead, Sidney E. 1975. *The Nation with the Soul of a Church*. New York: Harper and Row.

Meyer, John W. 1987. "The World Polity and the Authority of the Nation-State." In *Institutional Structure*, edited by George M. Thomas, John W. Meyer, Francisco O. Ramirez, and John Boli, 41–70. New York: Sage.

Meyer, John W., John Boli, and George M. Thomas. 1987. "Ontology and Rationalization in the Western Cultural Account." In *Institutional Structure*, edited by George M. Thomas, John W. Meyer, Francisco O. Ramirez, and John Boli, 12–37. Newbury Park, CA: Sage.

Niebuhr, Richard. 1929. *The Social Sources of Denominationalism*. New York: Henry Holt.

Novak, David. 1992. *Jewish Social Ethics*. New York: Oxford University Press.

Rawls, John. 1993. *Political Liberalism*. New York: Columbia University Press.

Rousseau, Jean-Jacques. [1762] 1954. *The Social Contract*. Translated by Willmoore Kendal. Chicago: Gateway.

Sandel, Michael J. 1996. *Democracy's Discontents*. Cambridge, MA: Harvard University Press.

Taylor, Charles. 1992. *Multiculturalism and "The Politics of Recognition."* Princeton, NJ: Princeton University Press.

Troeltsch, Ernst. [1911] 1992. *The Social Teaching of the Christian Churches*. 2 vols. Translated by Olive Wyon Louisville, KY: Westminster/John Knox Press.

United States White House. 2002. *The National Security Strategy of the United States of America*. Washington, DC.: President of the United States, vii, 31.

Walzer, Michael. 1980. "Dissatisfaction in the Welfare State." In *Radical Principles*, 23–53. New York: Basic Books.

Weber, Max. [1915] 1946. "The Social Psychology of the World Religions." In *From Max Weber*, edited by Hans Gerth and C. Wright Mills, 280. New York: Oxford University Press.

Wiebe, Robert H. 2002. *Who We Are*. Princeton, NJ: Princeton University Press.

Wuthnow, Robert. 1988. *The Restructuring of American Religion*. Princeton, NJ: Princeton University Press.

4

Faith and Law in a Multicultural World

Harold J. Berman

In the twentieth and twenty-first centuries, for the first time in the history of the human race, virtually all the peoples of the world have been brought into more or less continual interrelationships, often involving mutual legal rights and obligations. We live in a world economy, supported by a growing body of transnational law of trade and investment and finance. Through new technology we have virtually instantaneous worldwide communications, also subject to a body of transnational legal regulation. A multitude of transnational organizations and associations, formed to advance a myriad of different causes, work to introduce legal measures to reduce world disorder and overcome world injustices, to prevent destruction of the world environment and pollution of the world atmosphere, to prevent the spread of world diseases, to remedy violations of universal human rights, to counter worldwide terrorism, and to resolve ethnic and religious conflicts that threaten world peace. People from all parts of the world have come together in calling for the development of worldwide legal protection against these and other global scourges through the development of official and unofficial legal institutions. They have also come together to promote world travel, world sports, world leisure activities, and other kinds of good causes that affect all peoples and that require transnational regulation to be carried out in a just and orderly way.

The emerging world society and its accompanying body of world law are, to be sure, gravely threatened by extremists of the various world cultures. But the "clash of civilizations," in Samuel Huntington's (1996) phrase, is taking place against the background of intercultural communication and interaction. Even the antiglobalists form a global network. Even the terrorists are part of a transnational conspiracy.

This chapter explores some dimensions of the developing body of world law and its source in the emerging world society. It is concerned particularly with the belief system that undergirds world law, its spiritual foundations. For every system of law depends for its vitality on a set of fundamental beliefs concerning the nature of law, its functions, its sources. Such beliefs constitute not only a philosophy of law but also a commitment, a faith, a belief *in* and not just a belief *that*. Our inquiry, therefore, following an analysis of the nature and functions of world law and its source in world society, pertains to the existence among the major cultures of the world of a common faith in law as a process of just and orderly resolution of conflicts.

Among people who adhere to a belief in God as the ultimate source of law, especially among believers in Judaism, Christianity, or Islam, faith in law is part of religious faith. In cultures that adhere, on the other hand, to non-theistic religions, including Buddhism and Taoism, or to humanist philosophies such as Confucianism, which do not share a belief in divine law and do not exalt faithfulness to a higher law as a manifestation of divine will, it is nevertheless generally accepted that conflicts that are not resolved through reconciliation, submission, self-denial, or other spiritual means should be resolved by law rather than by force. In such cultures, when Buddhist enlightenment or Confucian harmony or other spiritual values have not succeeded in overcoming conflict or deterring antisocial acts, resort is to be had to formal institutional procedures of settlement. Faith in such procedures when other forms of settlement fail is, in fact, common to the operative belief systems of virtually all the world's various cultures. Legal systems, to be sure, vary widely among the peoples of the world, but all complex societies have some forms of legislation, administration, and adjudication, and everywhere these are accepted as authoritative. It is the thesis of this chapter that the universal belief in law constitutes an important element of the fundamental belief system—in that sense, the religion—of the emerging world society.

World Law

The term "world law" will, I believe, become more and more widely used as humanity moves through a new century and a new millennium. It will embrace, but not replace, the term "international law," introduced by Jeremy Bentham in the 1780s. Eventual acceptance of the term "world law" will reflect as deep a conceptual change as that which occurred when Bentham's "international law" replaced the traditional term "law of nations" (*jus gentium*).

Bentham contended that the term "law of nations" was objectionable because it combined three mutually contradictory elements: (1) natural law, defined as a body of legal principles derived from natural reason and common to all civilized peoples, which Bentham said was not law at all; (2) rules of mercantile and maritime law concerning private transactions that cross national boundaries, which Bentham said are governed by the applicable municipal law of one or another sovereign nation-state; and (3) "the mutual [legal] transactions between sovereigns as such," which alone, in Bentham's view, could be called both "inter-national" and "law" (Bentham 1970, 296; Janis 1984). As late as 1831, Bentham's neologism was called "a frightfully barbarous title" and "a vile pollution" (Hogg, 1831 in Hoeflich 1988, 115); yet it had already been widely adopted both in Europe and in the United States, and in time the positivist theory of international law that it reflected also came largely to prevail, at least in the United States (Boyle 1985, 18). In the twentieth and twenty-first centuries, however, the "frightfully barbarous title" has been stretched to cover matters that hardly fit within Bentham's nationalist and positivist concept.

Especially after World War II, scholars began to look for new names to designate areas of law that transcend "mutual transactions between sovereigns as such." The most ambitious effort to find a name that would correspond to the realities of a new world order was Philip Jessup's proposal in 1956 to replace the term "international law" with "transnational law." "The term 'international' is misleading," Jessup wrote, "since it suggests that one is concerned only with the relations of one nation (or state) to other nations (or states)." A term is needed, he said, to identify "the law applicable to the complex interrelated world community which may be described as beginning with the individual and reaching up to the so-called 'family of nations' or 'society of states.'" "The word 'international' is inadequate to describe the problem . . . the term 'international law' will not do." "[I] shall use, instead of 'international law,' the term 'transnational law' to include all law which regulates actions or events that transcend national frontiers. Both public and private international law are included, as are other rules which do not wholly fit into such standard categories" (Jessup 1956, passim).[1]

The breadth of Jessup's definition is counteracted to a certain extent by the word "transnational," which takes the nation-state as the basic point of reference. When Jessup himself gave examples of matters that would be covered by "transnational" law, they were usually problems that ultimately involved "mutual transactions between sovereigns as such." Indeed, the word "transnational" refers back to the era of sovereign nation-states and indicates that it is to be transcended.[2] It does not, however, give a new name to the new era that all humanity has now entered. The right name for the new era, I submit, is "emerging world society," and the right name for the law by which it is governed is "world law."[3]

Indeed, "world law" is a new name for the older *jus gentium*, the law of nations, the law of *gentes*, of peoples. In Bentham's day it included, in addition to what we now call public international law, not only mercantile and maritime law but also natural law, defined as concepts and principles of law common to all civilized peoples. To speak of "world law" is to go back to the older concept of a common law of mankind (Jenks 1958, 66–84).

A whole new body of world law has emerged since the end of World War II. It embraces, most obviously, a greatly expanded body of so-called public international law created by agreements of nation-states, including more than 20,000 international treaties and conventions and implemented in part by over a thousand international governmental organizations (IGOs).[4] Less obviously but equally significantly, it embraces also various kinds of transnational customary law that have been created by voluntary associations that cross national boundaries—voluntary transnational associations of persons involved in world economic transactions and global communications and technology, as well as in global cultural, scientific, scholarly, athletic, and other types of activities. In virtually all countries of the world, associations of people at various levels of political, economic, and social life are called upon, and will be called upon increasingly in coming generations, to help create unofficial legal structures and processes of peaceful interchange across cultural and territorial boundaries.

An example of a body of world law created initially not by governments but by voluntary associations on the ground, so to speak, is the customary law of transnational commercial transactions, the so-called law merchant. We live not only in an "international" economy of "foreign" trade but also in a "world" of interdependent, interacting economies. The law that governs a contract for the sale of goods, say, by a business firm in New York to a purchaser in another country may be not only New York law or the law of the other country but also world law. For example, the bill of lading, issued by the carrier to the seller and to be transferred to the buyer, will normally have the same legal character as a bill of lading in an export-import transaction between enterprises in any two countries in the world: it will constitute the carrier's receipt for the goods, evidence of the contract of carriage, and a transferable document of title. If payment for the goods is by letter of credit, such credit will normally be subject to the same rules that govern letter-of-credit transactions throughout the world. Similarly, payment by a negotiable instrument is subject to the same rules of negotiability that exist throughout the world. The exporters and importers of the world, the shipowners and other carriers of the world, the marine insurance underwriters of the world, the bankers of the world, and others who work with them, including their lawyers, form a world association whose members over the centuries have made, and continue to make, the customary law by which their various types of transactions and relationships are governed. Formally, the law applicable to a cross-border commercial transaction may be national law, but a national court—or, more likely, a transnational tribunal of arbitrators chosen by the parties—will enforce the contract terms, which are usually the customary terms used throughout the commercial world and, in that sense, constitute world law. Two centuries ago that body of law was considered to be part of the *jus gentium*, the law of nations.

The law of world trade is, of course, also regulated in part by public international law, including multilateral treaties and conventions such as that establishing the World Trade Organization, as well as by public controls of national states. But so far as its strictly commercial aspects are concerned, its primary source is in the patterns and norms of behavior of those who over the centuries have engaged in it.

Most other branches of world law are not as ancient and not as highly developed as cross-border mercantile and banking law, yet they exist. In the economic sphere a customary law of transnational investment and transnational finance is developing, supported (as are customary mercantile and banking law) by multilateral treaties and conventions. There is worldwide protection of rights of intellectual property. Protection of the world's environment is increasingly subject to transnational controls, as is protection of various kinds of universal human rights. Not only piracy and slavery, as before, but also torture and genocide are now universal crimes that may be prosecuted wherever the offender is captured. Moreover, the Statute of the new International Criminal Court, to which eighty-nine nations have subscribed, gives that court jurisdiction over persons charged with murder, enslavement, rape, apartheid, and various other "crimes against humanity" when committed as part of a widespread or systematic attack directed against any civilian population.

World Society

Business enterprises and other kinds of economic actors, coming together from all nations to conduct their common affairs and to establish common norms of intercourse and common institutions, constitute an important element of a world civil society. That is, they are people from different nations and different cultures who are associated with each other voluntarily and are not government officials or members of state or interstate agencies. Such groups of persons or enterprises are sometimes called "private" associations, though it must be understood that they also serve public interests, notably in establishing customary legal norms that may also constitute a basis for national and international legislation and judicial decisions. Other constituent elements of world civil society include multinational religious associations, information and news media, educational and research organizations, professional societies, sports associations, and a host of other types of voluntary associations "made up of individuals and groups without regard to their identities as citizens of any particular country and outside the political and public dominion of the communion of nations" (Christenson 1997, 724–31).

Within world civil society, a legal distinction is made between voluntary transnational associations of persons or organizations that carry on or support commercial, financial, and production activities, including, for example, the International Chamber of Commerce, with its membership of more than 50,000 business enterprises plus individual members from about 110 countries, and, on the other hand, voluntary transnational associations that are engaged in activities that are classified as not-for-profit. The latter are qualified to be registered with the United Nations as international nongovernmental organizations (INGOs). Of the approximately 35,000 INGOs so registered, approximately 6,000 are multinational not only in their interests but also in their membership. These 6,000, most of which have been founded since 1945, cover a huge range of activities. Most are highly specialized, drawing members worldwide from a particular occupation, technical field, branch of knowledge, industry, hobby, or sport (Boli and Thomas 1999; Lechner and Boli 2000; Barber 1995). Examples include organizations with specific economic, scientific, or artistic concerns, such as the International Tin Council, the International Union for the Study of Social Insects, and the International Council of Museums. Others have broader concerns and a larger membership— for example, the World Wide Fund for Nature (formerly the World Wildlife Fund), which in the 1990s grew in transnational membership from 570,000 to 5,200,000, and its sister transnational multi-million-member environmental protection organization Greenpeace. Others that are less numerous but perhaps equally widely known include Doctors Without Borders, a transnational association of more than 2,500 doctors, which provides emergency medical assistance to victims of disease in more than 80 countries, and which also works to rehabilitate hospitals and to introduce vaccination programs and water and sanitation programs; Amnesty International, which exposes violations of civil rights throughout the world and exerts pressures to rectify them; and the International Red Cross, the Scout Movement, and the International Olympic Committee, which need no introduction.

Being both not-for-profit and nongovernmental, INGOs generally represent neither the material nor the specific national interests of their members but rather the universal interests of the worldwide class of people whose cause they advocate. The numerous organizations whose cause is the equality of women, for example, purport to represent not merely the interests of their members but the interests of all women of the world (Berkovich 1999, 100). Similarly, the various INGOs that advocate protection of the environment or reduction of pollution of the atmosphere claim to speak not only for themselves but for all environmentalists worldwide. Likewise, Doctors Without Borders and the numerous other INGOs that are dedicated to raising standards of world health are not special-interest groups seeking to benefit themselves or the nations of which their members are citizens but are associations of public-spirited persons seeking to meet a universal human need. Hence particular IGOs, charged by the United Nations with such causes as advancing gender equality or protecting the world's environment or combating world diseases, frequently consider that INGOs whose interests coincide with theirs are qualified to participate in their deliberations and to assist in establishing their policies. And, indeed, INGOs have played an important role in such deliberations and in the establishment of such policies.

An example is the role of international nongovernmental environmental organizations in the intergovernmental formulation of environmental legislation (Frank et al., 1999, 94). After the introduction of the United Nations Environment Programme in 1972, environmental INGOs, which previously had been relegated to the status of outsiders, began to receive entry to the official IGO deliberations on the implementation of the program. Their numbers rapidly increased as official roles were designated for them and funds and other resources were made available to them. At the United Nations Earth Summit in Rio de Janeiro in 1992, nongovernmental organizations (NGOs) were granted official accreditation, thus giving them direct access to national delegations and the right to propose draft treaties. More than 1,400 nongovernmental associations were registered at the Rio conference, and some of them had a substantial influence on the decisions it adopted. The Rio Earth Summit issued an "Agenda" to achieve environmentally sustainable development by the twenty-first century, one of whose provisions, entitled "Strengthening the Role of NGOs," states that "the UN system and Governments should initiate a process, in consultation with NGOs, to review formal procedures and mechanisms for the involvement of these organizations at all levels from policy-making and decision-making to implementation."

Another example of the role of international NGOs in the formation of policies by IGOs is furnished by the World Health Organization (WHO), which was established in 1946 and now has a membership of 191 states. Its constitution articulates principles of world health, including the principle that "governments have a responsibility for the health of their people" and the principle that "enjoyment of the highest standard of health is one of the fundamental rights of every human being, without distinction of race, religion, political belief, or economic or social condition." WHO functions include the setting of global standards for health and cooperation with governments in strengthening national health programs. It is best known for its programs of gradual and total eradication of certain diseases, and it is credited with having played a major role in the total eradication of smallpox in 1977. It also monitors and responds to AIDS, tuberculosis, polio, and other world diseases. In setting standards to ensure the highest quality of biological and pharmaceutical preparations, it brings together world experts in many disciplines and, in the words of one commentator, is "at the center of a transnational Hippocratic society made up of physicians, scientists, and public health experts" (Fidler 1997, 15).

WHO has, in effect, an advisory council of nongovernmental organizations operating under "Principles Governing Relations between the World Health Organization and Nongovernmental Organizations," adopted in 1987 by the Fortieth World Health Assembly, in which representatives of NGOs participated. The principles provide that to enter into relations with the WHO, an NGO shall "normally be international in structure and/or scope and shall represent a substantial proportion of the persons globally organized for the purpose of participating in the particular field of interest in which [the NGO] operates" (World Health Organization 1987, sec. 3.2). Under the principles, an NGO receives certain privileges, including the right to be represented in a nonvoting capacity in WHO meetings, access to nonconfidential documents through WHO distribution facilities, and the right to submit memoranda directly to the WHO director-general, to be circulated subsequently to others at his discretion. Under the WHO-NGO principles, an NGO may also implement WHO programs that the NGO helped to design, may disseminate information concerning WHO and policies, and may cooperate with member states in implementing WHO programs (Balloon 2002).

A dramatic example of the impact of an international NGO on world health law is the role played by Doctors Without Borders in defeating the effort of American and other pharmaceutical companies to prevent the distribution of generic AIDS drugs in South Africa. The availability of such generic drugs would make AIDS treatment affordable to the 4.2 million South Africans who tested HIV positive, the 1,700 who suffered new infections each day, and the 68,000 infected babies born each year. In 1998, thirty-nine pharmaceutical companies brought suit in a South African court, relying on universally recognized legal principles, to prevent infringement of their patents. Doctors Without Borders started a worldwide campaign, called "Drop the Case," to petition the pharmaceutical companies to withdraw their suit. Eventually, the companies, under the consequent pressure of world opinion, did withdraw their suit, accepting, in effect, a principle that in countries whose populations suffer from world diseases that can only be combatted by the use of medicines that cost more than their populations can afford to pay, the patentees of such medicines will permit the circulation of less expensive generic drugs, although the circulation of such drugs would otherwise constitute an infringement of their legal rights (Fidler 2002, 150–58). Earlier this principle had been invoked in Brazil, where since 1996 virtually all AIDS patients have been given access to generic drugs manufactured in that country. Ultimately, the member states of the World Trade Organization adopted a decision that "least-developed country Members" will not be obliged, with respect to pharmaceutical products, to enforce foreign patent rights otherwise applicable under the international agreement on trade-related aspects of intellectual property rights (World Trade Organization 2002, IP/C/25).[5]

These examples support the point that activities and interrelationships of members of a world civil society—world citizens, as the members of INGOs have sometimes been called—are a source of an emerging body of world environmental law and world health law.

Occupying a special place among such world citizens are participants in world sports. In Prof. Boli's words (1992), "More than 200 sports are organized at the world level." Moreover, the rules of such sports—of football (soccer), boxing, baseball, basketball, and others—are the same throughout the world, and international competitions are usually regulated by world standards. In Olympic sports, the International Olympic Committee is the legislator, and according to its rules, disputes that arise in the course of the games may not be submitted to national courts but only to arbitrators chosen by the parties under the rules of the Arbitration Court of Sport in Switzerland. Worldwide participation of athletes in performing world sports and of spectators in the enjoyment of them is an effective symbol of a world society. In Boli's words, sports are "the most visible rituals dramatizing the world polity." "Sports competition," he writes, "has become a major source of [world] identity and [world] solidarity." Sports, he adds, "express and help shape the subjective axis of world culture, building and ritually displaying individual, national, and human moral value."

The role of world sports in symbolizing and effectuating a world society is shared by world music, world games such as bridge and chess, and a host of other hobbies and leisure activities. Such activities help to convert an emerging world society into an emerging world community, in which not only nongovernmental but also intergovernmental organizations increasingly play an important part. The coming together of the personnel of INGOs and the personnel of IGOs is an important step in this direction. Indeed, the personnel of IGOs themselves, the representatives of national governments who meet together regularly in the performance of intergovernmental tasks, tend to form close personal interrelationships and to consider themselves as participants in a common enterprise. In addition to IGOs, informal inter-governmental networks exist among financial regulators (central bankers, securities regulators, insurance commissioners, and antitrust officials). In the words of Anne-Marie Slaughter (2000):

> These transgovernmental organizations tend to operate with a min-imum of physical and legal infrastructure. Most lack a foundational treaty, and operate under only a few agreed objectives or bylaws. Nothing they do purports to be legally binding on their members and mechanisms for formal enforcement or implementation are rare. Instead, these functions are left to the members themselves. But

despite this informal structure and loose organization, these organizations have had an important influence on international financial
regulatory co-operation. (179)

Thus the distinction between a nongovernmental world civil society and a
world society of representatives of nation-states is not absolute, just as the
distinction between the civil society of an individual nation and the government of that nation is not absolute, and just as the distinction within world civil
society between not-for-profit organizations and business organizations is not
absolute. In a healthy world society, as in a healthy national society, there is
continual interaction between governmental and nongovernmental associations, as well as between economic organizations and charitable organizations.

Faith in World Law

The development of world law is sustainable only if the belief system that
underlies it and nourishes it also continues to be sustained and to develop.

Such a world belief system is not to be identified with religion in the
conventional sense of that term; that is, it does not include a common belief in
a transcendent or ultimate reality and is not embodied in a common ritual of
worship. It shares, however, important features of the world's major religions.
These include fundamental moral beliefs—that it is wrong to murder or to
steal or to lie or to break one's promises, that one should act responsibly
toward others, that children should respect parents and parents should care
for children, that it is right to aid persons in distress, that the dignity of all
persons should be respected, that every human being should be treated hu-
manely, and that (as summarized in the Golden Rule) "you should do unto
others what you would want them to do unto you." These and similar moral
principles are reflected in all the cultures of the world; they constitute a global
ethic, endorsed not only by Judaism, Christianity, Islam, Buddhism, Hinduism, Taoism, and other religions[6] but also by Confucianism and other humanist philosophies (Küng et al., 1986, xvi; Rost 1986; Lewis 1947;
Kluckhohn 1962).[7] Such moral principles form a part of the foundation on
which all social cohesion is built. In the words of Hugo Grotius, traditionally
considered to be the founder of modern theories of international law, the
universal law of nations is based on the existence of a fundamental quality of
sociability that is inherent in human nature itself and that is a fundamental
source of all law (Grotius 1957, sec. 6; Murphy 1982, 477).

It is true, of course, that in practice these ethical principles have repeatedly been violated by adherents of the various religious faiths. How can one
speak, for example, of Christian or Muslim love of neighbor, let alone love of
enemy, in view of violent attacks on each other by Christians and Muslims in

the name of their respective faiths? As Mark Juergensmeyer (2003) has shown, religious zealots of virtually all the major religious faiths have repeatedly invoked "terror in the mind of God" to justify violence against adherents of competing faiths. Yet these are distortions of the basic doctrines of all the major religions, and not only of their doctrines but also of their basic spirit. At the heart of all the major religions is the same faith in peace, in sociability, that is at the heart of all the major legal systems. It is this faith that is exploited by extremists who invoke divine support for war and enmity.

A common faith in law adds to the common ethical principles of the world's religions a commitment to formal institutional settlement of conflicts that disputing parties are unwilling or unable to settle amicably by mutual accommodation, including conflicts that arise from criminal acts as well as from civil offenses. The foundational ethic of such institutional settlement is the ethic of the hearing: a person charged with violation of a legal obligation has a right to be heard. A hearing, in law, must be fair; that is, it must take place before an impartial tribunal, with the opposing parties given full opportunity to present evidence to support their arguments pro and con. This often means that the parties should be represented by persons capable of eliciting such evidence and presenting such arguments. The decision of the tribunal must be based on general principles applicable to the issues in dispute. Time must be taken for such procedures and for deliberations by the tribunal. These and other fundamental principles of law are applicable not only in judicial proceedings but also in legislative and administrative proceedings. Moreover, they are applicable, in different forms, not only in official proceedings before official bodies but also in the unofficial settlement of conflicts within and between associations of all kinds—within and between families, neighborhoods, workplaces, or professional associations, within and between religious societies, within and between diverse ethnic groups, nations, cultures, and civilizations. It is out of the universal ethic of a fair hearing that substantive legal rights and duties—of contract, of property, of civil liability for injury, of punishment of crime, of business associations, of taxation and other public controls of the economy, of constitutional liberties, and the rest—have emerged in one form or another in virtually all cultures.

It is true that some of the world religions and philosophies, such as Buddhism, Taoism, Shintoism, and Confucianism, as well as certain branches of Christianity, have minimized the spiritual value of law, with its emphasis on formal procedures, on objective application of general principles of justice and order, and on the enforcement of rights. Yet no large complex society that adheres to a Buddhist or Confucian or other antinomian religious or philosophical faith has been able to survive without some forms of legal regulation of conflict. In that respect, the legal traditions of the world transcend the religious traditions. The global ethic of a fair hearing, expressed in the ancient Latin legal maxim *audi alteram partem*, "hear the other side," is a common article of faith among all the cultures of the world—often, to be sure, disregarded or abused in practice but nevertheless believed in as a sacred instrument of peaceful resolution of conflict (Glenn 2000, 282–94).[8]

A universal faith in law shares with religious faith not only a body of moral principles but also the element of faith itself. Faith adds to ethics a sense of commitment. Faith involves emotion—feelings of dependence, gratitude, and humility, and of purpose, obligation, and responsibility. It comes not only from the mind but also from the heart. It is our willingness to live out our beliefs, to sacrifice for them, even to die for them if necessary. Also, as the theologian H. Richard Niebuhr emphasizes, faith brings human beings together in communities of trust and loyalty. It has a social dimension. "Faith," Niebuhr (1960) writes, "is embodied in social institutions as well as in private intuitions, in corporate endeavors as well as in individual activities, in secular pursuits as well as sacred expressions" (38–48). World faith in law shares with world religions not only their ethical dimension but also their commitment to a common future of universal peace and universal justice. It is, indeed, what Jean-Jacques Rousseau called a "civil religion," based on "the sanctity of the social contract." Faith in law is more universal in its acceptance by world society than Rousseau's civil religion of individualism, democracy, and civil rights, or the twentieth century's civil religions of collectivism and state programs of social welfare, that stem primarily from Western historical experience of recent centuries.

If one thinks of law only in positivist terms as a body of rules laid down by political authorities and backed by coercive sanctions, one will not naturally be led to connect law with faith. Starting from such positivist assumptions, most legal scholars in recent generations, as well as most political scientists, sociologists, and social theorists, have stated that connections between law and religion that existed in earlier societies have been severed in modern times. With Max Weber, they have linked a "rational" model of law with a "bureaucratic" model of political power. The law of the modern state, they have said, does not reflect any belief in the meaning or purpose of life; instead, its tasks are finite, material, impersonal—to get things done, to make people act in certain ways. Legal man, like his brother economic man, has been portrayed as one who uses his head and suppresses his dreams, his convictions, his passions, his concern with ultimate purposes. Likewise, the legal system as a whole, like the economic system, is seen as a complex machine, a Weberian bureaucracy, in which individual units perform specific roles according to specific incentives and instructions, independently of the purposes of the whole enterprise.

Yet law itself, in all societies, encourages the belief in its own sanctity. It puts forward its claim to obedience in ways that appeal not only to the material, impersonal, finite, rational interests of the people who are asked to observe it but also to their faith in a system of justice that transcends social utility—in ways, that is, that do not easily fit the image of instrumentalism presented by the prevailing theory.

To say that the law of a society is closely linked with the society's belief system, that each is a dimension of the other, that they interact, requires not only a broad definition of law but also a broad definition of belief. If one defines belief, faith, not in terms of belief in God or in an ultimate transcendent reality or "ground of being" but, even more broadly, in terms of shared intuitions and convictions concerning the purpose and meaning of life, shared emotions (as well as shared thoughts) concerning spiritual values, concerning the nature and destiny of humankind—then legal relations, legal processes, and legal values cannot be excluded from its purview. Similarly, if one understands law to be not only a body of rules but also a process of social self-control through the balancing of order and justice, then it is apparent that law—law in action—is inextricably interconnected with intuitions and convictions concerning spiritual values.

The interaction of law and spiritual values is reflected in law itself: first, in the rituals of law—its solemn language, the formalities of legal procedure, its reliance, in our system, on oaths; second, in its emphasis on tradition, its continuity with the past, and its sense of ongoingness into the future; third, in its appeal to authority, whether it be the authority of the court or of the legislator, of precedent or of statutes, or of a written constitution; and fourth, in its universality, its justification of itself in axiomatic, a priori terms—that persons charged with an offense or an obligation should have a right to a fair trial by an impartial tribunal, that like cases should be decided alike, that crimes should be punished, that torts should be compensated, that contracts should be enforced—not only for pragmatic or utilitarian or philosophical reasons but because such basic legal norms represent an all-embracing spiritual reality, a purpose of life itself. These four aspects of law—its reliance on ritual, on tradition, on authority, and on universality—give law a sacred quality and link law with religion as matters of faith.

World law, like other forms of law, embodies and depends for its effectiveness on its acceptance of such jural postulates (as Roscoe Pound, following Josef Kohler, called them), all of which are supposed to be applied equitably, so as to temper justice with mercy in individual cases (Pound 1959, 8–15).

A viable world law, like viable national legal systems, also depends on a system of beliefs concerning the nature and sources of law and the relation of law to the fundamental values of the society which produces it and which it helps to regulate. Like society itself, law depends for its cohesion and vitality on what the great French sociologist Émile Durkheim called "collective conscience," that is, a society's consciousness of, and commitment to, the spiritual sources of its unity (Durkheim 1995; Bellah and Hammond 1980). Durkheim linked the collective conscience of a society with its religion, and linked a society's law with its collective conscience. If we speak, however, of a world society in which many different religions flourish, including so-called civil religions such as dogmatic socialism or dogmatic individualism—then the collective conscience that underlies and nourishes world law must be sought in a larger category of belief, a spiritual faith in processes that transcend the conflicts that divide the human race.

What, then, is the source of the faith that underlies and sustains the developing body of world law, for example, the commercial law of world trade? The answer usually given is that it is in the material self-interest of the merchants and bankers of the world to have a uniform law governing the transnational transfer of goods. And that, of course, in itself, is true. But self-interest hardly explains it. There is also a shared ethic, a shared belief that contracts should be honored, that promises should be kept. But even more important, there is also a shared faith in the society of merchants and bankers who make the trade terms and the credit terms and who come together periodically in the International Chamber of Commerce in Paris to revise them, a shared trust that the people who constitute the market will not degenerate into a body of scoundrels and thieves, a shared commitment to adhere to the multicultural worldwide legal tradition by which the interrelationships of mercantile and banking and shipping and underwriting enterprises are governed. In Lon Fuller's words, these are friendly strangers, whose joint activities are governed by a self-generated body of customary law, made in the first instance by the mutual understandings of persons engaged in "human interaction." Such law may be found in the typical terms of contracts between persons who do business with each other, which Fuller (1969) calls "contractual law." They anticipate that conflicts will arise among themselves, including conflicts that reflect their cultural differences, and they rely on their common law to resolve those conflicts in an orderly and just way.

May one say the same of the transnational law that is created not by voluntary associations of world civil society but by official intergovernmental agencies—that it embodies a shared faith in the community of nation-states, a shared commitment to adhere to the legal tradition by which the relationships of nation-states within that community are governed? As noted earlier, intergovernmental organizations created to implement international legislation themselves sometimes constitute associations of trust and dedication, but these are only in an early stage of development; one may expect that in coming generations their coherence and permanence will increase and, with that, the transnational customary law that grows out of their operations will come to increase in scope and in significance.

Important also is the body of international legislation itself, especially in areas of concern that have a spiritual dimension. Referring to such legislation, William George (1999) has called attention to the challenge that it presents to the world's religious communities to transcend the boundaries of their own belief systems, to reassess their views of women, of cultures and races, of global banking and finance, of nonhuman species, of outer space and celestial bodies, of the deep seabed, of migratory bird and fish populations, of the ozone shield, of radio frequencies, of the sun's radiation, of polar icecaps, of future generations, of intellectual property—all current or potential topics of international law."

"This suggests," George states, "that international law has...a transcendental or religious dimension or capacity" (488).

The fact that theological references have largely dropped out of international legal discourse does not mean, he adds, that religious persons cannot recognize the religious dimensions of much of the recent international legislation. He gives the striking example of the 1970 declaration of the United Nations General Assembly, quoted in the 1982 UN Convention on the Law of the Sea, that the open seas are "the common heritage of mankind," and that the exploration of the open seas and the exploitation of its resources shall be carried out "for the benefit of mankind as a whole." "If the earth, or a part thereof, is the heritage of humankind," George asks, "then what—or who—is the primordial benefactor?... And if the claim is that the goods of the earth are given to humankind as a whole, from what vantage point do people regard the whole if not from a transcendent viewpoint...?" "Common heritage of humankind, it seems, points to an 'Ultimate Reality'" (George 1999, 490–91).

Similarly, as Michael Perry (2004) has shown, the provision in the human rights covenants of the United Nations that those rights are based on "the inherent dignity" of all persons presupposes a universal source of such rights that transcends political authority (Perry 2005, 97–150).

In the words of the British scholar and former diplomat Philip Allott, quoted by George, there is "a pressing need" for "a spiritual horizon, the horizon of the interdependence of the human spirit, as human societies and human beings everywhere at last begin to take moral and social responsibility for the survival of and prospering of the whole of humanity" (George 1999, 496).

What is new, in Allott's statement, is the word "everywhere." After some six thousand years of human history, all the civilizations of the world have been brought into contact with each other. Especially in the second millennium of the Christian era, Western Christendom, through its merchants, its military, and its missionaries, made a world around itself. Now as we enter the third millennium of that history, the West is no longer the center. All humanity is joined together in a common destiny. Despite two world wars and their aftermath of terrible ethnic, territorial, and ideological conflicts, Saint Paul's extraordinary insight, that "every race of man" is "made of one blood to inhabit the whole earth's surface" (Acts 17:26), has not only been proved scientifically but has also become a historical reality. We are all faced with the alternative of worldwide mutual support or worldwide mutual destruction.

From a religious viewpoint, this is providential: that the eventual inter-action and association of all the peoples of the world with each other was intended from the beginning, that that is what world history has been all about, namely, to make the eventual communification of the human race a possibility, and that the God of history has now put it to us squarely: either you come together, or you will destroy each other.

The challenge may also be understood from a secular standpoint. In a world of diverse religions, diverse cultures, and clashing national, ethnic, and other loyalties and interests, a world where another major war could bring human history to an end—in such a world not only the peoples, the nations, but the people, the associations of world citizens, in order to survive, must come together to create a common law that will enable them to resolve their conflicts peacefully. Indeed, they have begun to do so.

Talcott Parsons, perhaps the leading sociologist of the mid–twentieth cen-tury, wrote in 1963 that "for the first time in history something approaching a world society is in process of emerging" (Parsons 1967, 298). This insight was undoubtedly influenced by the earlier writings of Durkheim, who, in the late nineteenth and early twentieth centuries, forecast that global expansion of the division of labor in the world economy would lead to political-legal regulation on a worldwide scale and that this would bring with it the universalization of beliefs and practices relative to sacred things (Bellah and Hammond 1980, 186). What I have added to these prophecies is that a universal faith in law among the various cultures of the emerging world society constitutes an essential element of a world civil religion. In the words of an ancient maxim, *ubi societas, ibi jus*, "where there is society, there there is law." Though not universal among transcendental religions, faith in law is common to some major world religions and to all secular political, social, and cultural belief systems. It offers the main hope for establishing world channels of cooperation and resolving world conflicts when less formal and more amicable means fail. Its sanctity is reflected, above all, in the shared spiritual values and the shared experience of the numerous associ-ations that constitute the emerging world civil society.

NOTES

1. The technical name for what is usually called simply "international law" is "public international law," which is the law agreed upon by the governments of nation-states, whether expressly or tacitly. The scope of this body of law has expanded enor-mously since the two world wars so that now it includes far more than matters of interstate relationships.

2. An important and widely used textbook entitled *Transnational Legal Problems* identifies as "transnational" the ways in which nations react to such problems as trade

and monetary flows, how they control immigration, how they regulate foreign conduct threatening national interest, and, in general, the way in which a nation's domestic policies "necessarily affect other countries and their nationals." "Such expression of an international legal system can be viewed as having a transnational character. Together with public international law and with regulation by international organizations, such phases of international law form a ... complex to which this book refers as ... 'transna-transnational law'" (Steiner, Vagts, and Koh 1994, iii–iv). Although this definition comes fairly close to what I call "world law," nevertheless "transnational" topics are treated by the authors almost entirely in the context of their significance for interstate relations.

Louis Sohn, who taught courses in United Nations law and in world organizations at Harvard Law School from 1947 to 1981, published in 1950 a pioneering textbook entitled *Cases in World Law*, devoted largely to the law of the United Nations and other interstate organizations. Sohn also published in 1956 an important book, coauthored with Grenville Clark, entitled *World Peace through World Law*, devoted primarily to the role of the United Nations and other interstate organizations in overcoming conflicts between nation-states. These were important early uses of the term "world law," largely confined, however, to various types of legal relations among nation-states.

3. The term "global law," which has been adopted by New York University School of Law, is less satisfactory because the word "global" carries only a geographic connotation, whereas the word "world" also carries the connotation of people and cultures.

4. IGOs play a variety of roles in international relations. Some tend to be mainly a forum for rule making, such as the World Trade Organization (WTO). Others, such as the World Bank, provide services. Other IGOs include the World Health Organization (WHO), the North Atlantic Treaty Organization (NATO), and the European Union (EU). Harold Jacobson (1979) describes the roles of IGOs as informational, normative, rule making, rule supervising, and operational.

5. The WTO Council for Trade-Related Aspects of Intellectual Property Rights ("Council for TRIPS") decided as follows: "Least-developed country Members will not be obliged, with respect to pharmaceutical products, to implement or apply Sections 5 and 7 of Part II of the TRIPS Agreement or to enforce rights provided for under these Sections until 1 January 2016." Sections 5 and 7 of part II of the TRIPS Agreement refer, respectively to patents and protection of undisclosed information.

6. Since 1933, hundreds of religious leaders from around the world have met periodically in the Parliament of the World's Religions to discuss the Declaration of a Global Ethic, which affirms "the fundamental unity of the human family on earth." The declaration, which was drafted initially by Hans Küng, states that "by a global ethic we do not mean a global ideology or a single unified religion behind all existing religions," but rather "a fundamental consensus on binding values, irrevocable standards and personal attitudes." The global ethical principles listed in the text are drawn from Küng's much longer list.

7. According to Küng, "Religion is a social and individual relationship, vitally realized in a tradition and in a community (through doctrine, ethos, and generally ritual as well), with something that transcends or encompasses man and his world: with something always to be understood as the utterly final, true reality (the Absolute, God, nirvana). In contrast to philosophy, religion is concerned at once with a message of salvation and the way to salvation." The recognition that most religions have

common features and share a common ethic provides an important basis for mutual understanding among adherents of different faiths but does not necessarily inspire or demand the kinds of spiritual commitment to the strengthening of a world society or the creation of a world community for which the Declaration of the Global Ethic calls. Clyde Kuckhohn and other cultural anthropologists have determined that the last six of the Ten Commandments have counterparts in all known cultures. Moreover, the summary of those six commandments in the Golden Rule, "Do unto others as you would have them do unto you," is found not only in the New Testament but also in the Talmud, and it has almost exact counterparts in Islam and in Buddhism, Taoism, Brahmanism, Confucianism, and Zoroastrianism. For the Christian version, see Matthew 7:12: "All things whatsoever ye would that men should do to you, do ye even so to them: for this is the Law and the Prophets." Cf. Judaism: "What is hateful to you, do not to your fellowmen. That is the entire Law: All the rest is commentary" (Talmud, Shabbat 31a). Brahmanism: "This is the sum of duty: Do naught unto others which would cause you pain if done to you" (Mahabharata 5, 1517). Buddhism: "Hurt not others in ways that you yourself would find hurtful" (Udana-Varga 5, 18). Confucianism: "Sure it is the maxim of loving kindness: Do not unto others that you would not have them do unto you" (Analects, 15, 23). Taoism: "Regard your neighbor's gain as your own gain, and your neighbor's loss as your own loss" (T'ai Shang Kan Ying P'ien). Zoroastrianism: "That nature alone is good which refrains from doing unto another whatsoever is not good for itself" (Dadistan-i-dinik 94, 5). Islam: "No one of you is a believer until he desires for his brother that which he desires for himself" (Sunnah).

8. Imperial China, for example, adhered to a Confucian philosophy that distinguished sharply between rigid formal law, called *fa*, viewed negatively, and informal altruistic morality, called *li*, viewed positively. This philosophy contributed to the absence, in imperial China, of a strong legal tradition and of a trained legal profession of counselors and advocates. There was, nevertheless, a substantial body of imperial law, both criminal and civil, which was enforced by imperial magistrates, before whom persons were brought to respond to charges of offenses, as well as a substantial body of local customary law with its own procedures for establishing channels of cooperation and resolution of conflict.

Hans Küng acknowledges that "the ethical acceptance of laws ... is the presupposition of any political culture" and that there should be an ethic that is not merely morally but also legally "binding and obligatory ... for the whole of human kind," and further, that "not human beings but laws should rule, and these should be constitutional" (Küng 1991, 34, 53). Other than listing some basic human civil and political rights, however, Küng does not attempt to identify principles of procedural and substantive law that in fact constitute a global legal ethic—perhaps because not all the world religions expressly endorse such principles.

BIBLIOGRAPHY

Allott, Philip. 1990. *Eunomia: New Order for a New World*. Oxford: Oxford University Press.

Balloon, Anthony M. 2002. "World Diseases, World Communities and World Health Law." Unpublished manuscript.

Barber, Benjamin R. 1995. *Jihad vs. McWorld: How Globalization and Tribalism Are Reshaping the World*. New York: Times Books.

Bederman, David J. 2002. *The Spirit of International Law*. Athens: University of Georgia Press.

Bellah, Robert Neelly. 1970. *Beyond Belief: Essays on Religion in a Post-traditional World*. New York: Harper and Row.

Bellah, Robert Neelly, and Phillip E. Hammond. 1980. *Varieties of Civil Religion*. San Francisco: Harper and Row.

Bentham, Jeremy. 1970. *An Introduction to the Principles of Morals and Legislation*. Edited by J. H. Burns and H. L. A. Hart. London: Athlone Press.

Berkovich, Nitza. 1999. "The Emergence and Transformation of the Women's Movement." In *Constructing World Culture: International Nongovernmental Organizations since 1875*, edited by John Boli and George M. Thomas, 100–126. Stanford, CA: Stanford University Press.

Boli, John. 1992. "World Polity Dramatization via Global Events." Paper presented at the New Ecumenical Research Association Conference "Religion, Peace and Global Order," Washington, DC.

Boli, John, Thomas A. Loya, and Teresa Loftin. 1999. "National Participation in World Polity Organizations." In *Constructing World Culture: International Nongovernmental Organizations since 1875*, edited by John Boli and George M. Thomas, 50–80. Stanford, CA: Stanford University Press.

Boli, John, and George M. Thomas, eds. 1999. *Constructing World Culture: International Nongovernmental Organizations since 1875*. Stanford, CA: Stanford University Press.

Boyle, Francis Anthony. 1985. *World Politics and International Law*. Durham, NC: Duke University Press.

Christenson, Gordon A. 1997. "World Civil Society and the International Rule of Law." *Human Rights Quarterly* 19:724–37.

Durkheim, Émile. 1995. *The Elementary Forms of Religious Life*. Translated by Karen E. Fields. New York: Free Press.

Fidler, David P. 1997. "The Globalization of Public Health: Emerging Infectious Diseases and International Relations." *Indiana Journal of Global Legal Studies* 5:11–51.

———. 2002. "A Globalized Theory of Public Health Law." *Journal of Law, Medicine and Ethics* 30:150–61.

Frank, David, Ann Hironaka, John W. Meyer, Evan Schofer, and Nancy Brandon Tuna. 1999. "The Rationalization and Organization of Nature in World Culture." In *Constructing World Culture: International Nongovernmental Organizations since 1875*, ed. John Boli and George M. Thomas, 81–99. Stanford, CA: Stanford University Press.

Fuller, Lon L. 1969. "Human Interaction and the Law." *American Journal of Jurisprudence* 14:1–36.

George, William P. 1999. "Looking for a Global Ethic? Try International Law." In *Religion and International Law*, ed. Mark W. Janis and Carolyn Evans, 483–504. The Hague: Martinus Nijhoff.

Glenn, H. Patrick. 2000. *Legal Traditions of the World: Sustainable Diversity in Law*. Oxford: Oxford University Press.

Grotius, Hugo. 1957. *Prolegomena to the Law of War and Peace.* Translated by Francis W. Kelsey. New York: Liberal Arts Press.

Held, David. 1999. *Global Transformations: Politics, Economics and Culture.* Oxford: Polity Press.

Hoeflich, Michael H., ed. 1988. *The Gladsome Light of Jurisprudence: Learning the Law in England and the United States in the Eighteenth and Nineteenth Centuries.* New York: Greenwood Press.

Hogg, Thomas J. 1988. "An Introductory Lecture on the Study of the Civil Law." In *The Gladsome Light of Jurisprudence: Learning the Law in England and the United States in the Eighteenth and Nineteenth Centuries,* edited by Michael H. Hoeflich, 96–117. New York: Greenwood Press.

Huntington, Samuel P. 1996. *The Clash of Civilizations and the Remaking of World Order.* New York: Simon and Schuster.

Jacobson, Harold Karan. 1979. *Networks of Interdependence: International Organizations and the Global Political System.* New York: Knopf.

Janis, Mark W. 1984. "Jeremy Bentham and the Fashioning of 'International Law.'" *Americal Journal of International Law* 78:405–18.

Janis, Mark W., and Carolyn Evans, eds. 1999. *Religion and International Law.* The Hague: Martinus Nijhoff.

Jenks, C. Wilfred. 1958. *The Common Law of Mankind.* New York: Praeger.

Jessup, Philip. 1956. *Transnational Law.* New Haven: Yale University Press.

Juergensmeyer, Mark. 2003. *Terror in the Mind of God: The Global Rise of Religious Violence.* Berkeley: University of California Press.

Kluckhohn, Clyde. 1962. *Culture and Behavior: Collected Essays.* New York: Free Press of Glencoe.

Küng, Hans, Josef Van Es S, Heinrich von Stictencron, and Heinz Bechert. 1986. *Christianity and World Religions: Paths of Dialogue with Islam, Hinduism, and Buddhism.* Translated by Peter Heinegg. Garden City, NY: Doubleday.

Küng, Hans. 1991. *Global Responsibility: In Search of a New World Ethic.* New York: Crossroad Publishing.

Lechner, Frank, and John Boli, eds. 2000. *The Globalization Reader.* Malden, MA: Blackwell.

Lewis, C. S. 1947. *The Abolition of Man.* New York: Macmillan.

McCoy, Michael, and Patrick McCully. 1993. *The Road from Rio: An NGO Action Guide to Environment and Development.* Utrecht: International Books.

McNamee, Bernhard L., and Timothy P. Terrell. 1994. "Transovereignty: Separating Human Rights from Traditional Sovereignty and the Implications for the Ethics of International Law Practice." *Fordham International Law Journal* 17:459–88.

Murphy, Cornelius F. 1982. "The Grotian Vision of World Order." *American Journal of International Law* 76:477–98.

Niebuhr, H. Richard. 1960. *Radical Monotheism and Western Civilization.* Lincoln: University of Nebraska Press.

Parsons, Talcott. 1964. "Christianity and Modern Industrial Society." In *Religion, Culture, and Society: A Reader in the Sociology of Religion,* edited by Louis Schneider, 273–98. New York: Wiley.

Perry, Michael J. 2005. "The Morality of Human Rights: A Nonreligious Ground?" *Emory Law Journal* 54:97–150.

Pound, Roscoe. 1959. *Jurisprudence*. St. Paul, MN: West.

"Principles Governing Relations between the WHO and Nongovernmental Organizations." 1987. *World Health Organization: World Health Assembly*, WHA 40.25.

Rost, H. T. D. 1986. *The Golden Rule: A Universal Ethic*. Oxford: G. Ronald.

Slaughter, Anne-Marie. 2000. "Governing the Global Economy through Government Networks." In *The Role of Law in International Politics: Essays in International Relations and International Law*, edited by Michael Byers. Oxford: Oxford University Press.

Steiner, Henry J., Detlev F. Vagts, and Harold H. Koh. 1994. *Transnational Legal Problems: Materials and Texts*. Mineola, NY: Foundation Press.

World Trade Organization [WTO]. 2002. "Council for Trade-Related Aspects of Intellectual Property Rights—Extension of the Transition Period Under Article 66.1 of the TRIPS Agreement for Least-Developed Country Members for Certain Obligation with Respect to Pharmaceutical Products—Decision of the council for TRIPS of 27 June 2002."

5

Property and Sacred Ordering in Global Civil Society

Jon P. Gunnemann

The idea of civil society emerged in seventeenth- and eighteenth-century Europe and America in response to a crisis in the social order in which the invocation of a single purpose or good—by the church or the king—to legitimate social order ceased to be plausible. "Commercialization of land, labor, and capital; the growth of market economies; the age of discoveries; and the English and later North American and continental revolutions—all brought into question the existing models of social order and authority" (Seligman 1992, 15). The ordering of social conflict now had to be negotiated, and authority had to be legitimated without reference to traditional sources. New social mechanisms evolved and were created to avoid tyranny or the chaos of war. These included market exchange, contract, new laws of property, debate and discussion, and emerging forms of self-governance both in small-scale associations and in the political order. "Civil society" refers to forms of association and interaction in which the conflict among a plurality of human ends is ordered relatively peacefully—which is to say, civilly.

Civil society was understood to occupy a place or space—including public squares, markets, and assembly halls—between the political (and ecclesiastical, in some accounts) courts and chambers and the merely private realm of the family, a space where individuals could freely reach agreements or make transactions. Whatever differences in later theories and assessments of civil society, metaphors of place and space remain central: civil society is situated "between" the state and the individual or "private" institutions such as the family; or it is said to "mediate" between individual and state. Civil society gives persons space for autonomous decisions, for free association, for free discussion of what people have in common, for community, for dwelling without fear. The founders of civil society were the bourgeoisie, a growing "middle" class, itself a spatial metaphor. The distinctive space of civil society, a "space between," reoriented its participants to the entire world.

The application of the idea of civil society to the global economy is both promising and problematic. That globalization has created (or is accompanied by) crises in social order not unlike those in seventeenth- and eighteenth-century Europe is grounds for the promise. Indeed, it can be argued that the crises of social order connected to globalization are but extensions of the early modern crises in the West, and that globalization began then, with the discovery of the New World and world trade routes. That the crises are occurring in the encounters of many different social orders and cultures, multiplying the number of competing ends and goods and compounding their conflict, is reason for caution. So, too, is the emergence of new and plural forms of power, political, economic, scientific, and technological. In a global context, the spatial metaphor of "between" is problematic: between what and what? Nevertheless, those who employ the idea hope that even in a global context the idea of civil society might offer insight into ways for a civil ordering of conflict.

I offer here a critical interpretation of the institution of property as one element in the ordering of conflict in civil society. Several reasons suggest this focus: for one, property arrangements were at the heart of every aspect of the social crisis in Europe that gave rise to the idea of civil society, and emerging new property arrangements were part of the new order. Looking at the ambiguity of property reminds us that civil society is always "a realm of conflict" (Walzer 2002, 38) and that the "harmonizations" of civil society are at best orderings that depend on people learning to negotiate and live with ongoing conflict and tension. Second, property orders the human habitat, creating spaces and boundaries in at least three dimensions: the individual's self-understanding and identity, social relationships, and the human relationship to the world of nature. Attention to these three dimensions of order illuminates aspects of order and disorder in the global context.

Third, because it orders the entire human habitat—understanding of self (identity), social relations, and relations to the natural environment—property also has a religious dimension. Put theologically (from a broadly Jewish and Christian perspective), property orders the human relation to God, but this religious ordering implies an interpretation of the whole human habitat in all three dimensions. The religious interpretation is complex. Religion can, as Marx argued, simply legitimate existing property arrangements. But religious commitments can also delegitimate existing property relations. These are claims requiring empirical and historical investigation, as well as normative analysis. The important theoretical points are that any property arrangement must be legitimated, and that the broad extent of property's ordering power means that its legitimations inevitably have religious and quasi-religious elements.

My argument is interpretive and normative, developing the preceding points in more detail and drawing out implications for current discussions of global civil society. I will use the metaphor of space for drawing connections among property, civil society, and religion in the ordering of the world. But the normative parts of the argument depend on the distinction between two models for understanding property: the *ownership model* and a *relational model*. I take up this distinction first.

Ownership versus Relational Models of Property

The State of Mississippi has worked hard in recent years to attract foreign investment to create jobs for a struggling economy, worsened by declining agricultural revenues. After years of wooing, including the offer of economic incentives totaling a billion dollars and 1,400 acres of land, Mississippi, competing with other southern states, staged a coup in attracting Nissan to build an auto plant, the largest industrial project in Mississippi history (ABC News 2002). But among the acres promised to Nissan was farmland owned for more than forty years by several African American farmers. While some accepted offers from the state to buy their land, Andrew and Matilda Archie and several other families refused to sell. The State of Mississippi went to the courts to invoke the right of eminent domain, a constitutional right of government to appropriate privately owned land in support of public good or need, arguing that the jobs to be created by Nissan were vital to the state's economy and hence counted as a "public good" (Ladd 2002).

The Archies resisted, and the battle came to public notice when ABC News reported it on national television. A sampling of views: Andrew Archie: "Why should I move for a parking lot? You wouldn't want me to take your land. That would be wrong." It would be especially wrong because his father bought the land in the 1940s when almost no land was owned by blacks. These farmers were among the first black landowners in Mississippi. Matilda Archie, noting that most of the black families who sold early had been frightened into doing so: "They took so much land from black people, it makes me sick how they got away with it." Stephanie Parker, a community activist: "They are being treated as sharecroppers and not shareholders in this billion-dollar deal." Alan Purdie, the attorney for the state: "Acquiring property for the use of economic development purposes is in fact a public use. We absolutely believe it is." Scott Bullock of the watchdog Institute for Justice, who filed briefs for the landowners before the Mississippi Supreme Court: "Nissan gets the land, the taxpayers in Mississippi get the bill, and these fine people get the boot" (ABC News 2002). Within days of the ABC report, the

State of Mississippi settled the dispute by offering much more than originally proposed to two of the families, and by agreeing to build the parking lot around the Archies' land (Ladd 2002).

Nissan and the State of Mississippi were working with an *ownership model* of property (Singer 2000; Nedelsky 1993; Underkuffler 1990; Underkuffler-Freund 1996). In the ownership model, property is conceived as something *external* to the owner, and property rights confer the power to dispose of the property as the owner likes. From this perspective and from the perspective of pure market theory—which assumes that all property is a *commodity* that can be given a price and alienated through exchange—the Archies' refusal to sell is irrational. All disputes about property should be resolvable by settling on the right price.

But the Archies' view that their land had no price is intelligible (rational) from the perspective of a *relational model* of property. The relational model understands property as a complex set of rights or entitlements that are deeply social in nature, and of which property as commodity is only a limited part. Property is an institution that orders society in multiple dimensions: it is in part constitutive of self-understanding and identity; it structures social relationships by specifying duties and obligations along with rights; and it orders the human relationship with the natural environment. The dispute between the Archies and the State of Mississippi was not a dispute about the relative value of the land but a clash of two incompatible views of the meaning of that land in relation to the owner, two incompatible views of what property is in all three of its ordering dimensions.

Ordering Identity

For the Archies, their father's purchase of the land imbued it with a symbolic meaning that was part of their identity, an identity that involved relations among their physical persons, the land, their family heritage, and a larger history of racial oppression in the United States. From their point of view, treating the land as a commodity with a price was irrational: it would have been a betrayal, for a price, of who they were, a selling of their birthright for bread and pottage.

Ordering Social Relationships

The State of Mississippi wanted simply to buy the land, a transfer of title from one owner to another. Scott Bullock, the lawyer who filed for the Archies, drew a more complex picture of the relations involved in this piece of property: Nissan gets the land, the taxpayers pay, and the Archies get the boot. But he only got it partly right. Nissan's shareholders—nameless and numberless—will get the profits from the deal; some taxpayers will get jobs, but many will not; the tax structure of the state will almost surely assure that the cost is not borne equitably; and some persons living close to the plant will benefit indirectly from the new prosperity while others will bear indirect costs in the form of increased traffic and pollution, noise, and other disutilities of having a manufacturing plant outside their living room windows. That is the way property relations are structured in our society.

In the ownership model of property, these different parties are interpreted as having claims that may pose *external* limits to a right of ownership. But in a relational model of property the tensions and conflicts are *internal* to the institution of property itself: each of these parties has entitlements, claims, and responsibilities in relation to the same piece of property (Singer 2002, 207–9). Property rights sort out these multiple claims by granting entitlements to some, assigning costs and burdens to others, creating boundaries that include some and exclude others. As Joseph Singer (2002) puts it,

> "What rights in fact do and have always done is construct relationships—of power, of responsibility, of trust, of obligation." Property law creates a setting in which individuals live their lives and interact with others. This setting partly consists of rules requiring individuals to respect the legitimate claims of others in controlling certain portions of the physical world. Other rules are designed to ensure that the property system as a whole functions well, with tolerable efficiency and justice. We should understand property as a social system. (208, citing Nedelsky 1993, 13)

This structuring of power is fundamentally *distributive*: it determines who gets what. Mississippi's claim that building the Nissan plant is a public good *might* lead to the proposal that, if so, the profits—or some of them—should be distributed to the taxpayers who pay for it, or to those paying other costs. But that would require a configuration of the relations of property rights different from the one we have, which privileges shareholders over other "stakeholders" in a capital good, or in locally generated wealth. The distributive nature of property rights means that property is inherently conflictual. To assign an entitlement to some is to exclude others from that entitlement; to draw a boundary protecting one person's claim coerces another person; to configure the relations of property in a particular way can be contested, and often is.

Property rights are best seen as a social arrangement whereby competing and sometimes deeply conflicting claims are resolved. Property includes individual entitlement, but a relational view of property understands that many parties claim entitlements to the same property. The legal sorting out of the plurality of interests and claims does not just protect individual interests but defines a particular "property regime," thereby constructing a social order. Because the human condition is plural, "Property is a form of power, and the distribution of power is a political problem of the highest order" (Singer

2002, 11). Any solution to that problem embodies "a vision of social life" (citing Nedelsky 1993, 13).

Ordering the Human Relationship to Nature

Nissan and the State of Mississippi understood land—one important part of nature—as "fungible," a commodity, while the Archies saw the land as part of their identity. For them identity was connected to place, a defined space in nature, distinguishable from any other.

The continuing struggle over rights of use of forestland—for example, between conservationists on one side and the logging industry on the other— shows differing and competing valuations of such land, and these differing valuations represent different meanings attached to "land" or "wilderness" or to nature itself. Again, viewed from the perspective of pure market theory or from an ownership model of property, the dispute between environmentalists and loggers can be resolved simply by setting the price right: offer enough for the trees, and the environmentalists will finally sell, or permit the trees to be sold. Like the Archies, environmentalists argue that some trees have no price, although the reasons they give are different. They might appeal, for example, to the "intrinsic value" of wilderness, or to "ecological balance," rather than to identity and history. Different interpretations of ownership orient and order people differently in relation to land, nature, and the entire environment—to their "habitat" both natural and cultural. Conversely, different interpretations of what is owned, or of those aspects of the human habitat on which people claim various entitlements, entail different understandings of property. Conflict over property rights is a conflict about the meaning of the human habitat.

A given property regime establishes, then, a defensible (but not uncontested) tension among competing claims and a complex set of relations and meanings. The question is, of course, what constitutes a defensible tension? How does it get decided, and by whom? In European history, "civil society" defined the place and the persons who made these decisions about property. The social evolution of "free cities," of public squares and markets, and of forms of self-governance by a new class of "free persons" (a "middle class" unattached to land and feudal relations) formed spaces and marked boundaries (not all persons were included, showing that the space was both physical and metaphorical) for the political decisions constructing defensible tensions among competing claims of entitlement. Market exchange itself was one device for the peaceful resolution of competing interests—a good reason not to rule out market institutions from inclusion in civil society—and the political theory of the "social contract" had its origins here. A new social vision was being constructed.

But in the contemporary global arena, not all of these elements are in place at the same time in any given context. At least the following problematics are salient. First, to the extent that globalization is driven by economic forces, the dominant model of property accompanying these forces is the "ownership model." The conflict between the Archies and Nissan/Mississippi is an example of how the export of global capital and property understandings—ironically from "Eastern" Japan to "Western" rural Mississippi—conflicts with local understandings of property. Transfer the location to the Amazon basin, or India, or to virtually any place outside the Western world, and the problems of cultural conflict are compounded. New property relations created by property as ownership are indifferent, if not hostile, to the local relations of property and hence deeply disrupt local social order and meaning. The introduction of property as merely ownership transforms the local basis for identity, the cultural meanings and social vision embedded in the local social order, and local understandings of the human relation to nature.

Second, if property as ownership obscures and undermines the other relations of property, then the entitlements historically secured in and through those relations must be secured by other means. Identity needs to be established through new forms of membership (including often new religious movements or radical forms of traditional religions); the right to dwelling may be secured by forms other than individual ownership of property; rights to the means of life itself—food, health care, income for these things—may often be detached from property as ownership, achieved rather through institutional membership (e.g., employment, cooperatives) or through membership in religious and social movements. The United Nations Universal Declaration of Human Rights specifies both civil and economic entitlements essential to human well-being, many secured historically through complex property relations but now understood as "rights" accruing to persons (and sometimes groups) in themselves.

Third, in all these problematics questions of meaning are central, pointing to intersections with religion. The metaphor of space illuminates these intersections.

Spaces, Boundaries, and Civil Society

When the Red Cross and other international relief organizations work to offer medical aid and provisions for ordinary people wounded and deprived of basic necessities in a region of war or civil conflict, they occupy a "humanitarian space" between hostile forces, theoretically a neutral and impartial ground between armed factions, groups, and nations (Ignatieff 2002). Such humanitarian space may be shrinking in the face of modern forms of ethnic conflict and terrorism (to cite a few examples: the use of Red Cross ambulances and uniforms by terrorists; military assaults on religious buildings that dissident militants use for protection; suicide bombings by pregnant women;

debates about military attacks on holy days), but to the extent that humanitarian work is respected by warring sides, the "space" created signifies a good recognized by both sides as transcending the conflict. Because of its symbolic potency—violation of it arouses widespread human horror and condemnation—humanitarian space is *sacred space*, a form of "sanctuary": it represents a domain to which no human power—personal, political, or economic—is entitled. Humanitarian space and sanctuary point to and protect ultimate values against the fallible and finite ends of human cultures. To violate them signals a descent from the ordinary barbarism of war into the cauldrons of holocaust and hell.

A continuous line runs from sanctuary and humanitarian space through the spaces of civil society and all spaces declared free from control by specified powers, to the space of the Archies' property. They have in common the designation of a safe zone, but they also have in common the precarious and fragile nature of their boundaries. From some vantage points, the very idea of such spaces and the boundaries around them is arbitrary, if not intellectually scandalous. From the standpoint of pure market theory, they are irrational blocks to pricing and exchange—or, more generously, "externalities" that somehow limit property as ownership. From the standpoint of secularization theory, such spaces are residues of premodern ways of thought. From the standpoint of ideological critique, many simply protect existing patterns of privilege, exclusion, and domination. From the standpoint of religious fanaticism, the spaces recognized by others have no standing. The sacred spaces of one culture may seem strange from the vantage point of another culture, and the sacred spaces of one time may look odd viewed from later in history. Indeed, the face of the earth is strewn with the ruins of boundaries and walls torn down, abandoned, forgotten.

But the drawing of lines around spaces and the designation of these spaces as "sacred," off bounds to secular interests, is one of the most fundamental of human activities because it protects people and what people value from various forms of tyranny. Without boundaries defining sacred space, there are no limits to political, military, economic, and other forms of power—there is only Hobbes's *bellum omnes contra omnia* or its despotic solution. It is precisely because certain spaces are protected from domination through the pursuit of finite human ends that they are religious in nature, or have a religious quality. To declare something *inviolable*, whether the interior of a church, an ambulance bearing a red cross, a person, a public meeting space, a portion (or all) of nature, is to interpret it as having meaning transcending political, economic, or other profane calculus. It is a religious act. Theologically, it declares that God too—and primarily—has a claim on this space.

An immediate objection is obvious: that the declaration of inviolability, the drawing of a line, the claim that a space is neutral, is itself not a neutral act but an act of power, whether made on religious or other grounds. This is exactly right. And the best we can say here is that civil society refers to spaces and forms of human association where the power to establish boundaries is itself limited or broadly shared, and where disputes about boundaries and spaces are resolved "civilly." Power does not disappear, nor does conflict. As with the relations of property, competing claims may be balanced, but any achieved balance may be contested. The religious claim of sacred space does not so much establish clear boundaries as remind us that there must be inviolable spaces and boundaries. Human life would be intolerable and brutal without them.

The idea of a boundary is the correlate of the idea of a space. If a boundary protects those within the walls, whoever builds and controls the walls can exercise extraordinary power and dominate those within, or use the space to extend power outside the walls. The castles along rivers in Europe often stand at strategic points on the slopes of a mountain where the river carves and flows through a mountain pass. The sites were strategic for military and defense purposes, but also for monetary purposes: the location, combined with means of force, permitted the lord or prince to exact fees from all who wished to pass by. Because rivers were the primary means of transport and commerce, a castle in this location had a monopoly position, controlling access between suppliers and markets, the basis for exacting "monopoly rents." When merchants were attracted to this capital space, the population grew, and fortified commercial towns sprang up.

Similarly, the development of sea trade and eventually global trade routes made port cities the new centers of power in a growing world market. Natural location was a capital asset. And as a place on the boundary, it was different kind of "space between," a *location* that controlled access to spaces vital to others. At the same time, *what* was being traded was decisive in matters of control. The Genoese gained world financial ascendancy in the late sixteenth century by investing in and gaining control of gold, silver, and other instruments of exchange (Braudel 1984, 166–69). What was of value—and this was a question both of human needs and of cultural meanings—defined the important spaces, and who had power over them. The force of monopoly control came from both market *location*—a space between—and *what was valued* in the market.

Religious institutions can also stand on the boundaries, and when they do, they may occupy monopoly positions, controlling access to grace, to meaning, and to material wealth. But religious beliefs can also critique boundaries (as Luther did with the doctrine of the "priesthood of all believers"); create boundaries that are protective of persons and groups (as in the Christian doctrine of the *imago dei* present in all human beings); critique finite institutions that, by claiming absolute control of the boundaries, essentially declare a divine right to define sacred space (as in all prophetic critiques of idolatrous claims to power, religious, political, or economic); and

by pointing to the relation of all that exists to God, recovering and nurtur-
ing obscured relational understandings of persons, society, and the natural
environment.

Religion offers interpretations of the spaces and boundaries created by
property arrangements and, in the West, by the associations and relations of
civil society. In a global context, the new spaces and boundaries created by the
ownership model of property often threaten existing religious interpretations
of the social order and the human habitat—the religious interpretations of
"land" in the Middle East offer only one example. It is an open question
whether a global civil society can emerge from these complex intersections of
property and religion, one that can lead to a defensible common sense of what
is inviolable, and to establishing the boundaries and institutions that protect
that inviolability.

Property and Identity in Global Civil Society

In the emerging global political economy, what do, and what should, property
relations protect with regard to the individual person's self-understanding and
identity? And against what does property protect? Cultural differences in
identity and self-understanding preclude any simple answer.

In the Western and especially the American political tradition, property is
intimately connected to individual liberty and to freedom from tyranny. This
liberty looks in two not entirely compatible directions: toward *political* liberty
and toward *economic* liberty. Politically, property creates a space for the individual in which neither the state nor any other person may interfere. John
Locke, whose *First Treatise of Government* is the classic text connecting property to liberty, stated the axioms for his larger argument thus:

> The *Natural Liberty* of Man is to be free from any Superior Power on
> Earth, and not to be under the Will or Legislative Authority of Man,
> but to have only the Law of Nature for his Rule.... This *Freedom*
> from Absolute, Arbitrary Power, is so necessary to, and closely joined
> with a Man's Preservation, that he cannot part with it, but by what
> forfeits his Preservation and Life together. (Locke 1988, §22–4)

From these axiomatic assumptions Locke argued against the absolute (divine)
power of kings or of the state, setting the stage for his argument that all
government is based on the consent of individual persons (who hold property). Property, which Locke understood chiefly as land, provides a *space* that is
inviolable, a space wherein no other person, including especially the state, has
any rights. (In the *First Treatise* Locke argued against Filmer's claim that kings
had inherited from Adam the right of absolute dominion over all the earth
and its inhabitants.) Those who emphasize this aspect of Locke's argument

see property as establishing the indispensable basis for citizenship, for membership in a political society committed to individual liberty and the mutual protection of the citizens' property.

Economically, the right of property is the right to use the property for one's needs and to dispose of the property in any way the owner sees fit, including the right to alienate it through sale or gift. Those who emphasize this aspect of Locke's argument emphasize economic liberty, the freedom to produce and to enter into exchange.

Economic liberty is consistent with property as *ownership*. It is consistent with political liberty insofar as both realize, and are necessary for, the fundamental right to the preservation of life. But political liberty and economic liberty are also vectors tugging in two directions: political liberty depends on the notion that some property is *inalienable*. One cannot alienate what is essential to life (the fundamental right), or that which prevents tyranny. The tension between the political and economic meanings of property is (or was) less acute in an idealized agrarian economy, where land is the paradigm for ownership, where everyone has land—Locke limits the right to property by the proviso that there must be enough left for all—and where owners exchange the fruits of their labor on the land. But in the real and global world, there is no easy harmony of the economic and political aspects of property.

In contemporary Europe and America, most rights offering protections against tyranny and entitlements to the means of life are secured through means other than landownership. Civil rights—political membership—are protected in the United States by the Constitution and the Bill of Rights. Rights to livelihood—so-called economic rights—are secured, if at all, by labor unions, home ownership, strong tenant rights, contracts guaranteeing tenure of employment, universal health plans, and the like, all relatively firmly established in the welfare states of Europe. But that all of these are far from guaranteed for a massive portion of the population of the United States indicates how far our own property regime is from realizing Locke's vision of property and liberty. If Locke's vision were to be realized in the United States, we would need to interpret it along the lines of Cowboy Bob Montgomery, a professor at the University of Texas who was accused in the 1950s of being a communist. When asked by a state politician whether he believed in private property, he answered, "Senator, I believe in private property so much that I think everyone in the state of Texas ought to have some" (Folbre 2001, 182). Or, given that ownership does not secure all the rights implied in Locke's conception, we would have to establish universal entitlements to health care, dwelling, and food, among other things.

But the individual liberty of the Anglo-American tradition is not a self-evident model for self-understanding and identity in the rest of the world. Moreover, self-understanding and identity—including liberal identity—are *formed* in relationships and spaces: families, tribes, communities, religious institutions, schools. One of the gross weaknesses of liberal thought in the Lockean tradition is its failure to offer an account of identity formation—fully formed free adults simply drop out of the sky, ready to appropriate property through their labor.

But it is possible to rescue a notion of freedom from tyranny, and of property's role in securing freedom, without subscribing to the full liberal account of the self. Like John Locke, Amartya Sen argues that freedom requires certain basic goods. These goods—Sen calls them "capabilities for flourishing"—are multidimensional and deeply social in nature. They include physical goods such as food and clothing, less tangible goods such as access to education and to the bases of social membership, freedom from violence, and freedom from preventable diseases. "The exercise of freedom is mediated by values" (Sen 2000, 9). Variations between communities in what is valued affect both the meaning of freedom and the degree of freedom that a person can actually exercise (Sen 2000, introduction and 88). The task is to identify sources of "unfreedom," those things that deprive people of capabilities, both relatively (with regard to their immediate context) and absolutely (in comparison to other human beings around the world) (Sen 2000, 22). The list of sources of unfreedom is long and complex, but it would be one task of participants in a global civil society to identify them and to create the spaces and boundaries to protect the freedoms and capabilities for flourishing.

Given the multiplicity of what people have reason to value in the cultural diversity of the global order, that task is daunting. Nevertheless, I venture the following points based on the argument so far:

(1) Freedom as an effective universal value must have roots in, and then be linked back to, local cultures and meanings. Locke's assumption of the inviolability of each person is based on the Calvinist doctrine of the *imago dei* impressed on each human being. This Christian teaching is at least a contributing factor in the articulation of the modern doctrine of human rights expressed in the UN Universal Declaration of Human Rights. The widespread acceptance of the declaration by the nations of the world creates a formal condition exerting continuing pressure on various political and economic structures to realize the civil and economic rights in legal and institutional structures. But the efficacy of this pressure, and the social forms emerging from it, will depend on the discovery of congruence between the formal commitment and the values and commitments present in a variety of religious and cultural traditions. (See Abdullahi An-Na'im's chapter on Islam and civil society in this volume as an example of work contributing to this end.)

(2) The efficacy of a universal commitment to human rights will depend equally on the actual development of laws and institutions establishing entitlements by creating spaces of inviolability and drawing the boundaries around them. This is the concrete institutional task of civil society. To take one example: Slum/Shack Dwellers International is a global network of

agencies and movements committed to securing and protecting adequate housing for the poor—the right to dwelling associated with property—in the face of an assault on their housing from the forces of globalization (Patel, Burra, and D'Cruz 2001). There are uncounted numbers of global agencies, nongovernmental organizations, and other movements, many of them religious or with religious affiliation, engaged in similar work, that is, aimed at securing entitlements typically connected to property rights.

But the securing of any one or several of these will not secure all. Moreover, if the formation of selves and identity requires community and space—space free from the domination of forms of power external to the community—the big question is, What forms of community will be decisive in forming selves in the new global context? Since all attempts to establish entitlements and mutual obligations in an emerging global society involve distributions of power—relations of property—the question is whether organizing efforts and spaces for formation will be effective in the face of the major forms of property and power now shaping globalization.

(3) If—and here follow several critical conditionals—the property rights being promoted as part of globalization entail a model of ownership understood chiefly in economic terms; if the forms of new global property are chiefly the instruments and structures of advanced capitalism with unlimited mobility and tremendous power; and if there is no tradition of political democracy and citizenship or of a bureaucratic state apparatus dedicated to securing economic rights, it is virtually certain that in newer, developing economies the emerging property regime will be destructive of local property arrangements and the forms of membership and identity they secure. The new property forms will also dominate spaces of identity formation. If the only alternative the new regimes offer is individual liberty, they will do little or nothing to secure either liberty or membership in a new social order capable of giving shape to globalization rather than being shaped by globalization. The Archies had the U.S. Constitution, a highly developed system of law on property rights, and a system of justice—including activist watchdog institutions and lawyers—to defend their property and their sense of who they were. Absent all these, local meanings, identities, property arrangements, and space for identity formation will almost surely be dominated by the "arbitrary power" of new forms of tyranny. In short, if "the exercise of freedom is mediated by values," the spaces for coming together to decide what we *should* value will be difficult either to form or to protect.

Property and the Ordering of Human Relations

In an idealized civil society, property arrangements structure entitlements, duties, and mutual responsibilities that represent a common social vision;

they also secure sufficient equality to permit voice in giving ongoing articulation to that vision. Some form of equality is a precondition for freedom and human capability; poverty and inequality are two great sources of unfreedom (Sen 2000, chaps. 4, 6). For the same reasons, the idea of civil society presses toward democracy.

But both civil society and democracy have historically required bounded spaces. The boundaries both determine who is to be counted as an equal member and help to structure the relations of property. Globalization threatens traditional boundaries while creating new ones. Insofar as globalization is driven by economic forces, including especially the flow of capital in pursuit of new resources, cheaper labor, and new markets for consumption, global economic institutions aim at removing all barriers to capital flow and trade—the vision of a "world without borders" and the target of protests against the World Trade Organization, the International Monetary Fund, and the World Bank. But capital is a form of property and therefore also requires bounded space, metaphorically and physically, and these new boundaries form the citadels of power.

In this environment, inequality exists on multiple *levels*: between capital-rich and capital-poor nations; between rich and poor within nation-states; and across the demographic sectors of new global cities. Inequality also takes multiple *forms*, involving not only the resources necessary for physical life—food, housing, health care—but also access to capital institutions, to knowledge, and to community structures that create "social capital," the social habits essential for modern forms of life, including the capabilities for political participation and democracy. There is no single focal point for thinking about equality and inequality, nor a single set of relationships for structuring social order. The relations that make for inequality or that might create equality cross borders and have multiple dimensions.

Religious rejections of globalization originate in the crumbling of walls that protect cultural identity and social and religious values, as well as in the perceived threat posed by the increased porosity of geographic and demographic borders. Jubilee 2000 and other global interfaith efforts aimed at international debt relief have struggled against new forms of international capital enslavement. Churches formed by liberation theologies (themselves hybrids of European and local meanings) in Latin America, Korea, and Africa resist the real impoverishment of people, the destruction of local ways of life, and the commercialization of culture. In various ways—some rejecting, some aimed at reform—religious groups have identified and opposed the worst excesses of global capitalism.

Constructing a new *civitas*, however, requires more than the identification of injustice and resistance to either threat or oppression. It requires constructing new property relations, new entitlements correlated with mutual obligations and responsibilities, that institutionalize equality. It also requires the building of social trust. Both of these in turn will depend on a common vision of the social order, the contours and lineaments of a global *civitas*.

If such a vision emerges, and new systems of entitlements, obligations, and mutual responsibilities come into being to express that vision, it will surely evolve from plural sources and at multiple social levels over a long period of time: a multidimensional constellation of local experiments and initiatives in ownership and production; international alliances for "fair trade" (putting producers and consumers in more direct contact); legal transformations protecting rights; attention to the cultural specifics of creating spaces for education, health, and other requisites of human trust and freedom.

There is a radical implication of the analysis I have offered thus far: these initiatives will evolve into something like a vision for a world *civitas* only if capital and its institutions become far more bound to geographic and demographic spaces than they currently are. Return to Nissan and Mississippi: Nissan is a capital institution, making a capital investment. But the new capital growing from that investment is fed by countless streams of input: taxpayer money directly in subsidies, indirectly in the creation of infrastructure; the labor of those who build and then work there; the legal and administrative framework and know-how of the State of Mississippi; the American consumer market; nature itself, in the form of land, energy, and other natural resources, and as a "sink" for energy and other waste disposal; and more. Repeat this exercise for the formation of the capital Nissan brings to the process—which would include technological knowledge often made possible by public funding of education and research—and we get some picture of the complexity of sources for capital formation.

Moreover, if property is an ordering of both entitlements *and* obligations, the property relations of capital represented by Nissan are radically asymmetrical. Legally, Nissan has primary obligations to shareholders (and creditors) and, through taxes (some waived in this case) to the state. Contractually, it has obligations to labor and suppliers and customers, but these are short-term. The other property relations are protected weakly, if at all, by law and have no direct claim on the capital—Nissan claims entitlements without symmetrically reciprocating responsibilities. Just as Nissan can choose to build a plant in Mississippi, it can choose to close the plant and leave with the capital. There is no enduring responsibility to the local community, no accountability, no matter how much the community has invested in it.

This is the central ambiguity of capital: capital is needed, essential for human flourishing. Because it is needed, it claims and is able to exact entitlements of many sorts from local and national governments. But the range of obligations it recognizes in its modern forms is narrow—indeed, as narrow as it can arrange. Capital and its institutions—the main forms of property in globalization—systematically escape local control. That is, capital systematically avoids being shaped into part of a social vision that allocates and distributes power, specifying both entitlements and enduring responsibility. Market capitalism dismantles boundaries and walls precisely because they represents ways of holding capital accountable to the relations that nurtured its growth.

In this sense, property in its modern capital forms presents a curious paradox: on one side it is without location, without boundaries, occupying no particular space and committed to no particular identity. As such, it seems itself a kind of "universal" entity, virtually godlike in status. But it is a false universality because the universality embraces none of the particular elements connected to it, bearing no enduring relationship to the particular human and natural sources of its composition. It claims entitlements but no responsibilities.

At the same time, capital constantly reorganizes the world, drawing new boundaries and restructuring social relations suitable to its own needs. Consider the global city. The energies of global capital have divided new global urban areas into distinct and increasingly separate residential areas paralleling distinct forms of work, each of which is itself a "city." The UN Report on global cities identifies five subcities: (1) the luxury city of those who make decisions about capital and development; (2) the gentrified city of professionals, managers, technicians, and college professors; (3) the suburban city of families of workers and managers in new manufacturing centers; (4) the tenement city of lower-paid workers and unskilled providers of service; and (5) the abandoned city of the very poor (United Nations 2001, 34). Physically and geographically, the ecological barriers separating these "cities" within the city make virtually impossible the formations of spaces and publics common to all. The separate zones block communication between the elite groups of global civil society and the agencies and movements working in other sectors to resist the elites. This urban ecological separation represents the deeper divide: capital institutions' property relations extend chiefly through the global channels of transportation and communication; they are not fundamentally accountable to the culture and social order in which they happen to reside for any given time.

I would argue that constructing the property relations adequate to the world(s) of globalization requires a high degree of local (read: urban, regional, national) control of capital, an accurate accounting of the sources of capital, and legal delineations of the responsibilities of capital institutions to local communities and cultures. Such accountability entails mutual relations of entitlements and obligation. These in turn require participation and voice on the part of the broadest possible number of those affected by the institution— some form of the "socialization" of capital. If civil society is the space where people debate and decide on the values that "mediate the exercise of freedoms," the dominating forces of capital must not be permitted to draw the boundaries of human spaces. They must be required to inhabit the same space with others, to join with others in negotiating the boundaries and relationships of that space, and to accept all the obligations entailed in these relationships.

The objection will be raised, as it always has been, that such control of capital creates inefficiencies. But efficiency is always relative to a specified *goal*. If the goal is simply unbridled growth, the objection may hold (bracketing concerns for long-term inefficiencies caused by environmental damage). And if the preceding analysis is correct, unbridled growth is an irrational goal. If the goal is, instead, to find a common vision of the global *civitas*, current patterns of accountability are not simply inefficient but destructive. In the absence of common space, common culture, and mutual obligations and trust, the only alternative is the commercialization of culture—cultural critics call this "Disneyfication" (United Nations 2001, 38)—as a "vision" to occupy and coordinate human time and space outside the workplace, and to provide aspirations for the poor.

Ordering the Human Relation to the Natural Environment

In recent years, a handful of multinational corporations have quietly bought up water rights across the globe, basically controlling the distribution rights to water for thousands of municipalities. Vivendi Universal, a French company known chiefly for its vast control of media, was until recently one of the largest, providing water services to more than 110 million persons and industries (including metropolitan Atlanta) in over 100 countries (*New York Times* 2002). Just behind the largest corporations are hundreds of smaller companies competing to control global water supplies. With population growth and increasing industrial and agricultural use, water has become an ever-scarcer resource. The battle over the control of water has been called a battle for "Blue Gold" (Barlow and Clarke 2002; Gleick 2000; Rothfeder 2001; De Villiers 2000), and the World Bank has said, "The wars of the next century will be about water." Fresh water, the paradigm abundant and therefore free common good in economic literature, has become a scarce commodity.

The irony of Blue Gold throws into bold relief the understanding of nature that has been prominent in much of Western culture and especially in economic thought. The roots lie in early modern characterizations of land and nature, and John Locke once again provides a deftly etched picture. Having posited that the Earth is given in common for all to use, he must account for how we appropriate portions of the Earth as our own property. For this he offers his famous labor theory of appropriation. Of the several accounts Locke gives of *what* we appropriate through labor, the example of water recurs several times:

> Though the Water running in the Fountain be every ones, yet who can doubt, but that in the Pitcher is his only who drew it out?

His *labour* hath taken it out of the hands of Nature, where it was
common, and belong'd equally to all her Children, and *hath* thereby
appropriated it to himself. (Locke 1988, §29)

A short time later he makes the explicit analogy of water and land, calling
them "perfectly the same":

No Body could think himself injur'd by the drinking of another Man,
though he took a good Draught, who had a whole River of the
same Water left him to quench his thirst. And the Case of Land and
Water, where there is enough of both, is perfectly the same. (Locke
1988, §33)

Locke makes two critical assumptions: the first is that both water and land
are so abundant that there is enough for all. Property so conceived is non-
coercive because it deprives no one of a similar right. His second assumption
is that land or Earth, like water, has no variation. This not only makes more
plausible his claim that there is enough land, or Earth's resources, for everyone but, by rendering land the same everywhere, it makes land—standing
in for all the resources and complexity of the Earth's ecosystem—*fungible*, a
commodity.

Locke's view of land and Earth's resources has been the common view
in most political economic thought since Adam Smith (with Malthusians a
dissenting tradition). Land conceived as one of the three inputs of production
(land, labor, capital) reduces the entire world of nature, the ecosystem with all
its fragile complexity, nothing more than a collection of fungible commodities
to be exploited for human use without cost to other human beings and
without cost—without harm—to the ecosystem itself. The human relationship to the Earth and the ecosystem becomes a commodity relationship, re-
placing Locke's theological metaphor of nature as a gift of God.

The struggle for Blue Gold is only the tip of a massive iceberg of the
commodification of nature. With all resources essential to human life—water,
food, clean air—increasingly scarce, and with the advances of science and
technology, there has been a rush to stake out property claims, in the sense of
ownership, to virtually every conceivable aspect of the physical world. One
major battleground in this "gold rush" is for intellectual property rights over
an immense range of natural resources. DuPont, a U.S.-based chemical giant,
"has filed approximately 150 applications for patents on genetic resources over
the past ten years with the European Patent Office" (Greenpeace 2001b).
Other corporations hold patents over the DNA codes of whole groups of
people, or even of individuals (Allen 2000). Monsanto, a huge multinational
company in seeds, food, and agribusiness generally, patents its own seeds;
develops sterile hybrids ("seed mules"), forcing farmers to by new seeds

annually from Monsanto; has sought patents (filing in more than one hundred countries) on the genetic characteristics of wild and cultivated soybeans in China (Greenpeace 2001a); and has also, according to some reports, developed plans to enter the market in buying rights to water supply and distribution. It this latter plan is carried out, Monsanto would effectively control the entire food chain in some parts of the world. Although many of these plans have met with resistance from both activist groups and government agencies, the goal of establishing increasing control over resources vital to human survival is clear.

There are two overlapping issues here: one is the issue of monopoly and the ability to extract monopoly rents over scarce resources—Vivendi and Monsanto as modern versions of the castles of medieval Europe or the Genoese in the sixteenth century—establishing a wall and then building a fortified gate on it to control access to resources essential for human life. The other is the question of the *meaning* of the resources, the understanding of the relationship between human beings and the environment in a context where environmental destruction proceeds at a pace seemingly outstripping the human capacity to control it.

The monopoly problem can be attacked from classical economic theory: monopoly rents are inefficient and should be disallowed. But my argument in the preceding section is much more radical: it would not permit capital institutions to create and to occupy the walls defining the human habitat. The understanding of the human place in relation to the natural environment is a question of deciding what we value, and how we value it, and why. With respect to ideas of property, the question is what portions of the natural order may be properly owned and freely exchanged, and what not.

There is no single, "right" interpretation of the natural order. But all the world religions—and most other religious traditions—understand nature in ways that rule out absolute ownership and commodification. Even though actual practices often betray these understandings, religion has the potential to play a powerful role in interpreting the natural human habitat. And the environmental crisis connected to globalization may serve as a catalyst for fruitful interreligious dialogue and possible cooperation in opposition to commodification and ownership. At the same time, many other voices will be involved in this global dialogue, each representing a particular interpretation of the human relation to nature.

The challenge is to forge some common agreements, if not on the full vision at least pragmatically, on ordering the human relation to the physical environment. And while critics of international property rights in seeds, water rights, and genetic codes frame the issue in terms of divergent moral groundings (including national sovereignty, the interpretation of DNA structures and vital portions of the food chain as "commons," religious convictions on the sacredness of nature), they show substantial common ground in the resistance to rights of private ownership and commodification. In all cases, private ownership is rejected as the *primary* way of ordering the human relation to the natural environment: capital institutions may not themselves create this order and then occupy the boundaries they create.

There is some empirical evidence supporting hope that the environmental crisis will be a catalyst for global dialogue and pragmatic consensus. It has already generated wide-ranging proposals, from the Treaty Initiative to Share the Genetic Commons that grew out of the Porto Allegro conference of NGOs in February 2002 (which draws analogies with the Law of the Seas Treaty), to proposals for international carbon dioxide taxes (taxing the largest producers of carbon dioxide to provide revenue for protecting rain forests). But the international accords necessary for such agreement require cooperation among the governments of nation-states and with international agencies, and the sheer complexity and competing interests render the needed common vision and accords difficult. Add to this the extraordinary power of capital institutions, and "war over water" may be the reality.

Summary Observations

(1) Based on a definition of civil society as "forms of association and interaction in which a plurality of human ends is ordered relatively peacefully," I have argued that an analysis of property relations can contribute to our understanding of the ongoing tension between conflict and harmony always present in civil society. I have used this analysis of property to delineate the multiple dimensions of conflict in globalization.

(2) The picture that emerges is one of a fragmentation of the entitlements and responsibilities historically associated with property in the West. The entitlements forming identity, securing membership in a civil order, and ordering the relationship to the natural environment continue to intersect, but the dimensions of ordering they represent have become increasingly variegated and complex. While this fragmentation has long been under way in advanced capitalist societies, it is accelerated and complexified in a global context.

(3) I have used the metaphor of space to illuminate the intersection of the ordering done by property and the ordering done by religious beliefs and practices. Property orders the human habitat in its multiple dimensions. Religion interprets that same habitat, sometimes legitimating, sometimes delegitimating the property arrangement. Both create spaces of protection, areas declared inviolable, free from tyranny. And both can be sources of domination and tyranny, and of conflict and chaos.

(4) If global civil society is to have meaning and efficacy in the direction of creating spaces for enhancing human freedom and the civil resolution of

conflict, it will need to address all the dimensions ordered by property. A major question is whether the movements and institutions associated with a global civil society—religious and secular—will work at cross-purposes, or whether they will evolve in a direction that permits some common vision of what it is people value, what needs protection, what kind of spaces and boundaries are needed. On any plausible interpretation of the complexity of factors involved, the evolution of a common vision will have plural roots.

(5) If religion interprets the whole human habitat, it potentially addresses all three dimensions of property relations and hence could play a major role in seeing these together rather than separately. But insofar as religious institutions and movements identify with or focus on only one of these dimensions—for example, on creating spaces for identity and self-understanding—they may ignore fundamental sources of unfreedom in the other dimensions, working at cross-purposes with those attending to other sources of unfreedom and permitting other, more powerful institutions to shape the human habitat.

(6) Insofar as property in modern capitalism—based on and promoting the model of ownership—recognizes no boundaries external to its own dynamics and needs (the point is as old as Marx), it is best understood as a "quasi-religious" force. Recognizing no sacred space, it both shapes and interprets the human habitat in all its dimensions, the true "mind" (Marx again) of globalization. It follows, I think, that an emerging civil society has two possibilities: either it will be shaped by and subservient to this property form and its religious usurpations; or it will bring capital under its control, which is to say, bring it within the spaces created by civil society, making capital fully accountable to the human and natural ecologies from which it draws its energies.

(7) It follows that economic and market institutions should not be ruled out as members of civil society in principle or by definition, even though it may be argued that with their current power they in fact control the boundaries and dominate civil space rather than being accountable within it. But the task is nevertheless to transform economic institutions, to "secularize" and "civilize" them by bringing them within the arena of accountable relations. Market exchange remains one of the most important mechanisms for the peaceful harmonization of plural ends *within* civil society; but the exchanges can only be just—and freedom protected—if property relations are just and the market bounded (Gunnemann 1985; Walzer 1983). Markets and capital must be bounded by and accountable to civil society.

(8) Political structures remain key players because government alone has the power to create law, shape property relations, and control capital. Global civil society, like classical civil society, appropriately occupies a space between persons living out either private or local purposes and larger governing structures. It is the space where people debate and decide what they have good reason to value together, and through this to influence government and law.

(9) By interpreting the human habitat, religion plays a major role in shaping those debates and decisions. At its worst, religion is but an extension of human power and pride, creating spaces and boundaries of unfreedom. At its best—and I realize the ambiguities of this value judgment—religion insists on the inviolability and interdependence of all human beings. In its sanctification of certain spaces as sacred, religion reminds citizens in the global *civitas* of the limits of human power in all its forms. In its affirmation of the natural habitat as divine gift, or mystery, or manifestation of divine glory, religion is a source for limiting and civilizing the powers that threaten life itself.

BIBLIOGRAPHY

ABC News, April 2, 2002. http://abcnews.go.com/sections/wnt/DailyNews/ nissano20402.html. Accessed April 5, 2002.

Allen, Arthur. 2000. "Who Owns Your DNA?" *Salon*, March 7. http://www .salon.com/health/feature/2000/03/07/genetic_test. Accessed June 28, 2004.

Barlow, Maude, and Tony Clarke. 2002. *Blue Gold: The Fight to Stop the Corporate Theft of the World's Water*. New York: New Press.

Braudel, Fernand. 1984. *The Perspective of the World*. London: Collins.

Chambers, Simone, and Will Kymlicka. 2002. *Alternative Conceptions of Civil Society*. Princeton, NJ: Princeton University Press.

De Villiers. 2000. *Water: The Fate of Our Most Precious Resource*. New York: Houghton Mifflin.

Folbre, Nancy. 2001. *The Invisible Heart: Economics and Family Values*. New York: New Press.

Gleick, Peter H. 2000. *The World's Water 2000–2001: The Biennial Report on Freshwater Resources (World's Water, 2000–2001)*. New York: Island Press.

Greenpeace. 2001a. "Greenpeace Attacks Monsanto's Biopiracy Plans." Press release, October 22, 2001. http://archive.greenpeace.org/majordomo/index-press -releases/1999/msg00295.html. Accessed June 28, 2004.

Greenpeace. 2001b. "Ratification Urgently Needed for Crucial Treaty on Genetic Resources." Press release, November 5, 2001. http://archive.greenpeace.org/ geneng/highlights/pat/FAO_4.htm#top. Accessed June 28, 2004.

Gunnemann, Jon P. 1985. "Capitalism and Commutative Justice." *1985 Annual of the Society of Christian Ethics*, 101–22. Washington, DC: Georgetown University Press, Society of Christian Ethics.

Ignatieff, Michael. 2002. "Mission Possible?" *New York Review of Books*, December 19, 73–74.

Ladd, Donna. 2002. *Donna Ladd Page*, "Mississippi Log." http://www.donnaladd.com/ misslog.html. Accessed April 10, 2002 (page no longer accessible, June 2004).

Locke, John. 1988. *Two Treatises of Government*. Ed. Peter Laslett. Cambridge: Cambridge University Press.

Nedelsky, Jennifer S. 1993. "Reconceiving Rights as Relationship." *Review of Constitutional Studies/Revue d'étude constitutionelles* 1:1–26.

New York Times. 2002. "As Multinationals Run the Taps, Anger Rises over Water Sold for Profit." August 26, Sec. A, p. 7.

Patel, Sheela, Sundar Burra, and Celine D'Cruz. 2001. "Slum/Shack Dwellers International (SDI)—Foundations to Treetops." *Environment and Urbanization* 13 (2): 45–59.

Rieff, David. 2002. *A Bed for the Night: Humanitarianism in Crisis.* New York: Simon and Schuster.

Rothfeder, Jeff. 2001. *Every Drop for Sale: Our Desperate Battle over Water.* New York: J. P. Tarcher.

Seligman, Adam B. 1992. *The Idea of Civil Society.* New York: Free Press.

Sen, Amartya Kumar. 2000. *Development as Freedom.* New York: Anchor Books, Random House.

Singer, Joseph William. 2000. *Entitlement: The Paradoxes of Property.* New Haven, CT: Yale University Press.

Underkuffler, Laura S. 1990. "On Property: An Essay." *100 Yale Law Journal* 100:127–48.

Underkuffler-Freund, Laura S. 1996. "Property: A Special Right." *Notre Dame Law Review* 71:1033–47.

United Nations Centre for Human Settlements (Habitat). 2001. *Cities in a Globalizing World: Global Report on Human Settlements 2001.* London: Earthscan Publications.

Walzer, Michael. 1983. "Money and Commodities." In *Spheres of Justice,* 95–128. New York: Basic Books.

———. 2002. "Equality and Civil Society." In *Alternative Conceptions of Civil Society,* edited by Simone Chambers and Will Kymlicka, 34–49. Princeton, NJ: Princeton University Press.

6

Religious Rejections of Globalization

Frank J. Lechner

Since it was first staged in Porto Alegre, Brazil, in 2001, the World Social Forum (WSF) has assumed a central role in the growing anti-globalization movement. Designed as a counterpoint to the World Economic Forum in Davos, the WSF has amplified the voices of globalization critics. Annually bringing together numerous groups from around the globe, it has served to link their efforts as part of a single movement. For all the differences among the participants, at the sessions held thus far they fervently contributed to the ritual denunciation of the ills of globalization and united behind a grand new vision, summed up in the slogan "another world is possible." But while the first installments of the forum were held on the campus of a Catholic university and a group representing Brazilian bishops was among the organizers, specifically religious voices were inconspicuous. The "other world" envisioned at the meeting, as reflected in the statement of principles issued at the first forum (WSF, 2001) and a subsequent charter proposed by the organizers, had no transcendent aura. As the WSF has become a key node in and symbolic focus of the opposition to globalization in its various guises, which itself has become one of the most vibrant sectors in global civil society, religion appears to play at best a minor role in this sector. Religious responses to globalization seem to contribute little to the overall globalization critique that is evolving in such venues. By examining those hitherto neglected religious responses in some detail, this chapter aims to provide a more complete picture of the evolving global critique of globalization and thereby to clarify one key element in global civil society.

The WSF, one could object after this introduction, is only one event among many. Since it is dominated by left-leaning activists, its secularist thrust does not convey an accurate view of this movement sector as a whole. Yet more comprehensive, academic reviews of global civil society confirm the impression left by Porto Alegre. For example, *Global Civil Society 2001* (Anheier, Glasius, and Kaldor 2001), which quite exhaustively catalogs a wide range of nongovernmental activity, reviews overall religious involvement in less than one page. Its analyses of particular movements within civil society rarely refer to religious groups, and when they do, as in the case of groups opposed to financial inequity (in chapter 3), this becomes an exception that proves the rule. If we broaden our perspective still further to encompass advocacy networks that are not directly engaged in critiques of globalization, but still part of the underlying WSF coalition, we again find few traces of religious involvement. Among the leading "activists beyond borders" working on issues such as human rights, the environment, and women's rights, identifiably religious actors are mostly missing (Keck and Sikkink 1998). Their networks contain hardly any religious nodes. Examining the "politics of resistance" against globalization (Gills 2000), another group of authors finds religious participation barely deserves mention; a single chapter on Islamic critiques is the lone exception (Pasha 2000). A collection of readings on the "global backlash" contains no readings pertaining to religious critiques or activism, lists religion in its index only in conjunction with labor rights, and includes only one article referring to religious influence in the antidebt movement (Broad 2002). According to all such accounts, entire swaths of global civil society, and critical responses to globalization in particular, seem to evolve along secular lines.

The apparent religious silence at the WSF and in global civil society is surprising for several reasons. If by civil society we mean all those forms of voluntary association outside of state and market, then religion constitutes the largest segment of global civil society. The Roman Catholic Church alone counts more members than all global advocacy networks combined. It is surprising, then, that religious association receives little attention in conventional overviews of civil society. But students of civil society could respond that they still adequately capture the absence of religious involvement in at least several civil society sectors. If this is the case, then it is surprising that religion should be so confined that the overall strength of global religion has no bearing on the crystallization of global concern about globalization. To this secular analysts could reply that globalization as a secular process calls for secular critique, so that globalization largely lies beyond religious purview. But this, too, would be surprising, for historically religious traditions have actively addressed the problems of the world. More recently and concretely, religious groups have been active in such "worldly" transnational efforts as the antinuclear/peace movement, and the Catholic Church is often credited with being at the vanguard of the "global human rights revolution" (Casanova

2001, 433). Given such precedent, if globalization is now widely regarded as the fount of problems of meaning and justice, then the absence of religious responses is puzzling.

Serious students of religion, by contrast with most civil society activists and observers, in fact have expected a much stronger religious voice on matters of globalization. As sociologists of religion have argued (Robertson 1992), religion as the authoritative source of comprehensive worldviews is bound to be intimately involved in debate about the direction of globalization. Insofar as globalization intensifies social problems already present in advanced industrial societies, religious contributions to discourse about such problems should become more salient (Beckford 1990). As a "disadvantaged modality" in global society, distinctively holistic religion should be a fruitful source of antisystemic activity addressing the "residual" problems of globalizing institutions (Beyer 1994, 104–5). Questions of meaning raised by globalization should thus provoke at least some religious responses. Why, then, do religious rejections of globalization seem to matter so little?

In this chapter, I propose to make these puzzles less puzzling by offering a double corrective. To WSF-style activists and civil society observers, I suggest that in the struggle about globalization religious actors are more important and religious voices more articulate than many have realized. I will show that and how at least some religious activists and leaders have been involved. To colleagues in the sociological study of religion, I suggest that expectations of religious involvement need qualification. While religious contributions do have specific strengths, their impact is contingent on other developments in global civil society. Empirically, this analysis yields a more detailed picture of the directions that "religious rejections of globalization" take. Analytically, it sheds light on the relative significance of religion in the formation of global civil society or at least one sector thereof.

To organize my argument, I distinguish three, empirically overlapping, aspects of global civil society. First, following Scholte's definition of global civil society as transborder civic activity that aims to change social order and focuses on global issues (Scholte 2000, 177, 180), I treat it as a form of movement activity by organizations independent of markets and states. Among the wide range of movements that constitute the antiglobalization front, one stands out for the prominence of religious contributions, namely, the movement to cancel the foreign debts of certain developing countries. Catholic and Protestant influences dominate in this effort. I argue that religion proved significant in framing the issues and organizing a coalition, but that with regard to the overall antiglobalization movement this role is the exception that proves the rule. The case thus only partially confirms Beyer's expectations about the distinct role of religion in addressing globally residual problems. Second, following Scholte's (2000) point that the expansion of global civil society depends on "global thinking," I focus on civil society as a form of discourse framing common concerns, that is, on the content of what gets discussed in the global public sphere. Here I analyze some specifically religious contributions to critiques of globalization. These contributions are not limited to Christian voices, and there is no single religious line. Yet in some respects religious critiques converge with the thrust of secular antiglobalization discourse. While religious contributions to the discourse have become more salient, as Beckford leads us to expect, they are not uniquely influential in identifying problems of globalization. Third, in a more philosophical vein, we can also regard civil society as a "moral project" (Thomas 2002, 50–52) or as a normative concept (Anheier, Glasius, and Kaldor 2001, 224), one that captures the emerging "awareness of a common framework of worldwide human society" (M. Shaw, quoted in Anheier, Glasius and Kaldor 2001, 224). On this score, religious conceptions of alternatives to ongoing globalization are especially pertinent, not only as rejections of dominant globalization models but also as ways of framing the normative core of civil society itself. In keeping with Robertson's expectations, a number of religious traditions are actively engaged in framing new world orders. A complete analysis of all "religious rejections" of globalization would of course have to delve into a range of different traditions, but as this brief synopsis already indicates, the scope of this chapter is more modest than the Weberian title suggests. It focuses on what I call the "global religious left," using selective references to the Islam*ist* "global religious right" for comparative perspective. Drawing a distinction between reformist and more radical "rejections" of globalization, the analysis leads to a paradoxical point about religion in global civil society: religious actions and voices that operate within a largely secular world order and seem subordinate to secular rules and concerns are nevertheless vital in undergirding a critical, independent "third sector" at a time when the very possibility of such a sector within world society is under challenge. This represents a case in which, in more ways than one, potentially divisive religion may have a civilizing effect.

Religion and Antiglobalization Activism: The Case of the Debt Movement

On November 6, 2000, President Bill Clinton signed a foreign aid bill fully funding debt relief for poor countries. The Office of Social Development and World Peace of the U.S. Catholic Bishops (2000) hailed the occasion by cheering, "We won on debt!" It attributed the "tremendous victory" to a grassroots campaign led by religious groups that had been based "on a quixotic belief that we could turn the Scriptural call of Jubilee into concrete commitments on debt by our government." Describing the range of activities in which Catholics had been involved, the office took some credit for the U.S. Catholic community, which had "played a central role in this victory." Somewhat later,

Presbyterians similarly noted their role in advocating debt forgiveness and their participation at all levels of the campaign from the beginning (Silverstein 2001). "Jubilee 2000," commented Rev. Gary Cook, "demonstrated once again the power of scripture to shape what we often call 'secular history.' "

The Clinton signing represented the culmination of an intense global campaign. When third world countries became burdened with debt in the 1980s, a loose group of nongovernmental organizations (NGOs) began to call for restructuring and forgiveness of external debt. In the United States, these included shifting and short-lived coalitions, such as the Debt Crisis Network (1985–90); in Europe, Oxfam and the European Network on Debt and Development (1990–) took a leading role, complemented by an African sister organization, AFRODAD, since 1994 (Donnelly 2000). But by the mid-1990s, it is fair to say, their actions had produced few tangible results. The effort to resolve the debt crisis only became a global movement when disparate efforts were connected as part of one campaign. Jubilee 2000, formed as a charitable trust in the United Kingdom in 1996, became the spearhead of a transnational advocacy network that used a specifically religious rationale to frame debt as a moral issue, organized the efforts of numerous groups into a single campaign, devised forms of protest drawing attention to their cause, exerted pressure on authorities to take effective action, and helped to turn debt relief into a tool of broader antiglobalization advocacy.

Religious organizations had addressed the debt issue prior to 1996. For example, the Pontifical Commission on Justice and Peace wrote in 1987 that "debt servicing cannot be met at the price of asphyxiation of a country's economy, and no government can morally demand of its people privations incompatible with human dignity" (cited in Donnelly 2000, 2). In the United States a 1989 study by the Presbyterian Church–USA entitled *The Third World Debt Dilemma* and a report by U.S. Catholic bishops, *Relieving Third World Debt: A Call for Co-responsibility, Justice and Solidarity*, were similarly critical. Church groups were among the debt activists since the 1980s. But religious involvement changed when a number of people applied the biblical concept of Jubilee to the problem of third world debt. Among the first to do so was the political scientist Martin Dent, who founded a group called Jubilee 2000 at Keele University in 1990, drawing on parallels with the nineteenth-century anti-slavery movement (Dent and Peters 1999, Chap. 3). After he met Bill Peters, a retired diplomat who headed the United Society for the Propagation of the Gospel, at a seminar in 1993, they joined forces to found Jubilee 2000 as a national organization in 1996. Though they quickly drew in secular groups, such as the UK Debt Crisis Network, the UK coordinator noted that "church groups were the initiators of the campaign and this has allowed it to spread very rapidly" (Rosen 1999). Their impetus came from the biblical injunction in Leviticus (25:10) to "hallow the fiftieth year and proclaim liberty throughout all the land to all the inhabitants thereof: it shall be a jubilee to you; and you shall return every man to his possession, and you shall return every man to his family." As Pope John Paul II interpreted the injunction in a message to a Jubilee 2000 gathering in 1999, the original Jubilee "was a time in which the entire community was called to make efforts to restore to human relations the original harmony which God had given to his creation and which sinfulness had damaged. It was a time to remember that the world we share is not ours but is a gift of God's love. During the Jubilee, the burdens that oppressed and excluded the weakest members of society were to be removed, so that all could share the hope of a new beginning in harmony, according to God's design" (John Paul II 1999b). Debt forgiveness thus fit divine design.

This new religious impetus behind the antidebt movement proved critical in several ways. By framing a policy issue as one of moral urgency, Jubilee created a new form of symbolic politics (Keck and Sikkink 1998, 16). It called upon new symbols and stories to make sense of an otherwise fairly arcane problem for a broad audience in developed countries, thus generating a certain amount of grassroots support (Donnelly 2000, 31). It provided a broad enough rationale to bundle the efforts of numerous groups under one ideological umbrella, thereby breathing new life into the old, loose network (Donnelly 2000, 3). The frame became the movement's primary resource, as it operated on a small budget (Busby 2001, 11). The religious factor was a necessary element in the success of the movement on two dimensions conventionally used to judge its success, namely, agenda setting and network building (Donnelly 2000, 31). The religious dimension of the campaign was decisive in very specific ways as well. When rock star Bono lobbied Senator Jesse Helms on behalf of debt relief legislation, his scriptural references were his trump card, moving Helms to unaccustomed tears (Busby 2001). Without Helms's support, the Clinton signing might not have occurred. That signing was only one of the movement's tangible results, since the G-7 had already adopted a debt reduction plan in Cologne in 1999.

More than debt relief alone was at stake in the antidebt movement. For radical elements in the Jubilee coalition, especially in southern Africa and Central America, legislative reform and cooperation with financial institutions presented a problem because they ultimately wanted to question inequitable approaches to development and repudiate debt altogether (Rosen 1999; Bond 2001; Broad 2002, 5.6). As one activist put it in Cologne, "Not just debt, but the whole neo-liberal model. Not just debt cancellation, but reparation for neo-colonial repression" (Donnelly 2000, 29). The leader of Jubilee UK recognized the radicals' "all-encompassing demands" as key elements in Jubilee's "progressive radical movement" opposing neoliberalism as based on "absolute freedom of capital to go wherever it wants and do whatever it wishes. What cancellation of debts would do is curtail those freedoms. It would make borrowing and lending more difficult" (Rosen 1999). Though she did not spell out how making borrowing and lending more difficult would help the interests of

the poor she presumably had at heart, her message was symbolically important, since it indicated the broader thrust of the antidebt movement as part
of rising antiglobalization activism. As one Catholic theologian commented,
"The hidden blessing of the debt crisis may be that it will force the world
toward a new global order, and there is more than a hint of this vision in the
realistically ambitious goals of Jubilee 2000" (Rosen 1999). The World
Council of Churches affirmed the point at its Harare meeting in 1998: "We are
called.... to seek new ways to break the stranglehold of debt, to redress its
consequences, and ensure that debt crises will never recur. This can only be
achieved through a new, just global order" (WCC 1998). The Jubilee vision, in
short, "challenges the triumphant claims of global capitalism" (Mihevc 1999).

Should we infer from this that since religion played a key role in antidebt
mobilization, and this mobilization was one platform for antiglobalization
activism, religion does contribute significantly to the antiglobalization movement after all? Catholic and Presbyterian activists have reason to see the debt
campaign as evidence of the power of religious forces. The religious role in the
antidebt movement provides a counterpoint to overly secular perceptions of the
antiglobalization movement. In reframing the debt campaign, religious activists did not simply reject the inequities of globalization but prophetically
imagined an alternative global policy. Yet the Jubilee record does not demonstrate that the "secular history" of antiglobalization activism is predominantly shaped by religious forces, and it would be wrong to overestimate
religious influence in this sector of civil society. The antidebt advocacy network
was one among others; within the network, many groups combined for different reasons. The Jubilee record does not support the most ambitious self-
interpretations among religious activists, since the course of secular history
was altered only slightly. The record also casts some doubt on Beyer's claim
that religion will concern itself with "residual" matters left unattended by
other global systems, for although Jubilee did heighten global concern about
debt, such concern had already been building in secular circles and also in
international financial institutions. The campaign may well have been successful to the extent that it amplified the thrust of debt reassessments in the
halls of government and lending institutions.

Notwithstanding the enthusiasm of Catholics and Presbyterians about
their accomplishments, many activists are not as sanguine about the results of
their efforts. At the WSF in Porto Alegre, the "International Peoples' Tribunal," convened by groups including the Jubilee South Brazil Campaign, issued a withering verdict (Social Justice Committee 2002). Denouncing the
debt as part of a profoundly unjust economic system, it declared external debt
"fraudulent, illegitimate and the cause of the loss of national sovereignty and
the quality of life of the majority of the population of the South." Not satisfied
with mere reforms, it called for tough action against the perpetrators of
economic crimes, in the interest of "justice of the peoples of the South and for

all humanity." If nothing else, the verdict confirmed what some Jubilee leaders also argued, namely, that action for debt relief was part of a larger critique of globalization. In this, too, religious actors have participated.

Religion and Antiglobalization Discourse

On his visit to Cuba in 1998, Pope John Paul II delivered a homily at a mass on José Martí Square in Havana in which he criticized, not surprisingly, systems that "presumed to relegate religion to the merely private sphere" and thereby prevented the expression of faith in the context of public life. Turning to a subject that must have been more congenial to Cuban authorities, he went on to lament "the resurgence of a certain *capitalist neoliberalism* which subordinates the human person to *blind market forces* and conditions the development of peoples on those forces" (John Paul II 1998, emphasis in original). The process was wrong in principle and unjust in practice: "From its centres of power, such neoliberalism often places unbearable burdens upon less favored countries. Hence, at times *unsustainable economic programmes* are imposed on nations as a condition for further assistance. In the international community, we thus see *a small number of countries growing exceedingly rich at the cost of the increasing impoverishment of a great number of other countries*; as a result the wealthy grow ever wealthier, while the poor grow ever poorer." The church, said the pope, has the answer in its "social Gospel," which *"sets before the world a new justice."* Read against the background of the pope's overall stance toward globalization, his critique of neoliberal market expansion in Havana was hardly intended to placate his hosts. Rather, it was one instance among many in which he applied key tenets of Catholic social ethics to the evils of globalization. As the U.S. bishops have noted, "The Third World debt problem exemplifies a recurring theme of recent Catholic teaching: the meaning and moral implications of increasing global interdependence" (U.S. Catholic Bishops 1999).

The rejection of ongoing globalization by the Catholic Church under John Paul's leadership has some distinctive features. There is something ironic about the anticapitalist rhetoric of a pope whose opposition to liberation theology was a hallmark of his early tenure. There is also a note of ambivalence in statements about the world economy that recognize ways it can become a force for good. In key respects, however, the pope's message converges with that of other Christian critics. These, in turn, converge with the central thrust of secular globalization critiques.

To describe John Paul II's stance toward globalization as a form of "rejection" at first blush might seem an overstatement. Apart from issues such as celibacy and abortion, church doctrine tends to be formulated in nuanced terms. With regard to globalization, the pope has noted that it is a "complex and rapidly evolving phenomenon," one that is in itself "neither good nor bad" (John Paul II 2001a), but "basically ambivalent" (2001b). Its ethical implications "can be positive or negative" (John Paul II, 1999a). Yet his Havana homily reflects a persistent and unmistakably critical diagnosis of globalization. The hallmark of globalization, from the point of view of Catholic social teaching, is that "*the market economy seems to have conquered virtually the entire world*," enshrining "a kind of triumph of the market and its logic" (John Paul II 2001a, emphasis in original). But if globalization is "ruled merely by the laws of the market to suit the powerful, the consequences cannot but be negative" (1999a). Among the negative consequences are "the absolutizing of the economy, unemployment, the reduction and deterioration of public services, the destruction of the environment and natural resources, the growing distance between rich and poor, unfair competition which puts the poor nations in a situation of ever-increasing inferiority" (1999a).

"Absolutizing" the economy is intrinsically wrong, the pope explained in the encyclical *Centesimus Annus*:

> If economic life is absolutized, if the production and consumption of goods becomes the entire of social life and society's only value, the reason is to be found not so much in the economic system itself as in the fact that the entire socio-cultural system, by ignoring the ethical and religious dimension has been weakened and ends up limiting itself to the production of goods and services alone.... Economic freedom is only one element of human freedom. When it becomes autonomous, when man is seen more as a producer or consumer of goods than as a subject, who produces and consumes in order to live, then economic freedom loses its necessary relationship to the human person and ends up by alienating and oppressing him. (John Paul II 1991)

From the pope's point of view, the consequences are equally worrisome. First, since markets are imperfect, they are bound to leave certain needs unsatisfied—the needs of those without the skills or resources to access the market, collective needs not amenable to market solutions, and immaterial human needs that cannot be left to its mercy (1991, nn. 33, 34, 40; 2001b). Second, without appropriate regulation by the community, markets do not serve the common good; when commerce knows no borders, the absence of such controls especially risks new forms of exclusion and marginalization (1991, n. 35; 2001a). Third, left to their own devices, world markets exacerbate inequality, as the pope noted in Havana; as wealth becomes more concentrated, weaker states lose sovereignty, thereby lagging farther behind (2001b). Fourth, "One of the Church's concerns about globalization is that is has quickly become a cultural phenomenon. *The market as an exchange mechanism has become the medium of a new culture*" (2001a, emphasis in original).

The Catholic concerns echo in similar statements by the World Council of Churches. Globalization was a key item on the WCC's agenda at its fiftieth anniversary meeting in 1998 in Harare, Zimbabwe. The meeting's official report, *Together on the Way* (WCC 1998), treats globalization as a threat. "The vision behind globalization," it says, "includes a competing vision to the Christian commitment to oikoumene." Like the pope, the WCC describes that vision as the "neo-liberal" faith in competitive markets and individual consumption that is bound to produce a "graceless system that renders people surplus and abandons them if they cannot compete with the powerful few" (WCC 1998, ch. 8.4). The consequences of this lamentable "unilateral domination of economic and cultural globalization" are once again dire as well: it contributes to "the erosion of the nation-state, undermines social cohesion, and intensifies the conquest of nature in a merciless attack on the integrity of creation." While new technologies may produce some "potentially positive" consequences, the reality of "unequal distribution of power and wealth, of poverty and exclusion" makes a mockery of neoliberal expectations. "The life of the people is made more vulnerable and insecure than ever before," the WCC declares. Growing interdependence also leads to greater concentration of power, fuels fragmentation of the social fabric of societies, and causes people to lose their cultural identity (8.4). "We have compromised our own convictions," a preparatory report concluded (WCC 1998). "We acknowledge the temptation we have to strive for our own inclusion in a world which has space for a privileged few." To resist the temptation, *Together on the Way* calls on churches to resist globalization.

After Harare, this became a common theme in the WCC's work. For example, the statement "Economic, Social and Cultural Rights" by a WCC commission to the UN Human Rights Commission (WCC 2001b) laments the way "traditional life styles of self-reliance have been undermined by integrating people into a market culture," opposes the "increasingly dominant role of economic mechanisms" and the concomitant concentration of power in the hands of a global elite, and cites with approval a WCC workshop's definition of the project of globalization as "a link in the chain of series of exploitative actions to appropriate the resources of the countries of the South by the countries of the North—first through slave trade then through colonialism and now through neo-liberalism." Thus, the WCC approach to globalization is even more emphatically negative than the pope's.

What, if anything, does this common Christian critique add to antiglobalization discourse? In many ways, Christian responses resemble their secular counterparts, as exemplified by WSF and other activists' statements and by kindred academic critiques (e.g., WSF 2001, 2002; IFG 2002; Broad 2002; Falk 1999). In both kinds of antiglobalization discourse, globalization is of course subjected to ritual denunciation. Both treat neoliberalism and the "absolutizing" of the world economy as the source of all troubles. Those troubles comprise a highly standardized list: decline of nations, undermining of cultures, ecological devastation, and so on. Inequality of wealth and power is the key shared concern. All sides of the oppositional discourse emphasize advocacy over analysis, attributing assorted problems, from poverty to fragmentation, to vaguely characterized globalization in broad-brush fashion. To be sure, motives differ (few WSF activists claimed to be moved by faith), and so does language (the pope's cautious phrases are mild by WSF standards). But the overall picture is one of convergence: with regard to globalization, the global religious Left and the global secular Left speak with one voice. Even as the problems of globalization become more salient from certain religious perspectives, as Beckford expected, the actual religious discourse largely follows a pattern set by secular critics. There is no single global problem that is defined mainly by religious actors from religious standpoints. Of course, this does not mean that religious voices therefore do not matter; it simply implies that they are only part of an intricate cacophony.

One could object that focusing on Christian antiglobalization discourse is misleading: many Muslims, after all, do define global problems from a distinctly religious perspective, and Islam does not converge in the manner just described. The objection is a bit too broad, since some liberal Muslim critics of globalization fit the general pattern. To give only one example, Chandra Muzaffar of the International Movement for a Just World takes globalization to task for aggravating global disparities (Muzaffar 1998). The objection is also too broad because, for all the various aims of movements across the Islamic world, they do embody a form of resistance to neoliberal globalization (Pasha 2000), to "colonization through the marketplace" (Sachedina 2002). It would therefore be a mistake to portray Islam as wholly divorced from non-Islamic globalization discourse. Yet it is fair to say that "widespread Muslim misgivings about globalization" have less to do with "an expression of opposition to global capitalism" and more with a "cry of desperation" about the perceived effects of Western dominance on Muslim societies (Kuran 2002). As the imam of the Masjid al Haram in Saudi Arabia put it, citing Qur'anic verses, globalization is a new form of colonialism, and Islam is its main victim (Hameed 2002). Islamist critiques of globalization, to generalize for the sake of brevity, stand out in several ways. The neocolonialist theme in Hameed's statement, though present in other responses, is a more prominent part of an explicitly anti-Western diagnosis of globalization. Like their counterparts on the religious Left, Islamists are concerned about the inequities of globalization, but their focus is obviously on the suffering of Muslims. To overcome the vices of neoliberal globalization they propose a new form of Islamic economics (Kuran 1997). More than other globalization critics, they challenge the existing secular order: "The revolt against the West is in substance a revolt against the dominant world order" (Tibi 2002: 84; cf. Murden 2002; Sachedina 2002). To put it mildly, globalization problems have become far more salient from an Islamist perspective in recent decades. Whether this is quite the kind of salience that fits Beckford's expectation, which draws on a Simmelian view of the autonomy of religion under conditions of secularization, is questionable.

Since the thrust and context of Islamist globalization critiques differ so greatly from others, their absence from standard WSF-style discourse is not surprising. Islamists obviously do not participate in the convergence noted earlier, yet they have one thing in common with their counterparts of the global religious Left. Beckford (1990, 12) already pointed to religion "striving for holistic contributions that defy compartmentalization of problems." As the next section shows, this is evident in several religious visions of the globe and their symbolic attempts to change civil society itself.

Religion and Alternative Visions of Globalization

When the Dalai Lama gave the commencement address at Emory University in 1998, the program quoted him as saying that "compassion can be put into practice if one recognizes the fact that every human being is a member of humanity and the human family regardless of differences in religion, culture, color, and creed. Deep down there is no difference." Like WSF activists, the Dalai Lama obviously believes "another world is possible," but the texture of his vision subtly differs from theirs. Of course, he has different reasons, and therefore justifies his worldview in different terms. His concern is not with any single issue; it is more encompassing. The core value at stake for him is not one that found expression at the WSF.

While the theme of compassion is characteristic of the Dalai Lama, his portrayal of humanity as a single family that strives for universal respect regardless of differences resonates with similar statements from leaders of other traditions. The convergence of religious views on a minimally shared global vision constitutes a distinctive contribution to the way civil society grapples with the implications of globalization. In the evolution of global civil society as a normative order, religious actors stand out in several ways. More explicitly than secular participants in civil society, they focus on the unity of the world, the interests of humanity, and the importance of accommodating cultural difference. Though some traditions show intriguing convergence in the framing of their actual worldviews, there is no full consensus.

One reason the pope described globalization as "ambivalent" (2001b) is that "for all its risks," it also "offers exceptional and promising opportunities, precisely with a view to enabling humanity to become a single family, built on the values of justice, equity and solidarity" (John Paul II 2000). Catholic leaders in fact see the universal church participating in globalization to advance a global moral project. This project starts from "the awareness that humanity, however much marred by sin, hatred and violence, is called by God to be *a single family*" (2000, emphasis in original). While the family metaphor resembles the Dalai Lama's, in the Catholic view the unity of humanity ultimately derives from common dependence on God, which provides a "new model of the unity of the human race" (John Paul II quoted in Martin 2001, 84). This conception of unity has moral implications. As the *Catechism* (n. 1911) states, "The unity of the human family, embracing people who enjoy equal natural dignity, implies a universal common good. The good calls for an organisation of the community of nations able to provide for the different needs of man." More concretely, "In our linked and limited world, loving our neighbor has global implications . . . and continuing participation in the body of Christ call[s] us to action for 'the least among us' without regard for boundaries or borders" (U.S. Catholic Bishops 1997). The whole church is called to global solidarity and responsibility. "To give positive bearings to developing globalization, a deep commitment to building a 'globalization of solidarity' is needed by means of a new culture, new norms and new institutions at national and international levels" (John Paul II 2001b). Central among the new norms, Catholic leaders have repeatedly stressed, must be universal respect for the human person (Martin 2000, 88–89), and here, again, Catholic views resonate with those of Buddhists.

The World Council of Churches, as we have seen, opposes the vision that currently undergirds globalization. It puts forth a competing one: that of the "oikoumene, the unity of humankind and the whole inhabited earth" (WCC 1998, 5.3). In *Together on the Way* it said that "the logic of globalization needs to be challenged by an alternative way of life of community in diversity" (5.3). The "catholicity" of the church may provide a model for the desired plurality within a single ecumenical movement (8.4). If the earth is to be treated as "home," then "people in very different situations and contexts" must "practice faith in solidarity and affirm life on earth together" (8.4). A subsequent WCC consultation in Fiji elaborated the vision of unity. Representatives of Pacific churches offered the "Island of Hope" as a "metaphor for the wholeness of life" (WCC 2001a). In contrast to prevailing features of globalization, that wholeness should be marked by "generosity, reciprocity and the sharing of communal resources." The meeting offered the churches as "places of sharing" on a journey toward "an alternative global family." In this way, the WCC brings to bear its traditional ecumenical commitments on the formulation of alternatives to globalization.

The statements briefly reviewed here fit sociological expectations. As Beyer and Beckford suggested, these views of world order are distinctly transcendent, holistic, and inclusive. As Robertson argued, it is precisely in formulating alternative views of world order that religion itself becomes more salient. The content of these views specifically fits one the images of world order he described. Buddhist, Catholic, and Protestant leaders portray a world Robertson captured in the image of "Global Gemeinschaft II." As repeated use of the family metaphor illustrates, a hallmark of this image is that *"only in terms of a fully globewide community per se can there be a global order"* (Robertson 1992, 78, emphasis in original). In such a community, as the preceding statements also suggest, distinct traditions will somehow be united in a new harmony (Robertson 1992, 81). The global religious Left envisions this harmony in an essentially ecumenical way, allowing for the expression of differences, and it therefore adopts what Robertson has called a "decentralized" version of the gemeinschaft model. Though globewide unity and solidarity ultimately must be rooted in common dependence on God, certainly in the Catholic view this decentralized version legitimates civil society as the critical sphere in which many actors from many different standpoints can work on reforming the thrust of globalization. While the rationale for the vision is obviously religious, it does not seek to define global civil society in exclusively religious terms. Civil society must make room for religion but should not itself be a religious edifice.

Liberal Muslims share this vision. They advocate a version of Islam that contributes to an inclusive "international morality" centered on human rights (Tibi 2002). They say that "in the midst of globalization, you have to reassert [Islam's] essence. And that is its universalism, its inclusiveness, its accommodative attitude" (Muzaffar 2002). Yet, notwithstanding Sachedina's claim about a "growing majority . . . in search of a tolerant creed to further human understanding beyond an exclusionary, intolerant, and even militantly institutional religiosity" (Sachedina 2002, 28), among contemporary Muslims such voices appear to be in the minority. More common is the Islamist version of "Global Gemeinschaft II," that is, the vision of an alternative Islamic world order brought about by defeat of the unbelievers, the spread of the *umma*, the return to first principles, and the reorganization of society under the sharia. As Sayyid Qutb envisioned, by ending the dominance of the West the "Islamic world revolution" will enable Islam to "take over and lead" (Tibi 2002, xv, 89, 187). Whereas the global religious Left vests its hopes in the vigor of global civil society, Islamists delegitimate any activity that does not serve the Islamic cause and therefore aim to eliminate civil society properly speaking. Whereas the global religious Left seeks to reform world order through civil society, the Islamist global religious Right seeks to transform world order by eradicating it. Religion thus has its greatest bearing on global civil society in the articulation of such contrasting visions, one sustaining a viable global "third sector," another challenging the very concept. The future viability of global civil society may well depend on which vision prevails.

Conclusions

With examples pertaining to three dimensions of global civil society, this chapter has tried to assess contrasting claims about the relative significance of religious contributions. While correcting misperceptions about the absence of religion in one sector of civil society, it also has qualified sociological expectations about the capacity of religious actors to address residual social issues, to define new problems, and to articulate compelling new visions of world order. Though to religious actors the overall argument may present a too-constricted view of religious influence, in this concluding section I also want stress a point that reinforces the significance of religion in global civil society. By contrast with Islamist responses to globalization, those I have broadly characterized as part of the global religious Left provide crucial legitimation for a free, independent global civil society critically engaged in reform from within the existing world order. Their prophetic participation in specific movements, their convergence with secular critics, and their articulation of a new form of global community infuse global civil society with symbolic support. In this way, they both "engage the demands" of global civil society and by "their very agency become implicated" in it (Thomas 2001, 532). Religious voices may have been absent at the WSF, but in the battle of ideas about civil society as a normative order the viability of WSF-style activism depends in part on the strength of larger visions that resonate with religious publics.

To retrace the steps in the argument briefly, by framing the moral rationale for debt relief and exerting political pressure, Christian groups played an important role in the antidebt campaign. They mobilized a previously disjointed network and set a clear policy agenda. They helped to achieve leverage with public officials and international organizations. Religious involvement was necessary to the success achieved by the Jubilee campaign. Yet religious groups did not create the issue; they constituted only one segment of the overall movement. Among those resisting the effects of globalization, the movement itself was a small part of a very large set of advocacy groups and networks. In the expanding scope of the antiglobalization movement, few "residual" issues are untouched, left for religious figures to address. Of course, religious actors are active in various branches of other, largely secular advocacy networks; there is precedent for their actions in earlier movements, such as the peace movement, that may be applied again in other areas. But the thrust of this argument is that the significance of religious involvement in the antidebt movement is the exception that proves the rule. We cannot infer from it that global civil society affords ample opportunity to religious groups to shape agendas and mobilize movements. The religious absence from the WSF is no accident.

Religious action on the debt crisis was related to broader religious critiques of the larger thrust of globalization. These critiques offer some distinct themes and rationales but, at least in the Christian orbit, converge to a large degree with the emerging antiglobalization consensus among progressive secular activists. On globalization the religious and secular Left tend to speak with one voice. Both reject, above all, the neoliberal version of globalization.

As a practical matter, this convergence is important in its own right, since it contributes to the crystallization of a certain kind of globalization critique. Yet because secular antiglobalization discourse proceeds on its own terms and encompasses many global problems, it is difficult to infer that the increased salience of religion in this overall discourse also demonstrates a distinctive religious capacity for the identification of new problems.

Religious critiques do stand out by the way they are embedded in larger visions of another world order. From their distinctively transcendent and "holistic" vantage point, religious voices, notably those on the religious Left, have begun to address the moral issues not addressed in equally systematic fashion by secular globalization critics. They call for universal solidarity, demand global religious freedom, inspire care for God's creation, and express the interests of humanity as such. Of course, the very slogan of the antiglobalization forces, "Another world is possible," indicates that secular thinkers do not hesitate to think in such grand terms. But even the brief examples given here suggest that religious actors think about "another world" more literally and precisely, guided by more definite, though still vague and general, overarching worldviews. In this way, ostensible rejection of globalization begins to turn into reformist reconstruction.

This chapter has shown that religious actors like the ones on the global religious Left studied here have not only been participants in civil society activism and contributors to civil society discourse but have also begun to articulate normative rationales for the structuring of civil society itself. As activists and critics, their relative significance has been modest in a rapidly expanding arena; in the rethinking of world order itself, their role is potentially more significant. Yet by their actions and their words, they sustain a lively third sector from which the state system and world markets can be critically addressed. Insofar as they shy away from utopian transformation, they provide a counterpoint to the less-than-civil Islamist rejection of globalization and its attempt at wholesale transformation of world order. If global civil society is to flourish, that attempt at transformation must be resisted, both from within the Islamic tradition (An-Na'im 2002; Hefner 2002; Berger 2003, this volume) and by the larger world religious communities.

NOTE

I am grateful to Alex Hicks, Mark Juergensmeyer, John Simpson, Regina Werum, members of the 2002 Halle faculty seminar and participants in the Sociology Department Fall 2002 seminar for their comments on earlier versions of this chapter, one of which was presented at the annual meeting of the Association for the Sociology of Religion in Chicago, August 2002. Research on this project was supported by the Halle Institute for Global Learning at Emory University. I thank Charles Jones and Velina Petrova for their research assistance.

BIBLIOGRAPHY

An-Na'im, Abdullahi A. 2002. "Religion and Global Civil Society: Inherent Incompatibility or Synergy and Interdependence?" In *Global Civil Society 2002*, edited by Helmut Anheier, Marlies Glasius, and Mary Kaldor, 55–73. Oxford: Oxford University Press.

Anheier, Helmut, Marlies Glasius, and Mary Kaldor, eds. 2001. *Global Civil Society 2001*. Oxford: Oxford University Press.

Beckford, James A. 1990. "The Sociology of Religion and Social Problems." *Sociological Analysis* 51:1–14.

Berger, Peter L. 2003. "Religion and Global Civil Society: An Overview." Paper presented at the Halle Institute Conference on Religion and Global Civil Society, Emory University, Atlanta.

Beyer, Peter. 1994. *Religion and Globalization*. London: Sage.

Bond, Patrick. 2001. "Strategy and Self-Activity in the Global Justice Movement." Institute for Policy Studies discussion paper. www.irc.org.

Broad, Robin, ed. 2002. *Global Backlash: Citizen Initiatives for a Just World Economy*. Lanham, MD: Rowman and Littlefield.

Busby, Joshua W. 2001. "Bono Made Jesse Helms Cry: International Norms Take-Up and the Jubilee 2000 Campaign for Debt Relief." Paper presented at the American Political Science Association meeting, San Francisco.

Casanova, José. 2001. "Religion, the New Millennium, and Globalization." *Sociology of Religion* 62:415–41.

Dent, Martin, and Bill Peters. 1999. *The Crisis of Poverty and Debt in the Third World*. Aldershot, UK: Ashgate.

Donnelly, Elizabeth A. 2000. "Proclaiming the Jubilee: The Debt and Structural Adjustment Network." Case study for the UN Vision Project on Global Public Policy Networks. www.globalpublicpolicy.net.

Falk, Richard. 1999. *Predatory Globalization: A Critique*. Cambridge: Polity Press.

Gills, Barry K., ed. 2000. *Globalization and the Politics of Resistance*. Houndmills: Macmillan.

Hameed, Saleh bin Abdullah. 2002. News article in Al-sharq Al-awsat. January 25.

Hefner, Robert. 2002. "The Struggle for the Soul of Islam." In *Understanding September 11*, edited by Craig Calhoun, Paul Price, and Ashley Timmer. New York: New Press. Accessed online at etn.sagepub.com/cgi/reprint/4/4/451.

IFG. 2002. "A Better World Is Possible! Alternatives to Economic Globalization." Summary of report by the Alternatives Committee of the International Forum on Globalization. www.ifg.org.

John Paul II, Pope. 1991. *Centesimus Annus*. Encyclical letter. www.vatican.va.

———. 1998. "Homily in the José Martí Square of Havana." www.vatican.va.

———. 1999a. "Ecclesia in America." Post-Synodal Apostolic Exhortation. www.vatican.va.

———. 1999b. "Message of the Holy Father to the Group Jubilee 2000 Debt Campaign." www.vatican.va.

———. 2000. "Message of His Holiness Pope John Paul II for the Celebration of the World Day of Peace." www.vatican.va.

————. 2001a. "Address of the Holy Father to the Pontifical Academy of Social Sciences." April. www.vatican.va.

————. 2001b. "Address of John Paul II to the Members of the Foundation for Ethics and Economics." May. www.vatican.va.

Keck, Margaret E., and Kathryn Sikkink. 1998. *Activists beyond Borders: Advocacy Networks in International Politics*. Ithaca, NY: Cornell University Press.

Kuran, Timur. 1997. "Islamism and Economics: Policy Implications for a Free Society." In *Islam and Public Policy*, edited by Sohrab Behdad and Farhad Nomani, 72–102. Greenwich, CT: JAI Press.

————. 2002. "The Religious Undertow of Muslim Economic Grievances." In *Understanding September 11*, edited by Craig Calhoun, Paul Price, and Ashley Timmer. New York: New Press. Accessed online of etn.sagepub.com/cgi/reprint/4/4/451.

Martin, Diarmuid. 2000. "Globalization in the Social Teaching of the Church." In *The Social Dimensions of Globalisation*, edited by Louis Sabourin (ed.), 82–93. Vatican: Pontifical Academy of Social Sciences.

Mihevc, John. 1999. "Starting from Scratch." *New Internationalist* 312 (May). Accessed online at www.newint.org/issue312/scratch.htm.

Murden, Simon W. 2002. *Islam, the Middle East, and the New Global Hegemony*. Boulder, CO: Lynne Riener.

Muzaffar, Chandra. 1998. "Globalisation and Global Equality." Paper presented at the seminar "Religions and Poverty Eradication," Tokyo. www.just-international.org.

————. 2002. Interview with PBS *Frontline*. www.pbs.org.

Pasha, Mustapha Kamal. 2000. "Globalization, Islam and Resistance." In *Globalization and the Politics of Resistance*, edited by Barry K. Gills, 24–54. Houndmills: Macmillan.

Robertson, Roland. 1992. *Globalization: Social Theory and Global Culture*. London: Sage.

Rosen, Fred. 1999. "Doing Battle against the Debt." *NACLA Report on the Americas*, 33(1): 42–5. July–August. Accessed Internet version: from expanded Academic Index: at http://infotrac.galegroup.com/itw/infomark/654/721/66694058w5/

Sachedina, Abdulaziz. 2002. "Political Islam and the Hegemony of Globalization: A Response to Peter Berger." *Hedgehog Review* 4:21–29.

Scholte, Jan Aart. 2000. "Global Civil Society." In *The Political Economy of Globalization*, edited by Ngaire Woods, 173–201. New York: St. Martin's Press.

Silverstein, Evan. 2001. "Presbyterians Were among Leaders of Jubilee 2000 Debt-Relief Campaign." *Presbyterian News Service*, January 12.

Social Justice Committee. 2002. "Submission to the International People's Tribunal on the Debt." Porto Alegre: World Social Forum. www.s-j-c.net.

Thomas, George M. 2001. "Religion in Global Civil Society." *Sociology of Religion* 62:515–33.

————. 2002. "Religious Movements, World Civil Society, and Social Theory." *Hedgehog Review* 4:50–65.

Tibi, Bassam. 2002. *The Challenge of Fundamentalism: Political Islam and the New World Disorder*. Berkeley: University of California Press.

U.S. Catholic Bishops. 1997. "Called to Global Solidarity: International Challenges for U.S. Parishes." United States Catholic Conference: Office of Social Development and World Peace, Nov. 12. Accessed online at www.parish-without-borders.net/global/2000.htm.

———. 1999. "A Jubilee Call for Debt Forgiveness." Statement by the Administrative Board of the United States Catholic Conference.

———. 2000. "We Won on Debt!!" Statement by the Office of Social Development and World Peace, December.

WCC. 1998. *Together on the Way.* Official Report of the Eighth Assembly of the World Council of Churches, Harare. Accessed online at www.wcc-coe.org/assembly/fprc2ce.html

———. 2001a. "Call to Churches: Resist Economic Globalization!" Office of Communication press update.

———. 2001b. "Economic, Social and Cultural Rights." Statement submitted to UNHCR by the Commission on International Affairs of the World Council of Churches.

WSF. 2001. "Porto Alegre Call for Mobilisation." World Social Forum. www.forumsocialmundial.org.br.

———. 2002. "Porto Alegre II Call of Social Movements." World Social Forum. www.forumsocialmundial.org.br.

7

Religious Antiglobalism

Mark Juergensmeyer

The televised images of the spectacular aerial assaults on New York's World Trade Center on September 11, 2001, stunned an audience around the globe. The world watched as the Twin Towers crumbled into dust in an awesome demonstration of the al Qaeda view of the world. Theirs was a world at war—and global warfare at that—a view that was echoed in the headlines and public pronouncements of America's political leaders in the days following the attack. But what kind of war did this act proclaim? It was not a war between states—Osama bin Laden scarcely commanded a cave, much less a political region—and it was not a contest between military powers. As the United States soon showed in its air strikes in Afghanistan, neither bin Laden nor his Taliban hosts could long withstand America's awesome military might. It was, in a sense, a religious war, in that bin Laden had proclaimed a jihad against America some five years before, and his several prior acts of terrorism—including attacks on U.S. embassies in Africa and an American naval ship in a Yemeni harbor—were attempts to bring that warfare to life. Yet his foe was not another religion. What he despised was nonreligion, the secular values of the West, the aggressive military and economic posture of modern societies, and the regimes of Saudi Arabia and other moderate Muslim states that bin Laden regarded as America's puppets. In that sense the Pentagon and the World Trade Center were apt targets, for they represented the power of the United States in all its military and economic glory.

But the World Trade Center was not just an American symbol. It was a *world* trade center, after all, and a sign of global economic strength. From its twin towers high above Manhattan's Wall Street, its economic tentacles truly had a global reach. Virtually every major financial center was represented in its offices. Its employees came from every corner of the planet. In the lists of the dead that were tallied after the buildings' collapse, citizens from eighty-six different nations were numbered among the victims. In choosing the World Trade Center as a target—twice, as it turned out, once in the less successful bomb attack in 1993 and again in the remarkable September 11 aerial assault—Islamic militants associated with the al Qaeda network showed that the new world order of Western-dominated economic globalization was their ultimate foe.

In an interesting way, the World Trade Center symbolized bin Laden's hatred of a certain kind of globalization. I say "a certain kind," since the al Qaeda network was both modern and transnational in its own way. Its members were often highly sophisticated and technically skilled professionals, and its organization was composed of followers of various nationalities who moved effortlessly from place to place with no obvious nationalist agenda or allegiance. In a sense they were not opposed to globalization, as long as it was of their own design. But they loathed the Western-style modernity that they imagined that secular globalization was forcing upon them.

Some twenty-three years earlier, during the Islamic revolution in Iran, the Ayatollah Khomeini rallied the masses with a similar notion, that America was forcing its economic exploitation, its political institutions, and its secular culture on an unwitting Islamic society. The Ayatollah accused urban Iranians of having succumbed to "Westoxification"—an inebriation of Western culture and ideas. The many strident movements of religious activism that have erupted around the world in the more than two decades following the Iranian revolution have echoed this cry. This anti-Westernism has at heart an opposition to a certain kind of modernism—its secularism, its individualism, its skepticism. Yet, in a curious way, by adopting the technology and financial instruments of modern society—and in some cases of religious nationalism, the modern notion of the nation-state—many of these movements have claimed a kind of modernity on their own behalf.

Understandably, then, these religious movements are ambivalent about modernity—whether it is necessarily Western and always evil. They are also ambivalent about the most recent stage of modernity (or postmodernity): globalization. On the one hand, these movements are reactions to the globalization of Western culture. They are responses to the insufficiencies of what is often touted as the world's global standard: the elements of secular, Westernized urban society that are found not only in the West but also in many parts of the former third world, and which are seen by their detractors as vestiges of colonialism. On the other hand, these religious movements point to alternative modernities with international and supernational aspects of their own. This means that in the future some forms of religious politics will

be global, some will be virulently antiglobal, and yet others will be content
with creating their own alternative nation-states.

Religious Rejection of Globalization

In those parts of the world that for much of the nineteenth and twentieth
centuries were under Western colonial control, economic and cultural globalization has often been perceived as an extension of colonialism. In the latter
half of the twentieth century, political independence did not mean a complete
liberation from European and American colonial powers. New forms of economic and cultural ties were emerging that yoked African, Asian, Middle
Eastern, and Latin American societies to the United States and Europe.

By the 1990s some of these ties had begun to fray. The global economic
market undercut national economies, and the awesome military technology of
the United States and the North Atlantic Treaty Organization (NATO) reduced
national armies to border patrols. More significantly, the rationale for the
Western-style secular nation-state came into question. With the collapse of the
Soviet Union and the postcolonial critique of Western democracy, the secular
basis for the nation-state seemed increasingly open to criticism. In some instances, such as in Yugoslavia, when the ideological glue of secular nationalism began to dissolve, the state fell apart.

The effect of what I have elsewhere called "the loss of faith in secular
nationalism" was devastating (Juergensmeyer 1993). Throughout the world,
it seemed, the old Western-style secular nationalism was subject to question,
and the scholarly community joined in the task of trying to understand the
concept in a post–cold war and transnational era (Connor 1994; Gottlieb 1993;
Kotkin 1994; Smith 1995; Tamir 1993; Young 1993). Part of the reason for
secular nationalism's shaky status was that it was transported to many parts
of the world in the cultural baggage of "the project of modernity" (Habermas
1987, 148)—an ascription to reason and a progressive view of history that
many thought to be obsolete. In a multicultural world where a variety of views
of modernity are in competition, the very concept of a universal model of
secular nationalism became a matter of lively debate.

Globalization challenged the modern Western idea of nationalism in a
variety of ways. These challenges have been varied because globalization is
multifaceted: it includes not only the global reach of transnational businesses
but also their labor supply, currency, and financial instruments. In a broader
sense it also refers to the planetary expansion of media and communications
technology, popular culture, and environmental concerns. Some of the most
intense movements for ethnic and religious nationalism have arisen in nations where local leaders have felt exploited by the global economy—as in Iran
and Egypt—or believe that somehow the benefits of economic globalization

have passed them by. The global shifts in economic and political power that occurred following the breakup of the Soviet Union and the sudden rise and subsequent fall of Japanese and other Asian economies in the past fifteen years have had significant social repercussions. The public sense of insecurity that has come in the wake of these changes has been felt especially in areas economically devastated by the changes, including those nations and regions that had been under the dominance of the Soviet Union.

These shifts led to a crisis of national purpose in less developed nations as well. Leaders such as India's Jawaharlal Nehru, Egypt's Gamal Abdel Nasser, and Iran's Reza Shah Pahlavi once tried to create their own versions of America—or in some cases a cross between America and the Soviet Union. But a new, postcolonial generation no longer believed in the Westernized vision of Nehru, Nasser, or the Shah. Rather, it wanted to complete the process of decolonialization by asserting the legitimacy of their countries' own traditional values in the public sphere and constructing a national identity based on indigenous culture (Chatterjee 1993). This eagerness was made all the more keen when they observed the global media assault of Western music, videos, and films that satellite television beams around the world, and which threatens to obliterate local and traditional forms of cultural expression.

In other cases it has been a different kind of globalization—the emergence of multicultural societies through global diasporas of peoples and cultures, and the suggestion of global military and political control in a "new world order"—that has elicited fear. It is this fear that has been expoited by bin Laden and other Islamic activists, and which made it possible for al Jazeera television and other popular media outlets in the Islamic world to portray America's military response to the September 11 attacks as a bully's crusade rather than the righteous wrath of an injured victim. In some parts of the Muslim world, the post–September 11 U.S. coalition against terrorism was seen as an excuse for expanding America's global reach. The U.S. invasion and occupation of Iraq in 2003 seemed to confirm their worst fears.

Perhaps surprisingly, this image of America's sinister role in creating a new world order of globalization is also feared in some quarters of the West. In the United States, for example, the Christian Identity movement and Christian militia organizations have been fueled by fears of a massive global conspiracy involving liberal American politicians and the United Nations. In Japan a similar conspiracy theory motivated leaders of the Aum Shinrikyo movement to predict a catastrophic World War III, which their nerve gas assault in the Tokyo subways was meant to demonstrate (Asahara 1995).

As far-fetched as the idea of a "new world order" of global control may be, there is some truth to the notion that the integration of societies, communication among disparate peoples, and the globalization of culture have brought the world closer together. Although it is unlikely that a cartel of malicious schemers has designed this global trend, the effect of globalization on local societies and national identities has nonetheless been profound. It has undermined the modern idea of the nation-state by providing nonnational and transnational forms of economic, social, and cultural interaction. The global economic and social ties of the inhabitants of contemporary global cities are intertwined in a way that supersedes the idea of a national social contract—the Enlightenment notion of "peoplehood" as John Lie (2004) describes it. In the Enlightenment view, peoples in particular regions are naturally linked together in a specific nation-state. In a global world it is hard to say where particular regions begin and end. For that matter, in multicultural societies it is hard to say how one should define the "people" of a particular nation.

This is where religion and ethnicity step in to redefine public communities, sometimes forcibly. The fading of the nation-state and the disillusionment with old forms of secular nationalism have produced both the opportunity for new culture-based politics and the need for them. The opportunity has arisen because the old orders seem so weak; and the need for political identity persists because no single alternative form of social cohesion and affiliation has yet appeared to dominate public life the way the nation-state did in the twentieth century. In a curious way, traditional forms of social identity in some cases have helped to rescue one of Western modernity's central themes: the idea of nationhood. In the increasing absence of any other demarcation of national loyalty and commitment, these old staples—religion, ethnicity, and traditional culture—have become resources for national identification. In other cases, the cultural identities are transnational.

The Revolutionary Character of Antiglobalization

In the contemporary political climate, therefore, religious activists have provided a solution to the perceived insufficiencies of Western-style secular politics. As secular ties have begun to unravel in the post-Soviet and postcolonial era, local leaders have searched for new anchors to ground their social identities and political loyalties. What is ideologically significant about these religious movements is their creativity. Although many of them have reached back in history for ancient images and concepts that will give them credibility, theirs are not simply efforts to resuscitate old ideas from the past. They offer contemporary ideologies that meet present-day social and political needs.

In the context of Western modernism this is a revolutionary notion—that indigenous culture can provide the basis for new political ideologies and institutions, including resuscitated forms of the nation-state. The movements that support these views are, therefore, often confrontational and sometimes violent. They reject the intervention of outsiders and their ideologies and, at the risk of being intolerant, pander to their indigenous cultural bases and enforce traditional social boundaries. It is no surprise, then, that they get into trouble with each other and with defenders of the secular state. Yet even such conflicts serve a purpose for the movements: it helps define who they are as a people and who they are not. They are not, for instance, secular modernists.

Since Western-style secular modernism is often targeted as the enemy, that enemy is most easily symbolized by things American. America has taken the brunt of religious and ethnic terrorist attacks in recent years in part because it so aptly symbolizes the transnational secularism that the religious and ethnic nationalists loathe, and in part because America does indeed promote transnational secular values, and it benefits from them. For instance, America has a vested economic and political interest in shoring up the stability of regimes around the world. This often puts the United States in the position of being a defender of autocratic secular governments. Moreover, the United States supports a globalized economy and a secular culture. In a world where villagers in remote corners of the world increasingly have access to MTV, Hollywood movies, and the Internet, the culturally objectionable images and values that have been projected globally have often been American.

So it is understandable that America would be disdained. What is perplexing to many Americans is why their country would be so despised. The demonization of America by many religious groups fits into a process of undermining the legitimacy of secular authority. In doing so, it often appropriates traditional religious images, especially the notion of cosmic war. In such scenarios, competing ethnic and religious groups become foes and scapegoats, and the secular state becomes religion's enemy. Such satanization is aimed at reducing the power of one's opponents and discrediting them. By humiliating them—by making them subhuman—religious activists assert the superiority of their own moral power.

During the early days of the Gulf War in 1991, the Hamas movement issued a communiqué stating that the United States "commands all the forces hostile to Islam and the Muslims," singling out then-president George Bush, who, it claimed, was not only "the leader of the forces of evil" but also "the chief of the false gods."[1] As late as 1997, Iranian politicians, without a trace of hyperbole, could describe America as the "Great Satan." This rhetoric first surfaced in Iran during the early stages of the Islamic revolution when both the Shah and President Jimmy Carter were referred to as Yazid (in this context an "agent of satan"). "All the problems of Iran," the Ayatollah Khomeini elaborated, are "the work of America" (Khomeyni 1977, 3). By this he meant not only political and economic problems but also cultural and intellectual ones, fostered by "the preachers they planted in the religious teaching institutions, the agents they employed in the universities, government educational institutions, and publishing houses, and the Orientalists who work in the service of the imperialist states" (Khomeini 1985, 28). The vastness and power of such a conspiratorial network could only be explained by its supernatural force.

The Global Agenda of Antiglobalists

Although the members of many radical religious groups may appear to fear globalization, what they distrust most are the secular aspects of globalization. They are afraid that global economic forces and cultural values will undercut the legitimacy of their own bases of identity and power. Other aspects of globalization are often perceived by them as neutral or, in some instances, useful for their purposes.

Some groups have a global agenda of their own, a transnational alternative to the modern nation-state system. Increasingly terrorist wars have been waged on an international and transnational scale. The international network of al Qaeda is a case in point. One of its affiliated movements, Gamaa i-Islamiya, literally moved its war against secular powers abroad when its leader, Sheik Omar Abdul Rahman, moved from Egypt to Sudan to Afghanistan to New Jersey. It was from the Jersey City location that his followers organized a bombing attack on the World Trade Center on February 26, 1993, that killed six and injured a thousand more. One of Osama bin Laden's operatives, Ramzi Youssef, who was also convicted of complicity in the 1993 World Trade Center bombing, mastermined the "Bojinka Plot" that would have destroyed a dozen American airliners over the Pacific during the mid-1990s; Youssef moved from place to place throughout the world, including operations in Pakistan and the Philippines. Algerian Muslim activists brought their war against secular Algerian leaders to Paris, where they have been implicated in a series of subway bombings in 1995. Moroccan activists were implicated in the 2004 train bombings in Madrid, Spain. Hassan Turabi in Sudan has been accused of orchestrating Islamic rebellions in a variety of countries, linking Islamic activists in common cause against what is seen as the great satanic power of the secular West. In addition to the acts directly attributed to his leadership, Osama bin Laden, from his encampment in Afghanistan, was alleged to have funded other acts of terrorism conducted by groups around the world.

These worldwide attacks may be seen as skirmishes in a "new Cold War," as I once described it (Juergensmeyer 1993), or, more ominously, a "clash of civilizations," as Samuel Huntington (1996) termed it. It is possible to imagine such a clash if one assumes—as many Muslim activists do—that Islam and other religions are civilizations comparable to the modern West, and that secular nationalism is, in the words of one of the leaders of the Iranian revolution, "a kind of religion" (Banisadr 1981, 40). He went on to explain that it was not only a religion but one peculiar to the West, a point that was echoed by one of the leaders of the Muslim Brotherhood in Egypt (el Arian 1989).

Behind this image of a clash of cultures and civilizations is a certain vision of social reality, one that involves a series of concentric circles. The smallest are families and clans; then come ethnic groups and nations; the largest, and implicitly most important, are religions. Religions, in this sense, are not just bodies of doctrine and communities of believers but shared worldviews and cultural values that span great expanses of time and space: global civilizations. Among these are Islam, Buddhism, and what some who hold this view call "Christendom" or "Western civilization" or "Westernism" (Shitta 1989). The so-called secular cultures of places such as Germany, France, and the United States, in this conceptualization, stand as subsets of Christendom/Western civilization. Similarly Egypt, Iran, Pakistan, and other nations are subsets of Islamic civilization. From this vantage point, it is both a theological and a political error to suggest that Egypt or Iran should be thrust into a Western frame of reference. In this view of the world they are intrinsically part of Islamic, not Western, civilization, and it is an act of imperialism to think of them in any other way. Proponents of Islamic nationalism, therefore, often see themselves as a part of a larger, global encounter between Western, Islamic, and other cultures. This view of a "clash of civilizations" is not confined to the imaginations of Samuel Huntington and a small number of Islamic extremists but underlies much of the political unrest at the dawn of the twenty-first century.

An even more extreme version of this global cultural clash is an apocalyptic one, in which contemporary politics is seen as fulfilling an extraordinary religious vision. Some messianic Jews, for instance, think that the biblical age that will be ushered in at the time of the return of the Messiah is close at hand. It will occur when the biblical lands of the West Bank are returned to Jewish control and when the Jerusalem Temple described in the Bible is restored on its original site—now occupied by a Muslim shrine, the Dome of the Rock. Several of these activists have been implicated in plots to blow up the shrine to hasten the coming of the kingdom. One who served time in prison for his part in such a plot said that the rebuilding of the Temple was not just a national obligation but also a critical moment for the sake of the redemption of the world (Lerner 1995).

Religious activists who embrace traditions such as millenarian Christianity and Shiite Islam, which have a strong sense of the historical fulfillment of prophecy, look toward a religious apocalypse that will usher in a new age. American Christian political activists such as Jerry Falwell and Pat Robertson are animated by the idea that the political agenda of a righteous America will help to usher in an era of global redemption. The leader of Aum Shinrikyo, borrowing Christian ideas from the sixteenth-century French astrologer Nostradamus (Michel de Nostredame), predicted the coming of Armageddon in 1999. Those who survived this World War III—mostly members of his own movement—would create a new society in 2014, led by Aum-trained "saints" (Asahara 1995, 300).

Activists in other religious traditions may see a righteous society being established in a less dramatic manner, but some Sunni Muslims, Hindus, and Buddhists have, in their own ways, articulated hopes for a political fulfillment of a religious society. They believe that "dhammic society can be established on earth," as one activist Buddhist monk in Sri Lanka put it, by creating a religious state (Thero 1991). These forms of religious politics are more than nationalist, therefore, since they envision the world as caught up in a cosmic confrontation, one that will ultimately lead to a peaceful world order constructed by religious nations. The result of this process is a form of global order radically different than secular versions of globalization, yet it is an ideological confrontation on a global scale.

The Future of Religious Antiglobalism

As we have seen, radical religious movements are ambivalent about globalization. To the extent that they are nationalistic, they often oppose the global reach of world government, at least in its secular form. But the more visionary of these movements also at times have their own transnational dimensions, and some dream of world domination shaped in their own ideological images. For this reason we can project at least three different futures for radical revision in a global world: one where religious politics ignore globalization, another where they rail against it, and yet another where they envision their own transnational futures.

Nonglobalization: New Religious States

The goal of some religious activists is the revival of a nation-state that avoids the effects of globalization. Where new religious states have emerged, they tend to be isolationist. In Iran, for instance, the ideology of Islamic nationalism that emerged during and after the 1979 revolution, and that was propounded by the Ayatollah Khomeini and his political theoretician, Ali Shari'ati, was intensely parochial. It was not until some twenty years later that new movements of moderate Islamic politics encouraged Iran's leaders to move out of their self-imposed international isolation (Wright 2000). The religious politics of Afghanistan, especially after Taliban militants seized control in 1995, were even more strongly isolationist. Led by former students of Islamic schools, the religious revolutionaries of the Taliban established a self-contained autocratic state with strict adherence to traditional Islamic codes of behavior (Marsden 1998). Their willingness to harbor Osama bin

Laden and his al Qaeda network led to their obliteration in a hailstorm of American air strikes in October and November 2001.

Other movements of religious nationalism have not been quite as isolationist and extreme, however. In India, when Hindu nationalists in the Bharatiya Janata Party (BJP; "Indian People's Party") came to power in 1998—a regime of religious nationalism that lasted until it was toppled by a resurgent secular Congress Party in 2004—some observers feared that India would become isolated from world opinion and global culture. The testing of nuclear weapons as one of the BJP's first acts in power did little to dispel these apprehensions. But in many other ways, including its openness to economic ties and international relations, the BJP maintained India's interactive role in the world community. Credit for this was due, in part, to the moderate leadership of the BJP prime minister, Atal Bihari Vajpayee, one of the country's most experienced and temperate politicians.

If other movements of religious and ethnic nationalism come to power, will they behave like the Taliban or the BJP? Observers monitor developments in Pakistan, Egypt, Algeria, and elsewhere for signs of antiglobal sentiment should the considerable strength of religious politics in those regions lead to the establishment of religious states. When Abdurrahman Wahid, a Muslim cleric, edged past the daughter of Indonesia's founder in 1999 to become for several years the country's prime minister, observers wondered whether he would usher in an era of religious nationalism. In this case, however, the fears were unfounded. The actions of his government showed Wahid's brand of Islam to be moderate and tolerant, and committed to bringing Indonesia into the world community and the global economic market.

Guerrilla Antiglobalism

In other regions of the world it is not the creation of new religious states that is at issue but the breakdown of old secular states with no clear political alternative. In some instances, religious and ethnic activists have contributed to these anarchic conditions. In the former Yugoslavia, for instance, the bloodshed in Bosnia and Kosovo was caused by the collapse of civil order as much as by the efforts to create new ethnic and religious regions. Because these situations have been threats to world order, they have provoked the intervention of international forces such as NATO and the United Nations.

It is, however, world order that many of these religious and ethnic nationalists oppose. In Iraq, for instance, Islamic insurgents opposed to the U.S. occupation have targeted not only the U.S. military and its Iraqi supporters but also members of the UN Mission and international relief agencies. The Iraqi insurgents, like religious activists elsewhere in the world, have imagined the United States and the UN to be agents of an international conspiracy, one that they think is hell-bent on forming a homogeneous world society and a global police state. It was this specter—graphically described in the novel *The Turner Diaries*—that one of the novel's greatest fans, Timothy McVeigh, had hoped to forestall by attacking a symbol of federal control in America's heartland. His assault on the Oklahoma City federal building and other terrorist attacks around the world were acts of what might be considered "guerrilla antiglobalism."

The largest guerrilla band of antiglobalists has been the *jihadi* network associated with Osama bin Laden's al Qaeda organization. Its vendetta against secular globalization led by America and the secular West has led to the bombing of U.S. embassies in Africa in 1998 and the USS *Cole* in Yemen in 2000, the catastrophic events of September 11, 2001, the attack on Bali nightclubs in 2002, the Madrid train bombings in 2004, and numerous attacks associated with the U.S. occupation of Iraq.

These acts were performances of power often meant for a wide television audience, especially the Middle Eastern audience that receives its news through al Jazeera television. The purpose of such dramatic terrorist acts was to demonstrate to the Muslim public that there was a vast global war going on, one in which America and its form of globalization represented the forces of evil, while the forces of good were identified as a transnational Muslim populace led by heroic figures such as Osama bin Laden. His many videotaped appearances on al Jazeera television portrayed a gaunt, renunciatory figure leading his battles in exile. Sometimes he was portrayed standing in front of a cave—a picture that was likely intended to invoke in the Muslim imagination an image of the Prophet himself during his time in the desert. Bin Laden pictured himself as a guerrilla antiglobalist in a cosmic war, one with enduring sacred dimensions.

Transnational Alliances

The far-flung reaches of the *jihadi* movement also exemplify another dimension of contemporary religious activists: their transnationality. Members of the al Qaeda cells have come from such places as Algeria, Egypt, Palestine, and Pakistan, as well as bin Laden's native Saudi Arabia. Many were forged together into a multinational fighting force in the crucible of the Afghan war against the Soviets. The political goals of this pluralist fighting force were not to create any one specific Islamic state—even the Taliban's Afghanistan was ultimately dispensable—but to project an image, albeit an inchoate one, of a transnational Muslim empire. In one of his videotaped diatribes after the onset of the American bombing in Afghanistan in October 2001, bin Laden refers to the "eighty years" that the West had oppressed the Middle East. The time frame is significant because it seems to refer to a signal event in the Muslim world in the 1920s, the final ending of the Ottoman Empire. In an interesting way, bin Laden was invoking the images of old Muslim dynasties in projecting his own image of an alternative globalization, one of Muslim values and presumably his own imperial leadership.

In addition to bin Laden's imaginary alternative globalization, there is the real possibility of religious states bonding together to create their own transnational entities, a sort of Muslim version of the European Union, for instance. According to one theory of global Islamic politics that circulated in Egypt in the 1980s and 1990s, local movements of Muslim politics were meant to be only the first step in creating a larger Islamic political entity—a consortium of contiguous Muslim nations. In this scenario, religious nationalism would be the precursor of religious transnationalism.

Yet another kind of transnational association of religious and ethnic activists has developed in the global diasporas of cultures and peoples. Osama bin Laden's al Qaeda network illustrated this form of transnationality. Members of the movement had taken up long-term residence and infiltrated the socially disgruntled immigrant Muslim communities of Germany, Belgium, Spain, Great Britain, Canada, and the United States. In the al Qaeda network, as in other patterns of expatriate association, rapid Internet communication technologies allow members of ethnic and religious communities to maintain a close association despite their geographic dispersion.

Increasingly open and password-protected Web sites have been the meeting places for new religiously militant cyber communities around the world. These "e-mail ethnicities" are not limited by political boundaries or national authorities. Expatriate members of separatist communities—such as India's Sikhs, and both Sinhalese and Tamil Sri Lankans—have provided both funding and moral support to their compatriates' causes. In the case of Kurds, their "nation" is spread throughout Europe and the world, united through a variety of modern communications technologies. In some cases these e-mail communities long for a nation-state of their own; in other cases, such as al Qaeda, they are prepared to maintain their nonstate national identities for the indefinite future.

Modernity, Identity, Power, and Globalization

Each of these futures of religious antiglobalism contains a paradoxical relationship between certain forms of globalization and renascent religious activism. It is one of history's ironies that the globalism of culture and the emergence of transnational political and economic institutions enhance the need for local identities. They also create the desire for a more localized form of authority and social accountability.

The crucial problems in an era of globalization are identity and control. The two are linked, in that a loss of a sense of belonging leads to a feeling of powerlessness. At the same time, what has been perceived as a loss of faith in secular nationalism is experienced as a loss of agency as well as identity. For these reasons the assertions of traditional forms of religious identities are linked to attempts to reclaim personal and cultural power. Many of the acts of religious terrorism that have been perpetrated at the beginning of the twenty-first century can be seen as tragic attempts to regain social control through acts of violence. Until there is a surer sense of citizenship in a global order, therefore, religious visions of moral order will continue to appear as attractive though often disruptive solutions to the problems of modernity, identity, and belonging in a global world.

NOTE

1. Hamas communiqué, January 22, 1991, quoted in Jean-François Legrain, "A Defining Moment: Palestinian Islamic Fundamentalism" (Piscatori 1991, 76).

BIBLIOGRAPHY

Anderson, Benedict. 1983. *Imagined Communities: Reflections on the Origin and Spread of Nationalism*. London: Verso.

Asahara, Shoko. 1995. *Disaster Approaches the Land of the Rising Sun: Shoko Asahara's Apocalpytic Predictions*. Tokyo: Aum.

Banisadr, Abolhassan. 1981. *The Fundamental Principles and Precepts of Islamic Government*. Translated by Mohammad R. Ghanoonparvar. Lexington, KY: Mazda.

Barber, Benjamin R. 1995. *Jihad vs. McWorld*. New York: Times Books.

Chatterjee, Partha. 1993. *The Nation and Its Fragments: Colonial and Postcolonial Histories*. Princeton, NJ: Princeton University Press.

Connor, Walker. 1994. *Ethnonationalism: The Quest for Understanding*. Princeton, NJ: Princeton University Press.

el Arian, Essam. 1989. Author's interview with Dr. Essam el Arian, Member of the National Assembly, Cairo, January 11.

Gottlieb, Gidon. 1993. *Nation against State: A New Approach to Ethnic Conflicts and the Decline of Sovereignty*. New York: Council on Foreign Relations.

Habermas, Jurgen. 1987. "Modernity: An Incomplete Project." In *Interpretive Social Science: A Second Look*, edited by Paul Rabinow and William M. Sullivan, 141–156. Berkeley: University of California Press.

Huntington, Samuel P. 1996. *The Clash of Civilizations and the Remaking of World Order*. New York: Simon and Schuster.

Juergensmeyer, Mark. 1993. *The New Cold War? Religious Nationalism Confronts the Secular State*. Berkeley: University of California Press.

———. 2003. *Terror in the Mind of God: The Global Rise of Religious Violence*. 3rd edition. Berkeley: University of California Press.

Khomeini, Imam [Ayatollah]. 1985. *Islam and Revolution: Writings and Declarations*, Translated and annotated by Hamid Algar. London: Routledge and Kegan Paul. (Orig. pub. 1981).

———. 1977. Collection of speeches, position statements [translations from "Najaf Min watha 'iq al-Imam al-Khomeyni did al-Quwa al Imbiriyaliyah wa al-Sahyuniyah waal-Raj'iyah" ("From the Papers of Imam Khomeyni against Imperialist, Zionist and Reactionist Powers")]. Translations on Near East and North Africa, no. 1902. Arlington, VA: Publications Research Service.

Kotkin, Joel. 1994. *Tribes: How Race, Religion and Identity Determine Success in the New Global Economy*. New York: Random House.

Lerner, Yoel. 1995. Author's interview with Yoel Lerner, member of the Yamini Israel political party, Jerusalem, August 17.

Lie, John. 2004. *Modern Peoplehood*. Cambridge, MA: Harvard University Press.

Marsden, Peter. 1998. *The Taliban: War, Religion and the New Order in Afghanistan*. London: Zed Books.

Piscatori, James, ed. 1991. *Islamic Fundamentalisms and the Gulf Crisis*. Chicago: Fundamentalism Project, American Academy of Arts and Sciences.

Shitta, Ibrahim Dasuqi. 1989. Author's interview with Professor Ibrahim Dasuqi Shitta, professor of Persian Literature and adviser to Muslim students at Cairo University, January 10.

Smith, Anthony D. 1995. *Nations and Nationalism in a Global Era*. London: Polity Press.

Tamir, Yael. 1993. *Liberal Nationalism*. Princeton, NJ: Princeton University Press.

Thero, Rev. Uduwawala. 1991. Author's interview with Rev. Uduwawala Chandananda Thero, member of the Karaka Sabha, Asgiri chapter, Sinhalese Buddhist Sangha, in Kandy, Sri Lanka, January 5.

Wright, Robin. 2000. *The Last Great Revolution: Turmoil and Transformation in Iran*. New York: Knopf.

Young, Crawford, ed. 1993. *The Rising Tide of Cultural Pluralism: Nation-State at Bay?* Madison: University of Wisconsin Press.

8

The Islamist Alternative
to Globalization

Carrie Rosefsky Wickham

In *Jihad vs. McWorld*, Benjamin Barber uses the term "jihad" as a shorthand for the militant defense of local ethnic and religious identities in a world increasingly dominated by Western—and, in particular, American—secular consumer culture. Though used to denote the general phenomenon of ethnic and religious particularism, Barber's reference to the Islamic tradition of holy war is deliberate, since, as he portrays it, Islamic fundamentalism is a quintessential example of the defensive reaction against modernity, secularism, and cosmopolitanism that has surfaced in other regions and cultures.[1] Barber's vision of an epic struggle between the forces of "jihad" and "McWorld" may offer a compelling overarching paradigm for globalization and its discontents, but it also distorts and obscures the complexity of contemporary responses to globalization, not least of all within the Muslim world itself. Islamist groups may be united in their opposition to the global spread of Western culture, but they differ sharply in their characterization of the Arab-Islamic cultural heritage that is to be preserved. While some Islamists juxtapose an "authentic" local tradition against a diametrically opposed and wholly alien modernity, other Islamists do not reject modernity so much as seek to reconstruct it on Islamic foundations. In so doing, the latter have incorporated the principles of civility, pluralism, and tolerance into their agendas, creating a bridge to secular proponents of democracy and civil society in the Arab world and the West.

Heralded as the rise of a "modernist," "liberal," "democratic," or "moderate" Islam, the new Islamist political discourse (*al-khitab al-islami al-jadid*) represents a significant break from and challenge to the dominant "revivalist" (or "fundamentalist") discourse promoted by many state-sponsored Muslim clerics in the Arab world, as well as by many leaders in the Islamic opposition.[2] While the "modernist" current has yet to be fully embraced by the region's main Islamic opposition groups, it has facilitated the shift of at least some Arab Islamists toward a constructive engagement with the emerging norms and networks of global civil society. We should not exaggerate the ideological shift represented by Islamic modernism, nor underestimate the extent to which it differs from the call for secular democracy. Nevertheless, the agenda of the modernists merits a serious examination, not as proof that Islamism and secular concepts of pluralism and democracy can be reconciled (because at least in present formulations of Islamism, they cannot),[3] but as a means to explore whether, to what extent, and in what ways such ideas as pluralism, toleration, and civility can be integrated within a broader project of Islamic reform.

This chapter examines the construction of an Islamist version of modernity in the platform of the Egyptian Wasat (Center) Party. The Wasat Party was formed in 1996 by a prominent group of activists who broke away from Egypt's largest Islamic political organization, the Muslim Brotherhood. Since that time, its bid for legal Party status has been rejected three times by the Egyptian government's Political Parties Committee (most recently in October 2004), and it remains confined to the margins of Egyptian political life. Nevertheless, in the Arab context, the Wasat Party platform is one of the clearest and fullest elaborations of the modernist Islamist worldview and, as such, indicates both the extent and the limits of the ideological innovation that has occurred within the region's Islamic movement over the past decade.

The Wasat Party's call for resistance to Western cultural domination echoes that of other Islamists past and present, including Hassan al-Banna, who founded the Muslim Brotherhood in Egypt in 1928, and Sayyid Qutb, the Brotherhood ideologue whose political tract *Signposts*, originally published in 1964, continues to inform the thinking of many Islamists in the Arab world. Yet in other ways the Wasat Party platform constitutes a striking departure from the "revivalist" strand of political Islam represented by al-Banna and Qutb and their disciples today. One dimension of this ideological change is particularly relevant for our purposes. Historically, the major ideologues of the Muslim Brotherhood portrayed Islam as a comprehensive, self-contained system wholly independent of—and inherently superior to—the ideologies and institutions of the West. Hence for al-Banna and Qutb, among others, the first priority was to defend Islam from the threat of Western cultural domination rather than to critically reassess the Islamic tradition itself. By contrast, the centerpiece of the Wasat Party platform is its call for Islamic civilizational reform, which must include the rejection of Islamic legal rulings and interpretations ill-suited to the needs and sensibilities of the community, or *umma*, in modern times. Further, the Wasat platform presents the legacy of Arab-Islamic civilization as one of pluralism and tolerance rather than religious rigidity and extremism. Hence it advocates the application of such principles in a modern context not as an imitation of the West but as a restoration of the fundamental principles of Arab-Islamic culture. By incorporating some of the norms of civil society into an Islamic civilizational framework, the Wasat platform *indigenizes* them, thereby investing them with a cultural authenticity they would otherwise lack. At the same time, it opens an area of common ground between the Wasat Islamists and secular advocates of civil society and democracy, creating the potential for new forms of dialogue and cooperation. In sum, the embrace of a "modernist" Islamic platform has facilitated the integration of some of Egypt's Islamists into broader civil society networks at both the local and the global level, creating new realities on the ground that defy the "clash of civilizations" paradigm, which portrays the cultures of Islam and the West as diametrically opposed.

To examine such issues in greater depth, let us look more closely at the Wasat Party's agenda.

The Revival of the *Umma*: An Islamist Conception of Civil Society?

In January 1996, a prominent group of activists in the Muslim Brotherhood, Egypt's largest Islamic political organization, announced their plans to form a new Party called the Wasat Party. Headed by Abu Ayla Madi Abu Ayla, a thirty-seven-year old Islamist engineer, the Wasat Party claimed to assume a middle (or "center") position between those promoting a rigid defense of Islamic tradition and those ready to jettison that tradition in its entirety in favor of values and institutions imported from the West. While affirming the core values of Arab-Islamic culture, the Party emphasized that civilizational reform (*al-islah al-hadari*) was needed to stimulate the community's political, economic, and spiritual advancement in modern times.[4]

The Wasat Party's initial application for Party status was rejected by the government's Political Parties Committee in 1996, a decision that was subsequently upheld on appeal in court. Two years later, Wasat Party leaders drafted a new and expanded platform and submitted it to the government in a second bid for legal recognition. The 1998 platform opens with an affirmation of the Arab-Islamic identity of the Egyptian *umma*, or community, and states that "this civilizational reference—Arab-Islamic—is the framework which must not be departed from, and from which derives all visions and programs and models" ("The Papers of the Egyptian Wasat Party," 17).[5] (Although in the Islamist political lexicon the term umma conventionally refers to the "community of believers," that is, to Muslims exclusively, the Wasat platform defines membership in the *umma* in terms of a shared civilizational reference and hence broadens the term to include Egypt's Coptic Christians.) As stated in this opening section, the primary aim of the Wasat Party is to revive the social and political role of the umma following a century in which it was forced to the margins of public life. For the Wasat Party founders, the restoration of the *umma* as an agent of its own destiny has a dual meaning. First, it signifies a strengthening of the role of individuals and associations vis-à-vis the state, a discourse that parallels the call for the empowerment of "civil society" in the West. Hence the opening section asserts:

> The role of the umma and the initiative of individuals and associations have become in the last century far weaker than they were, and much weaker than they should be, and hence the Party is oriented toward a revival of the role of the umma, every individual and association in it, in new and innovative forms, so that the umma is restored to its role as an active being in various civilizational activities, as the source of authority and as the authentic repository of the Shari'a and the constant protector of it. ("The Papers of the Egyptian Wasat Party," 17)

Along the same lines, the platform states in a later section that "the state must not take the place of the people in the launching of activities, and must not engage in that which individuals or associations or institutions of the umma are obligated or capable of doing" ("The Papers of the Egyptian Wasat Party," 26). However, in its call for a revival of the autonomous organizations of the umma, the platform avoids the direct Arabic translation of civil society (*al-mujtama' al-madani*) with its secular, liberal, and Western connotations. Instead, it uses the descriptive term *ahli*, from the root *ahl*, denoting "family or kinship ties," as a general reference to the communal institutions—that is, mosques, religious charities, guilds, and kin-based associations—that played an active role in the public affairs of the *umma* in times past.[6] Despite these differences in terminology, the "new" political Islam represented by the Wasat Party approximates the Western civil society discourse in its call for an active citizenry to assume responsibility for social and political functions recently monopolized by the state.[7]

The Wasat Party's call for a revival of the *umma* has a second meaning as well. As the Party portrays it, the umma is essentially a cultural unit, a repository of the core values of Arab-Islamic civilization. Hence a revival of the umma also entails a restoration of the inherited values that have been pushed aside over the past century in favor of values and models of behavior imported from the West. Yet rather than call for a return to traditional Islamic values and beliefs, the platform calls for an indigenous process of cultural renovation, which, it contends, is necessary for the *umma*'s development. Hence it states that inherited patterns and values "must be reconstructed on new foundations, in order for their existence to develop, and regain their former authority, and play their role in a comprehensive social renaissance" ("The Papers of the Egyptian Wasat Party," 17–18). After delineating its vision of an energized and active umma, the Wasat platform lays out its plan for the fundamental reform of Egypt's constitutional order. What is interesting in this regard is the incorporation of the principles of pluralism, popular sovereignty, and popular representation into a broader political framework based on the application of Sharia, or Islamic law. The Wasat Party's conception of a modern Islamist political system is examined in the following section.

Revisioning Sharia Rule: The Wasat Party's Definition of an Islamic State

The Wasat Party does not support the separation of religion and state. On the contrary, like other Islamist groups, it seeks to establish a political system based on the application of Sharia, or Islamic law. The Party notes that this general Islamic frame of reference is a point of consensus for all Egyptians as a result of their shared history and culture. For the country's Muslims, it is a basic requirement of their faith, while for its Copts it is a reference to the Arab-Islamic civilization to which they belong ("The Papers of the Egyptian Wasat Party," 19). While the Wasat Party identifies the Sharia as the principle source of legislation, it portrays the Sharia as an inherently flexible set of juridical rulings and interpretations that reflect the circumstances of the umma in different eras and are thus open to revision over time. The platform proceeds to advocate the articulation of a constitutional framework based on the Sharia that expresses the general consensus of religious experts as well as of the general public, to be submitted to the representatives of the umma for their ratification.

What will the application of Sharia involve in practice? The platform first asserts that the specific rules contained in the texts (al-nusus) must be applied to all Muslims. From the context it is obvious that this refers to the sacred texts of Islam that are based on divine revelation, but it is worth noting that which texts fall into this category is not specified, that is, whether it refers only to Qur'anic verses or also to the hadith, that is, the narrative accounts of the words and deeds of the Prophet and his companions, and in the latter case, which hadith are to be considered authoritative. In cases where such rulings contradict the beliefs of non-Muslims, the platform asserts that non-Muslims will be governed by their own religious laws (shari'atu). The platform goes on to explain that the sacred sources (al-usul) determine the realm of what is permitted (al-masmuh), and this is space designated for human legal reasoning and the development of positive laws applicable to all ("The Papers of the Egyptian Wasat Party," 20).

The platform emphasizes that the scope for human legislation is in fact quite broad, and that the task of articulating new laws through *ijtihad* (human reasoning) falls to Muslims and Christians alike. It then proceeds to justify this unorthodox claim by reiterating that Muslims and Christians are members of a single umma and therefore equal in rights and responsibilities:

> In the Islamic civilizational project, Muslims and Christians stand on equal footing, in belonging and roles and authenticity. They are the children of a single umma, and a single civilization despite their religious differences. Not only are their rights equal but so are their obligations in the renaissance of the umma and its administration and its defense and the protection of its sacred elements, Islamic and Christian alike. ("The Papers of the Egyptian Wasat Party," 21)

The platform then explicitly challenges the traditional Islamist rulings have have declared the highest positions in government off-limits to non-Muslims:

> And no one should be denied the right to occupy any position whatever on the basis of religious belonging. And all the pronouncements pertaining to authority which are built on religious differences require the exertion of new interpretation which looks at them in light of the nature of the political system which prevailed at the time in which they were issued from the Prophet or his Companions or Islamic jurists. ("The Papers of the Egyptian Wasat Party," 22)

Along the same lines, the platform rejects traditional Islamic rulings that degrade the civil and political rights of women. Like the more conservative Islamists aligned with the "revivalist" strand of Islamic thought, the Wasat founders emphasize the special obligations of women to care for the family. Yet unlike the "revivalists," they contend that women are equal to men in their political rights and duties, and as such are entitled to occupy all positions in government, including those of head of state and judge. The platform details such positions in a section entitled "On the Family and Women," which begins with this assertion: "Our Party views the family as the primary unit of society, and if it is healthy, then so is the social body as a whole, and it is the repository of the values of the umma and its skills and experiences" ("The Papers of the Egyptian Wasat Party," 28). The platform observes that this emphasis on the family, as opposed to the individual, is one of the prime factors distinguishing Arab-Islamic civilization from Western civilization, and goes on to assert that the status of women should be viewed through the institution of the family:

> Hence the woman's relation to the man is that of the mother who has rights over the man, and she is the daughter, and she is the sister deserving of care and honor, and she is also the wife who is a source of advice and compassion, and women are the partners of men, and

they are half of society and half of the umma, and hence there is no cause for conflict between men and women. ("The Papers of the Egyptian Wasat Party," 28–29)

The platform further notes that the care of the family is the first of a woman's primary duties, "since there is no one else who can take her place in this regard." At the same time, however, it contends that traditional Islamic views that treat women as the possession of men or as beneath men in value, ability, or social status are "superficial and must be changed immediately and through all available means" ("The Papers of the Egyptian Wasat Party," 29). The Party then elaborates a strong defense of gender equality in the public sphere:

The Party affirms that women are fully equal to men in their civil and political rights and obligations, and hence it is a woman's right to occupy all political positions, with the Party heedful of the position of modern Islamic interpretation involving the abandonment of the old concept which linked the assumption of political office to private individual characteristics. And hence it is the right of a woman, indeed it is her duty, to be a voter, or a candidate, or a member in a representative assembly, and to assume all public and professional tasks and positions, just as it is incumbent upon her to participate and take an interest in public life in all its dimensions and forms. ("The Papers of the Egyptian Wasat Party," 29)

Having examined the party's discourse on rights, let us now move to its conception of the broad contours of an Islamic state.

The platform's section "The Foundational Principles of the Political System" identifies three core principles on which an Islamic political system should be based. The first is "pluralism" (al-ta'addudiyya). Indeed, the platform asserts that "the most important civilizational principle of our umma, and hence of the public order of the umma, is pluralism"; it elaborates that "we mean pluralism in its many dimensions, not just political pluralism, because the umma has been based throughout history on religious, cultural and social pluralism, as well as other types." Challenging the "revivalist" argument that internal dissension weakens the umma from within,[8] the platform insists that "pluralism within a single civilizational framework" has in fact been a source of the umma's strength ("The Papers of the Egyptian Wasat Party," 24). The second stated principle is "The umma is the source of authority." The platform asserts:

The Party sees the umma as the first and the original and the only source of authority. And we mean by this that the state is not the source of authority, but rather is an agency to which powers are delegated by the umma, and hence the state comes after the umma. And thus the constitution is the constitution of the umma, and not

the constitution of the state, and the laws which supplement it belong
to the umma and not to the state. And the state itself is subject to
the constitution and these laws. ("The Papers of the Egyptian Wasat
Party," 24)

The platform notes that the party's respect for the supreme authority of
the *umma* leads to its affirmation of the peaceful alternation of power, "which
means that the choice of the umma is the basis, for it is the umma which
chooses its delegates, in what should be a genuine choice free of coercion or
material or psychological pressure." It specifies that the members of the
umma should select their representatives based on knowledge of their character, qualifications, and previous experience, rather than on the basis of
electoral promises and propaganda. And those to whom the *umma* has delegated its authority must conform to the conditions of their office and pursue
the instructions and interests of their constituents; if they do not, their constituents can remove them ("The Papers of the Egyptian Wasat Party," 24).

Based on this exposition of key sections of the Wasat Party platform, what
broader conclusions can we draw about the political project of modernist Islam?[9]
The modernist Islamist project echoes the concerns of secular proponents of
democracy and civil society in several ways. Of relevance here is the clear anti-
authoritarian bent of the Wasat Party's political discourse, that is, its call for
a strengthening of private and civic initiative; its designation of the *umma*
(community)—rather than the state—as the source of all sovereign power; and
its emphasis on the rule of law (and, in particular, on the subordination to the
law of those at the apex of the state). While not equivalent to calls for the empowerment of "civil society," the modernist Islamist project arguably reflects a
similar ethos. Further, in its redefinition of the *umma* in cultural and historical
(rather than religious) terms and its explicit rejection of traditional Islamic
rulings that assign an inferior status to non-Muslims and women, the Wasat
platform moves Islamist discourse closer to a modern concept of democratic
citizenship. Finally, in its emphasis on the broad scope for *ijtihad* (i.e., the use of
reason to apply Islamic principles to modern times); its stress on the equal rights
and duties of all members of the *umma* to participate in *ijtihad*; and its recognition of both the inevitability and the desirability of conflicting views and
opinions, the Wasat Party platform directly challenges the "revivalist" push
toward ideological conformity and opens the door to the acceptance of genuine
contestation between different programmatic alternatives.

Yet if the modernist Islamist project parallels the secular discourse on
"civil society" in some ways, it departs from it in others. First and foremost, in
its call for the application of Sharia, the Wasat Party platform grants absolute
authority to specific rulings contained in the sacred "texts" (*nusus*), which, as
the product of divine revelation, are beyond revision. The exact implications of
this cordoning off of the "revealed" elements of Sharia are unclear because the

identity of the rulings and the textual sources in question is never specified. Moreover, apart from the *identity* of the revealed sources, the platform's presumption of unanimity about their *intent* is problematic, since individual Qur'anic verses and hadith can be (and have been) interpreted in different ways. The setting aside of a corpus of revealed law also dilutes the force of popular sovereignty by denying the representatives of the *umma* the authority to alter rulings contained in the sacred texts (or to challenge their interpretation). Further, even in the wide areas in which *ijtihad* (reintepretation) is permitted, the platform leaves some important issues unresolved. In particular, it fails to specify who has the authority to reinterpret traditional Islamic rulings, what methods they should employ, and how conflicts of interpretation should be adjudicated.

Further, the citizenship rights accorded by the Wasat Party to members of the umma are restricted by the obligation to conform to the religious laws of their particular confession (Islam, Christianity, etc.) Hence, while the Wasat Party explicitly rejects those traditional rulings that accord non-Muslims and women an inferior legal and political status, they continue to discriminate between the rights and obligations of citizens on a communal basis. In effect, this denies the right of the nonobservant or nonbelieving Muslim (or Christian or Jew) to opt out of conformity with his or her confession's religious behavioral codes.

Finally, the platform's insistence that legislation occur within an "Islamic frame of reference" (*al-marja'iyya al-islamiyya*) or, as it is phrased elsewhere in the platform, must be consistent with "the enduring values of the umma" (*thawabet al-umma*) narrows the scope for ideological and political pluralism in an Islamic state. That is, differences of opinion are legitimate and permissible only insofar as they do not transcend a fixed set of cultural boundaries, fixed because—as portrayed here—the "enduring values" of the community are not open to revision. While the platform never provides a detailed and comprehensive definition of such values, it does emphasize two constitutive principles of Arab-Islamic civilization: the identity of the family, rather than the individual, as the primary social unit; and the religious character of Arab-Islamic culture. In sum, the Wasat Party platform retains a concept of personhood defined in terms of membership in kinship and religious groups and, as such, as enmeshed in a web of social duties and obligations that cannot be abandoned at will. Further, by defining certain cultural traits as "essential" features of Arab-Islamic identity, the Wasat Party platform removes them from the realm of human contention and debate, in effect according them the same transcendent status it grants to revealed law.

The Wasat Party's project of Islamic civilizational reform represents an intermediate position between cultural continuity and change. Its platform can be said to incorporate such "modern" ideas as pluralism, popular sovereignty, and popular representation into a religious political framework, yet this synthesis remains an awkward fit. As noted earlier, the Wasat platform does not acknowledge—let alone address—the tension between its support of pluralism and other civil society norms, on the one hand, and its commitment to the application of revealed law, on the other. Moreover, in its emphasis on preserving the core values of the Arab-Islamic community, or *thawabet al-umma*, the Party elevates certain temporal cultural traits to an immutable status, thereby placing an upward ceiling on cultural change. Such features of the Islamic project do not necessarily detract from its popular appeal; on the contrary, they may enhance the project's appeal by burnishing its mantle of authenticity. What the foregoing analysis rather suggests is the tension between the Wasat Party's defense of Arab-Islamic culture, on the one hand, and its efforts to reinvent it, on the other.

The defensive aspect of the Islamic reform project is in large part a response to what Islamists see as the projection of Western power in Muslim societies. Articulated by Hassan al-Banna and his contemporaries as a rejection of "Western political, economic, and cultural imperialism," this defensive discourse has been transmuted in recent years into an Islamist critique of globalization. How are the dimensions and consequences of globalization depicted by the proponents of a "modernist" Islam, and what do they propose as an alternative? To address these questions, let us examine the treatment of globalization in the Wasat Party platform.

Globalization in Islamist Political Discourse

The final section of the Wasat platform, titled "External Relations and National Security," delineates the party's perspective on the emerging global order and the place of the *umma* within it ("The Papers of the Egyptian Wasat Party," 51–62). The section begins by pointing to the "new international situation" that has emerged since the collapse of the Soviet Union and the end of the cold war. In this new situation, the Party asserts, the United States aspires to create a unipolar system in which it is the dominant power, but the framework of this new system has not yet solidified. The platform contends that in the emerging order, international relations are dominated by economic competition, in which each of the world's major powers—that is, the United States, the European bloc, Japan, and China—seeks, at the expense of the others, to achieve economic gains that will enhance its own strategic political and military positions.

In this new environment, the *umma* must work to strengthen its own economic power to assume an effective role in the new international order. To do this, the platform recommends the development of an Arab-Islamic economic union to facilitate trade between Arab and Muslim countries and enhance their ability to compete effectively with other global economic powers.

The creation of an Arab-Islamic economic bloc will also make it easier for member states to assume the "difficult" positions necessary to defend their strategic national interests, for example, in the Arab-Israeli conflict.

The platform takes a critical stance toward the huge disparity in living standards between the North and South, and it condemns the imposition of uniform economic policies by the World Bank, the International Monetary Fund, and other international institutions on countries with different needs and circumstances, in ways that only increase the pressure on their lowest-income groups. In this light, the platform affirms the "extreme importance" that the *umma* must give to the autonomous investment of its own wealth and the optimal allocation of its own economic resources.

In addition to strengthening its position in the global economy, the *umma* should work to strengthen the institutions of international community, such as the United Nations, and deepen the *umma*'s relationship with them. Since the global information revolution has made isolation impossible, the *umma* should seek new opportunities for dialogue and cooperation with other members of the international community, to identify common interests and minimize points of tension. The platform affirms that the *umma* should respect international treaties and covenants and favor peaceful methods of conflict resolution. At the same time, it should work to strengthen international laws that support the right of all peoples to self-determination and, in particular, to select their own representatives in free and fair elections. It should also insist that international laws guarantee the right of all peoples to lead a life of dignity, and hence "a people who have committed no crime should not be subjected to economic boycotts or enforced starvation, or deprived of their legitimate right of self-defense, or of their right to resist those who attack them" ("The Papers of the Egyptian Wasat Party," 51–56).

In sum, the Wasat platform calls for the constructive engagement of the *umma* with the institutions of the global community, combined with efforts to strengthen its own weight and influence within it. At the same time, the platform takes a principled stand against the tendency of the world's most powerful nations (and, in particular, of the United States) to act unilaterally in defense of their own interests, particularly when doing so violates the rights of less powerful groups and peoples. The strengthening of international law is thus supported as a means to restrain the world's most powerful nations from imposing their will on weaker nations by force.

If members of the Arab-Islamic *umma* must resist foreign domination in the economic and political spheres, they must do so in the cultural sphere as well. The platforms states that the Wasat founders are deeply alarmed by "the efforts by some Western agencies (*jihat*) to impose a single global culture based on Western examples, or what is called globalization (*al-'awlama*)" ("The Papers of the Egyptian Wasat Party," 57). The platform explains that the party's opposition to globalization stems from two sources. The first is its "clear violation of one of the most important human laws and that is the diversity of people in terms of race and language and custom and way of life." Second, this stance is a response to the negative aspects of the Western value system itself. As the platform elaborates:

> Our alarm derives in part from the content of some of these values which threatens the social peace when social norms are jeered at and the pillars of the family are uprooted, and which threatens the psychological well-being of the individual when he is confronted with extreme pressure, especially in the material domain, and forgets his social role or even his family role, and ends up in an abyss and in private turmoil; and which threatens the economic peace when competition which is unregulated and is based on monopolies and on the destruction of the basic rights of low-income groups becomes harsher and more relentless according to a purely materialistic rationale. ("The Papers of the Egyptian Wasat Party," 57)

Hence, the platform concludes:

> We feel it is our obligation to confront this process of globalization and focus on the necessity of respecting the particularities of all nations and the modes of conduct which distinguish them, and to work to preserve them and avert efforts to dissolve them. And in this way international endeavor will be based on a foundation of cooperation across cultures in a framework which respects their diversity, oriented toward an exchange of human skills, not toward the domination of some states or peoples over other states or peoples. ("The Papers of the Egyptian Wasat Party," 57)

The Wasat platform's critique of globalization contains several interesting elements. First, at a time when some commentators in the West define globalization as involving the spread of such "universal" (and hence culture-neutral) values as pluralism and human rights, the Islamists portray it as involving the coercive spread of a single cultural model, and hence as a direct violation of pluralism in the global sphere. Indeed, the Islamists portray their opposition to globalization as a *defense of pluralism*, meaning a pluralism of distinct civilizations or cultures, rather than a pluralism of values, beliefs, and lifestyles within a single civilizational framework. Yet if the Wasat Islamists condemn globalization as the imposition of one cultural model at the expense of its rivals, they reject the Western model not only because it is "Other" but also because it is inherently flawed. In particular, the Wasat platform equates Western culture with excessive individualism and materialism; contends that such values lead to the dissolution of family and communal ties; and argues that the latter is the cause of a broader range of social ills. The platform elaborates on the dangers of Western individualism in the section on family and women:

And the party's view of the family [as the primary social unit] is linked to its understanding of the difference between Islamic civilization and Western civilization, in that the latter is based on the individual and nurtures in him a solitary individualist orientation; and linked to this is the easy disintegration of the marriage relationship and of the family more generally, and the absence of effective supervision of youth—to which the family is entrusted—and hence a situation in which youth fall prey to drug addiction and devastating illnesses, the most dangerous of which is AIDS, which reveals the ugly side of the civilization of the West, which it tries to hide but cannot. ("The Papers of the Egyptian Wasat Party," 28)

Hence the Islamist critique of globalization is predicated on a particular understanding of Western civilization. First, the latter is portrayed as a unitary cultural model rather than as a complex synthesis of diverse and contradictory elements. Second, this unitary model is described as seriously flawed, and hence inappropriate as a universal exemplar.

The Wasat platform's defense of Arab-Islamic civilization reflects a similar dual logic. The platform highlights the particularism of Arab-Islamic culture and calls for its preservation as one culture among many. In this sense, the Wasat Islamists may be said to advocate a model of "civilizational pluralism" as an alternative to the global spread of Western culture. At the same time, however, the Wasat platform offers the values of Arab-Islamic civilization as a model for others to follow:

The umma has a distinguished civilizational project which it should be thoroughly informed of, and we are certain that we have human and civilizational values which we should offer to the peoples of the world, like respect for human diversity, and an interest in getting to know other peoples, and interacting with them on a foundation of mutual respect, and social solidarity and equality and a lack of racial discrimination and above all the consecration of the dignity of the human being, in addition to other elements which characterize our umma. ("The Papers of the Egyptian Wasat Party," 56)

While they defend their own cultural model on particularist grounds, the Wasat Islamists also present it as worthy of broader application.

Islamism and Global Civil Society

In *Many Globalizations: Cultural Diversity in the Contemporary World*, Peter Berger points to the "increasingly significant phenomenon of *alternative globalizations*; that is cultural movements with global outreach originating outside the Western world and indeed impacting on the latter" (Berger and Huntington 2002, 19). As Berger and Huntington observe, local responses to the global spread of Western (and predominantly American) culture are not limited to accommodation or rejection; instead, they may involve the construction of "alternative modernities" combining participation in global economic and political systems with the self-conscious affirmation of indigenous culture. Berger and Huntington note that the Islamic movements in Turkey and Indonesia are good examples of this phenomenon and concludes that "throughout the Muslim world today, even in Iran, such visions of an alternative Islamic modernity are gaining influence" (2002, 21).

The platform of the Egyptian Wasat Party represents one version of the "alternative modernity" proposed by Islamist activists in the contemporary Muslim world. As demonstrated earlier in this chapter, it seeks to preserve the "core values" of Arab-Islamic civilization while at the same time urging an autonomous and self-directed process of cultural adaptation and change. The broader implications of this intellectual reformation of the Islamist agenda remain open to debate. To some observers, the key question is whether or not the new Islamist discourse signals a reconciliation of Islamism with the norms of global civil society—that is, with support for democracy, pluralism, and human rights. Based on the foregoing analysis of key sections of the Wasat Party platform, what broader conclusions can we derive about the character of the new political Islam?

In its emphasis on civilizational pluralism in the global sphere, and its call for greater tolerance of contending views and opinions within the umma itself, the new Islamism represents a qualitative break from the "clash of civilizations" paradigm that continues to inform the thinking of many Islamists in the Arab world today. As noted previously, the Wasat Islamists do not see Islam and the West as diametrically opposed civilizations headed on a collision course. While different in some fundamental ways, the platform suggests, the members of Arab-Islamic civilization and Western civilization share some important values and interests and thus should engage in dialogue and cooperation when this is possible and resolve their conflicts peacefully when it is not. If the Wasat platform represents a significant break from "revivalist" Islamist thinking on such issues as the scope for pluralism or relations with the West, it does *not* indicate the Islamist embrace of secular Western values and institutions as appropriate models for the Muslim world. Moreover, the Wasat platform's incorporation of such values as pluralism and popular representation within an Islamic political framework remains problematic because they conflict with its emphasis on the fundamental obligation of all Muslims to adhere to rulings that—as they see it—are clearly defined in the Qur'an and the narrative records (hadith) of the speech and practice of the Prophet Muhammad. By placing such rulings beyond the reach of human reasoning or *ijtihad*, the Wasat Islamists establish an upward limit on how much of the Arab world's cultural legacy can be reformed. Similarly, by demanding fidelity to the core values of Arab-Islamic civilization, or *thawabet al-umma*, they add a second major constraint on the scope of legitimate reform. According to both criteria, one of the major principles that is not open to revision is the essentially religious—as opposed to secular—character of the Arab-Islamic *umma*, and hence of any government that truly represents it.

The modernists within the Islamic camp are not secular democrats, nor are their concerns directly parallel to those of "new social movements" in the West. Nevertheless, the rise of an Islamic discourse advocating pluralism, tolerance, and the empowerment of an active and autonomous citizenry has opened up new possibilities for dialogue and cooperation between Islamists and their secular counterparts at home and abroad. Indeed, one of the most interesting trends in Egyptian opposition politics over the past decade is the unprecedented participation of Islamists and secular counterparts in various non governmental organizations-sponsored conferences, salons, and seminars on democratic themes. While they remain divided on some important issues, such as the role of religion in the constitutional framework of the state, the Wasat Islamists and secular civil society activists in Egypt have found some areas of common ground and begun to develop relationships of familiarity and trust.

Such relationships have paved the way for new initiatives that cross partisan lines. For example, after the Wasat Party's second bid for legal status was denied, a group of Wasat Islamists and secular Egyptian activists and intellectuals applied to the Ministry of Social Affairs for permission to form a new association (*gama'iyya*). In April 2000 they achieved a modest breakthrough when their application was approved. According to its chairman, the independent Islamist lawyer Muhammad Salim al-'Awa, the new association, known as the Egyptian Society for Culture and Dialogue, "supports the culture of dialogue in a society in which violence prevails" ("The Little NGO That Could," 2000). Its charter calls for holding seminars and conferences, conducting and publishing original research, and assisting in other ways to "strengthen the values of intellectual pluralism and cultural opening and encourage the country's development in various fields." In addition to holding annual conferences on general themes such as "Freedom of Expression" (May 2001) and "Citizenship in a Changing World" (May 2002), the association has provided an institutional forum for prominent Islamist intellectuals to lecture on various aspects of the new Islamic thought.

Recent Developments

The founders of the Wasat Party persist in the effort to gain a legal foothold in Egypt's political system. In May 2004, six years after their last attempt, the

Wasat group submitted a third application for Party status. In October 2004, the government's Political Parties Committee once again rejected their request, a decision that Party leaders will appeal in court. Party leader Abu Ayla Madi Abu Ayla (2004a) claims to be undaunted by this latest setback, explaining that "we never expected the committee to approve it, but rather hoped to obtain a favorable verdict in court." As Party leaders prepare their third legal appeal, they remain guardedly hopeful that this time the judges will rule in their favor.

In the six years since the Wasat Party's last bid for legal status, its membership base has expanded to two hundred members, including forty-nine women and seven Coptic Christians. And in the summer of 2004, it released a new and expanded platform that addresses the same themes covered here but in greater detail and with a marked increase in analytic sophistication.[10] According to Party founder Abu Ayla, such changes reflect both the continued maturation of the Party leadership's understanding of Islam and the input of a number of independent, younger-generation Islamist intellectuals who were invited to participate in writing the document for the first time. A full treatment of the third platform exceeds the scope of this chapter, but it is worth noting that the platform indicates a deepening of the party's commitment to a global ethic of tolerance and cooperation. Of particular interest here is the platform's closing paragraph, which rejects the "clash of civilizations" paradigm as a means of ordering relations between the Muslim world and the West. This final paragraph reads in full:

> The founding members believe that the essence of religion is human connectivity and cooperation based on justice, righteousness and charity and, hence, that any call to war—unless for the legitimate purpose of self-protection from enemy powers or resistance to occupation—contradicts the spirit of religion and faith. We therefore do not agree with the ideas put forward by those western intellectuals and thinkers, and by the extremists in the Arab world, who speak of "the clash of civilizations." We refuse this idea of a "clash" and support the principal current in both the Arab and Western world, namely, the current to which belong all reasonable human beings worldwide who object to the idea of a "clash of civilizations" and who call for the cooperation, mutual knowledge and complementarity of all cultures. ("Wasat Party Platform" 2004)[11]

The Wasat Party platform thus indicates that the religion of Islam furnishes a discursive platform not only for defensive reactions to globalization (or "jihad", in Barber's shorthand) but also for constructive engagement with other peoples and religions in the establishment of a global order founded on the recognition of our shared humanity and oriented toward universal values of justice and peace. It goes without saying that Barber's "jihad" versus "McWorld" paradigm fails to account for this trend or acknowledge its significance.

The Wasat Party's evolving commitment to cross-partisan dialogue and cooperation is not simply a matter of rhetoric. In recent years, the Wasat Islamists have become increasingly visible and active members of civil society networks linking them with secular activists and intellectuals in the pursuit of common goals. For example, Abu Ayla and other Party leaders have assumed a high-profile role in recent citizens' initiatives to accelerate Egypt's progress toward democratic reform. On June 24, 2004, a statement urging comprehensive democratic reform cowritten by Wasat Islamists and secular democrats was published in the Egyptian daily *al-Misri al-Yawm*, together with the names of five hundred prominent Egyptian politicians, academics, journalists, actors, and artists who supported it. As Abu Ayla recounts,

> The idea for this statement came up at a Ramadan break-fast in November 2004. We decided that if we were going to oppose reforms imposed from the outside, then we must develop our own vision of reform. Six of us [representing different political trends] were selected to form a committee to prepare a joint statement. So we wrote the statement and got five hundred people to sign it. The signers included Islamists, leftists, nationalists, and liberals. The government was really shocked. (Abu Ayla, 2004b)

Future plans include the preparation of a democratic national charter (a committee for which was established in September) and eventually, the drafting of a new constitution.

At the same time, the Wasat Islamists have accepted numerous invitations to participate in international workshops, seminars, conferences, and meetings organized to promote understanding and cooperation between the Muslim world and the West. For example, Abu Ayla joined Islamist leaders from other Arab states in the ongoing, multiyear "U.S.-Europe-Arab Dialogue" organized by the Washington-based International Institute for Sustained Dialogue; participated in an informal, civic-based German-Egyptian dialogue in 2003–4; attended the December 6–8, 2003, conference "The Role of Islamic Groups in the Political Reform Process in the Middle East" cosponsored by the Kuwaiti publishing house Dar al-Watan and the Carnegie Endowment for International Peace; and recently held discussions at his Cairo office with American embassy officials and staff members of the Foreign Affairs Committee of the U.S. Congress. Such initiatives, and Abu Ayla's participation in them, are not unique but rather reflect a wider trend, namely, the emergence of a growing web of transnational networks linking Muslim and secular activists and intellectuals with a shared commitment to pluralism, democracy, and human rights.[12]

Interestingly, such nonreligious networks are now being complemented by faith-based initiatives to promote cross-cultural understanding between Muslims and the West. For example, in 2002 the Presbyterian Church (USA) founded the Interfaith Listening Project, designed to encourage Muslim-Christian understanding. The project brings Christian and Muslim religious leaders from countries around the world to the United States to speak with church members in local communities, where they are lodged not in hotels but in family homes. Among the participants in the second cycle of the Listening Project from September 23 to October 7, 2004, who spoke with Presybterian church members in western New York, Indiana, Iowa, and Kentucky, was Abu Ayla of the Egyptian Wasat Party. Abu Ayla's decision to visit the United States was a controversial one, given high levels of anti-American sentiment in Egypt and the broader Arab-Islamic world. Yet, as Abu Ayla explained, he decided to accept the invitation on the strength of his conviction that such citizen-based initiatives represent a positive step toward healing America's relations with the Muslim world. As he told Presbyterian church members in towns across middle America, "We have a misunder-standing, we harbor negative images of each other, and together we need to solve this" (Abu Ayla, 2004a).

Civil Networks and Civil Islam

The rise of a "modernist" current of Islamic political thought has facilitated the integration of some Islamist actors into local and global civil society networks. Participation in such networks has helped Islamist leaders over-come their former isolation and, in so doing, increased their receptivity to new ideas and augmented their tolerance of values and beliefs that differ from their own. As a result of ongoing exchanges with activists and intellectuals across the ideological spectrum in Egypt and abroad, Abu Ayla notes that his own thinking and that of his peers has evolved toward a recognition that "we have a human understanding of Islam" and that "we don't monopolize the Truth." Such language is echoed in the preface of the Wasat Party's latest platform. While calling for the application of Sharia, it emphasizes that the party's interpretations of it are human and as such "may or may not be correct" and hence are "open to debate, criticism and revision and change depending on time and place." Further, their interactions with political, re-ligious, and civic leaders outside the Islamist camp have prompted Islamist actors to articulate and prioritize transcendent human values that exceed the bounds of religion, culture, and race. As the preface of the new platform states, the Wasat Party's project of reform "should be open to the world and should participate in the global movement seeking to activate the values held in common by all members of humanity."[13] The Wasat Party initiative thus underscores the internal complexity and diversity of Islamist responses to globalization, and the distortion produced by paradigms that reduce them to a call for jihad. While the jihadist response merits close attention, do the alternative ways in which Islamists understand and engage with the global order deserve not recognition as well?

NOTES

1. Barber quotes Hassan al-Banna, the founder of the Egyptian Muslim Brotherhood, as representative of the Islamic fundamentalist position: "Al-Banna's indignation goes to the very heart of Jihad's campaign against the modern, the secular, and the cosmopolitan. It captures the essence of fundamentalism as it has existed since the seventeenth century, growing up alongside the devil modernity to which it has played angel's advocate for Puritans and Muslims, Buddhists and born-again Baptists alike" (Barber 1995, 210–11). Barber briefly acknowledges the presence of more moderate and democratic forms of Islam but does not reflect on how they relate to his broader paradigm in which Islamism is an expression of jihad.

2. For a discussion of the "revivalist" strand of Islamic thought, see the introductory essay in Kurzman (1998, 5–6).

3. To be clear, the question here is not whether Islamism and secularism can be reconciled *in principle*, but whether current formulations of Islamist ideology are compatible with secular democratic ideals.

4. In its call for civilizational reform, the Wasat Party builds on a longer tradition of Islamic modernist thought associated with such late nineteenth-century and early twentieth-century Arab Islamist thinkers as Khayr al-Din and Muhammad 'Abduh (Hourani 1983).

5. The Egyptian Wasat Party (the group's second Party initiative, as distinct from its first, which was known simply as the Wasat Party) was announced in the spring of 1998, and its platform was likely published in the same year. The platform of the Wasat Party is a forty-nine-page document that is divided into eleven sections, preceded by an introduction (pp. 5–12) and succeeded by an appendix on internal procedures and a list of Party members (pp. 63–87). The text of the platform begins on page 13 and concludes on page 62. This chapter focuses on those sections of the platform that concern the broad contours of an Islamic political system; the nature of citizens' rights and obligations; and the relationship of the Arab-Islamic community with the West. Other sections of the platform, such as those on the environment, social justice, technology, and tourism, are not covered here. The platform is not available in English, and all translations from the Arabic are my own.

6. The preference for *al-mujtama' al-ahli* as an "authentic" alternative to *al-mujtama' al-madani* is a feature of the new Islamist discourse more generally. Sami Zubaida discusses the Islamist conception of civil society (Zubaida 1992, 5) and the primacy of "civil society" in the thinking of the new Islamists (Zubaida 2001, 24).

7. This emphasis on an active citizenship is a more general feature of the new Islamic thought. As Sami Zubaida notes, for the thinkers of the new Islamist current (which he refers to as a "third way," distinct from both conservative and radical Islam), Islam is not essentially about the state, but about the community (*umma*). They

proceed to identify the community with a "civil society of actively participating citizens." (Zubaida 2001, 24).

8. As Richard Mitchell notes, "Perhaps no other theme so preoccupied Banna as the disunity of Muslims and the consequent weakening of the community." Mitchell also emphasizes the Muslim Brotherhood's "basic intolerance of dissent" (Mitchell 1969, 323, 325–26).

9. For an extended treatment of the Wasat Party's Islamic reform project, see Wickham's "The Path to Moderation: Strategy and Learning in the Formation of the *Wasat* Party in Egypt" (Wickham 2004).

10. The third Party platform was released in June 2004, after the main text of this chapter was written.

11. English translation of the Wasat Party's 2004 platform. For this first time, both English and Arabic versions of the platform are available to the public. Both can be found on the party's new Web site: www.alwasatparty.org.

12. Two American organizations with an important role in creating bridges between Islamist and secular democracy activists are the Washington-based Center for the Study of Islam and Democracy and Dialogues: Islamic World-U.S.-The West, a program of the World Policy Institute of New School University in New York.

13. Comments made by Abu Ayla Madi Abu Ayla during an interview with the author in Cairo, Egypt, in July 1997 and reiterated on numerous occasions since then. Abu 'Ayla credits his extensive interactions with civic and political leaders outside the Islamist camp, both as assistant secretary general of the Engineers' Syndicate in the early 1990s and later as the Wasat Party's founder, for this evolution in his understanding of Islam. Other Wasat Party leaders express the same idea. For example, in a published interview, Islamist lawyer and Wasat Party activist Esam Sultan noted, "I am not able to say—no one in the *Wasat* Party is able to say that the program of the *Wasat* Party, this is Islam. But I can say that the program of the *Wasat* Party is my understanding of Islam.... It is possible for you to agree or disagree with me about it" (Shadid 2001, 267).

BIBLIOGRAPHY

Abu Ayla Madi Abu Ayla. 2004a. Author's interview with Abu Ayla Madi Abu Ayla, Louisville, Kentucky, October 10.
————. 2004b. Author's interview with Abu Ayla Madi Abu Ayla, Amman Jordon, June 26.
Barber, Benjamin. 1995. *Jihad vs. McWorld*. New York: Random House.
Berger, Peter L., and Samuel P. Huntington, eds. 2002. *Many Globalizations: Cultural Diversity in the Contemporary World*. New York: Oxford University Press.
Hourani, Albert. 1983. *Arabic Thought in the Liberal Age: 1798–1939*. New York: Cambridge University Press.
Kurzman, Charles, ed. 1998. *Liberal Islam: A Sourcebook*. New York: Oxford University Press.
"The Little NGO That Could." *Cairo Times*, April 13–19.
Mitchell, Richard. 1969. *The Society of the Muslim Brothers*. New York: Oxford University Press.

"The Papers of the Egyptian Wasat Party (*Awraq Hizb al-Wasat al-Misri*)." Year and publisher unlisted.

Shadid, Anthony. 2001. *Legacy of the Prophet: Despots, Democrats and the New Politics of Islam.* Boulder, CO: Westview Press.

"Wasat Party Platform." 2004. www.alwasatparty.org.

Wickham, Carrie Rosefsky. 2004. "The Path to Moderation: Strategy and Learning in the Formation of the *Wasat* Party in Egypt." *Comparative Politics*, January, 205–28.

Zubaida, Sami. 1992. "Islam, the State and Democracy: Contrasting Conceptions of Society in Egypt." *Middle East Report* 179, pp. 2–10.

———. 2001. "Islam and the Politics of Community and Citizenship." *Middle East Report* 221, no. 4. pp. 20–8.

9

Intercultural Understanding in a Community School

Elizabeth M. Bounds and Bobbi Patterson

The small ring formed spontaneously in the morning sunlight. Four children joined hands and began to circle and sing. Differences of accent and skin color were no differences at all.... On a school playground in Avondale, a Sudanese girl, a Croatian boy, an Iraqi boy and an American girl played together during a break from their classroom work. A simple moment, yet also a miracle.

This image of a beloved community of children encapsulates the ideals of the International Community School (ICS), a new public charter school located six miles from the center city of Atlanta, Georgia. The image is central to the school's introductory brochure, which speaks of the "miracle" that the school wants to foster, through the four "key planks" of its educational program: academic excellence, service-oriented education, community in diversity, and family and community partnerships. Its intention, stated in the school's basic informational packet, is to bring refugee, immigrant, and local U.S. children together in one educational environment, while also helping both children and their families to "access the support services they need to excel in a multi-cultural society" (International Community School Informational Packet 2003).

Mixing cultures in a public institution is not in itself new, but the wide global span of the children's backgrounds points to the new breadth of global migration as it shapes and is shaped by entrance into a society such as the United States, itself formed by complex mixes of previous immigrations, both voluntary and involuntary. This tiny school is part of what is now being called a new or emerging "global civil society." The religious resonances of the image of the "beloved community" along with the language of "miracle" demonstrate the centrality of spirituality in the core values of the school. ICS prefers the term "spirituality" over "religion." Spirituality conveys an inclusivity of various traditions and expressions of faith that the administrators, faculty, and staff of ICS understand to be fundamental to the formation of this microcosmic global civic space. All contributors to this volume are asking what are or might be the differing roles of religion in these global civic structures. Does religion in its various forms and dynamics enable connections? Does it divide and destroy? For us, the International Community School is a case study offering some responses to these questions. Many of the other chapters in this collection focus on the macro-levels of globalization. In contrast, we focus on the local and particular, asking what can happen as globalized social, political, and religious structures shape one experimental school intentionally trying to foster a civic space of shared global values. This exploration of what we have begun to understand through our initial encounters and conversations offers, we believe, some insights into the complexity of globalized religious interactions and suggests caution about any easy generalizations. We will start on the ground, at one of the meetings held to prepare for the opening of the school.

The Story of the Chimes

The first parents' meeting we attended was on a rainy Saturday morning in March 2002 in Avondale Estates, an exurb of Atlanta. It was held in the fellowship hall building of Avondale-Patillo United Methodist Church, behind the main sanctuary, chapel, and Sunday school buildings. The church has been very public about its role in supporting the school. The A-frame architecture of the space was wood paneled, with a fireplace on the south wall and an industrial kitchen on the north side, with a serving area buffering it from the large open space that served as the meeting space. Within this larger space were a grand piano in the northwest corner and several long tables with fruits, sweet rolls, milk, coffee, and juice on the eastern wall. There were dozens of metal folding chairs laid out to form two different spaces. The larger space had two or three concentric circles of chairs, with a podium at the northern end in front of the kitchen serving area. The smaller space had about eight circular tables set up with eight chairs each.

People milled about, waiting for the meeting to start: a group of Vietnamese women, dressed somewhat professionally for a Saturday morning; an African man with his little boy; some Bosnian couples with small children; an African man in a work uniform accompanied by a young white man. Several African American women, some with men and children, chatted together. There were also young white parents from Avondale, newly arrived and longtime locals, all casually dressed. Each of these groups was having conversations among themselves.

Around 9:40 an older white woman in a denim skirt and sandals who had been warmly greeting almost everyone in the room called people together in the circle of chairs. Slight and gentle-looking, she evidently was a leader. This was Sister Jane,[1] a Dominican nun who had lived in Atlanta for more than ten years and who had spent most of her career in education. She, along with a few others in the room, had written the grant that made this occasion possible—one that had resulted in permission from DeKalb County to establish a federally funded charter school specifically to serve refugee children, mostly from the neighboring community of Clarkston, as well as a selected group of other DeKalb County children. Our meeting that Saturday was the third public meeting for parents and other interested persons to be involved in all that needed to be done for the opening of the school in August.

As we settled in our chairs, Sister Jane introduced Gloria, a middle-aged African American woman in a more formal blue suit. She represented the Friends of International Community School Board and began the meeting with the blessing "This is the day the Lord has made. Thank God." She continued, expressing gratitude for the commitment displayed here and concluding with, "We will see many miracles." After her statement, she turned again to Sister Jane, who, she said, would lead us in a meditation. Picking up a pair of Tibetan hand chimes, Sister Jane told us that "we [the ICS community] value quiet," which reminds us of the sacred. She invited us to sit in silence as she rang the bells three times to enable us to become quiet. With each sound, we were asked to become quieter inside. Then she rang the bells slowly, each time slightly louder than before. Out of the quiet, she asked us to reflect on our own education, focusing on "what about it would you like to pass on to your children." After a few moments of silence, we were invited to talk with our neighbors about our thoughts.

For a while the room buzzed with small conversations. Some groups spoke in their native languages. Other, culturally mixed groups slowly struggled through broken English. Sister Jane asked the groups to express in a word or short phrase their responses to the question. Their answers included the following: safety, bonds, art, desire, dedicated teachers, patience, community, values, hands-on learning, protection, tenacity, fun, love of learning, self-esteem building, protection, acceptance of self and others, love of other languages and other cultures, diversity, and freedom to experiment and to express.

During these discussions, Sister Jane suggested that there would need to be some translation of what was being said for the Bosnians and perhaps others in the room. The principal, Jack, the former head of a prestigious private international school in Atlanta, was introduced, along with an assistant teacher from Bosnia whose previous work had been with one of the refugee resettlement programs in Clarkston. The floor was open for questions.

Most of the questions focused on the details of the first day of school, uniforms, the after-school program, and so on. One parent asked if there would be religious instruction, to which Jack, a middle-aged white man dressed in jeans and a shirt, quickly responded, "No, there is no religious instruction at this school," although, he said, there would be learning about different religions, and there would be a "concern for spirituality" (with the use of the bells as an example). He emphasized the importance of studying religions in the contemporary world to cut down on "stereotypical ideas" about both the religions themselves and the people who practice them. As Jack spoke, the room filled with the mumblings of translations.

In later conversations with some of the original organizers of the school, we discovered that there was even more occurring around questions of religion and spirituality than had met our eyes. The original vision had been to found a Christian school, since many of those involved were committed Christians who were eager to model an inclusive way of being Christian. However, they had come to realize that many Muslim, Hindu, and Buddhist parents would never send their children to any school that called itself "Christian" because they would be concerned about proselytism. However, the organizers had agreed that religious understanding would be an important contributor to the kind of intercultural exchange they wished to foster. Moreover, they valued an inclusive spirituality as part of the processes of the school. However, developing such an inclusive spirituality was not, they were discovering, easy.

At an early meeting with representatives from various refugee groups, a candle had been lit. A Bosnian woman told Sister Jane and her colleague that the only time Bosnians used candles was for funerals. At the end of the meeting, Sister Jane asked everyone to get in a circle and hold hands, and the Muslim men told her about the prohibition of men touching the hands of women. After doing so, they would need to purify their hands. These elements were subsequently avoided, and Sister Jane and others always asked participants what would be appropriate for them, and they were very responsive and helpful in their answers. Clearly, there were no easy answers when seeking practices of spirituality appropriate to such a multicultural space. But all involved in ICS were committed to finding ways to share their deepest beliefs for the sake of the children and the school.

Creating Global Space

As the two of us sat in this planning meeting, we began to realize that the International Community School is a new kind of public space in the making where there is a mixing and re-formation directly connected to the impact of globalization. This school is a transnational space, "a diaspora of cultures and peoples around the world," as Mark Juergensmeyer suggested to us in a conversation. Its participants are embedded in "complex, multistranded social relations that link together societies of origin and settlement" (Levitt 2001, 6). What could we learn by observing the formation of this space, including its religious aspects? Reading in different literatures about globalization, we recognize our privilege to be exploring a global civil society in microcosm. Historically, schools have been settings in which cultural formation occurs. They are the spaces where entrance into a society is mediated. But in the global context, this mediation is not a simple assimilation to a dominant national culture. What is exciting about this space is how it demands attention to multiple cultures and religions. Embodied in this school are multiple social forces. ICS may provide an example of a space in which teachers, students, and parents negotiate a global citizenry reflecting pluralized transnationalism.

As societies become more complex, increasingly elaborate institutions mediate the relationships between persons and their places and among persons themselves. Scholars from many disciplines connect the notion of civil society to these mediating institutions or spaces. Here conflicts can be resolved and connections can be formed. Historically under conditions of modernization, civil society as a concept represented the institutionalizing requirements and processes for forming a national identity. But in today's global contexts, these earlier assumptions focused solely on nation-based civil societies are being challenged. The civic spaces of any nation are now influenced by forces that span the globe. Globalization, remarks Saskia Sassen (1998), "generates contradictory spaces, characterized by contestation, internal differentiation, continuous border crossings" (xxxiv). Much of the current discussions about global civil society focuses predominantly on the actions of elites working through voluntary/NGO associations. For example, Anheier, Glasius, and Kaldor (2001) in their definition of global civil society emphasize actors who are "engaged in negotiations and discussions about civil matters with governmental, inter-governmental, and other transnational actors at various levels and the business sphere" (4).

Yet what we find in the emerging space of ICS is not about global elites. The parents and students of ICS have not voluntarily joined this new global space. Neither are they part of a privileged business, intellectual, or governmental class. As refugees, they bring their stories and identities to this new space, to ICS, in which both will be negotiated. The emerging experience and definition of civil society in this kind of global context, then, concentrates on negotiation of individual and communal identities. While partially determined, of course, by broad global changes, these local spaces have their own integrity, processes, and counterinfluences on current ideas about civil society. The participants in ICS are certainly "agents of globalization...crafting multiple modes of global capitalism itself" (Freeman 2001, 1029, 1031), but they are not the barons of global capital and power that many expect. Their capital includes social and religious elements crucial to their survival amid forces far beyond their control with which they must cope. At ICS, we see families not as passive pawns but as active agents in a different and emerging global civil society. They continually react, adjust, respond, create, and re-form their identities and lives, now part of the ICS space and story (Bourdieu and Wacquant 1992, 130).

As scholars of religion, we were specifically intrigued to explore how religion did and did not contribute to this emerging global civil society at ICS. We recognized that in U.S. public school systems, problematics involving religion's presence or absence remain. Officially at ICS, a public charter school, religious instruction is not offered, as Jack made clear. However, the mission of ICS is rooted in cultural encounters that are understood to be inescapably religious—a reality underlined in the negotiations over a common expression of spirituality related earlier in this chapter. Most of the refugee families whose children attend ICS have little consciousness of the American or modern way of dividing between religion and culture. Many Sudanese Christians, Somalian and Iraqi Muslims, and Bosnian Muslims whose children are now at the school have known violent persecution because of their religious identities central to their cultural self-understanding. But these religious-cultural identities sustained them as they were forced to give up homes, jobs, and neighborhoods and come to the United States.

While they do bring these religious experiences and identities to the school, the primary concern of these parents is to have their children educated. They value education not only because it will aid their children's assimilation but also because it eventually will provide the economic stability needed to keep their faith alive. Realizing that the school values religious traditions, they also find social support for their beliefs and practices They accept the multireligious vision, possibly as part of what they understand as an "American way of life," and send their children to study religious traditions during school hours and in the after-school program. With firsthand experience of the ways in which religion is both scourge and haven, most families at ICS understand the importance of exploring how religion shapes the deepest levels of identity. What they seek at the school is a place in which their religious identity is respected, accepted, and heard. At ICS, globalization, religion, and civic life interconnect.

The school has been able to include teaching about religion by highlighting specific religious festivals such as Ramadan, Christmas, and Hannukah. Bulletin boards designed by classroom teachers reflected shared learning about each of these significant religious experiences. We were told of an time when some Russian Jews came to the school during Hannukah. As they were touring the school, they looked into a kindergarten classroom and saw that the teacher was holding up a book about Hannukah and reading it to the children. This group also noted the bulletin boards. Then we went to the ESL class, where the teachers were telling the children about this special Jewish time. They explained the menorah and how to make a dreidel. The school had no notion that these people were going to appear on that day. Needless to say, they were very touched personally and by the educational valuing of religious life and practice. One day the principal observed three or four children from different countries standing together outside but apart from others. He stood to watch them, and when they got on their knees and touched the ground with their foreheads, he realized that they were praying to Allah. After this brief practice, they immediately got up and went off to play with their friends. Such outward expressions of spiritual devotion are honored at ICS. Another example of this is that many Muslim staff members and almost all others take their various holy days off. ICS views this as a good learning experience for everyone. Additionally, many Muslim staff members fast during Ramadan, which the school views as a reminder of the sacred in their midst. One member of the school staff was so impressed with this Muslim devotion that she decided to wear her ashen sign of the cross on Ash Wednesday. Usually, she did not show this sign, but now she felt that the school was creating a culture of respect for religious practices. The interchange about religion among the staff thrives.

Such interactions have led to a significant amount of mutually created and mutually corrective dialogue around religion. This dialogue partially shapes a new language and a new space, along the lines of the envisioned "beloved community." One analysis of this dialogue could focus on the relative positive or negative impacts of religion in this shared civil space and conversation. Alternatively, we have been interested in how the freedom to express religious identity and difference is identified as valued and then negotiated. Because of these interests, we will first address the global refugee situation, including issues of religion and emerging global cultures and civil societies and their expression in Clarkston, Georgia; we will then turn to the local expression of these issues at the International Community School.

Clarkston and Diaspora

Regardless of differing definitions of globalization, there is agreement that national economies and societies in the late twentieth and early twenty-first centuries are connecting in new and complex ways. Perhaps the most visible connections are those made by persons, human bodies who are now moving more rapidly and more frequently among nations. These transnational migratory movements are resulting in growing diasporas of persons who, through the power of modern communication and transportation, can stay connected in unprecedented ways with both their communities of origin and others in diaspora. These migrations may be due to direct coercion and violence in their communities of origin or to indirect violence or pressure of economic restructuring (Levitt 2001, 7–8). Since the 1960s, immigration to the United States has been rising sharply, with most immigrants coming from Asia, Latin America, and the Caribbean. Sassen (1998) identifies "political, military, and economic linkages with the United States . . . that, together with overpopulation, poverty or unemployment induce emigration" into the increasing number of low-wage service jobs available here (40).

Atlanta is now very much part of these diasporas. It can (and does) claim itself as a global city, a term that signifies not only the presence of international business and financial connections but also the presence of "cultures from all over the world [that] are de- and re-territorialized" (Sassen 1998, xxxi). While many of those coming from other countries have been economic immigrants and migrants, a significant group have been refugees. Since 1981, more than forty-eight thousand refugees have come to Georgia and often are first settled in Atlanta (Bixler 2002a, F5). Most of the Atlanta-bound refugees have been given their first U.S. homes in apartment complexes in Clarkston, Georgia. Many longtime Atlantans view Clarkston as a peripheral place. Perched at the edge of the burgeoning metropolis, this formerly sleepy, southern town bristles with new suburbanization and economic development. Until recently, Clarkston maintained many of its original patterns and racial homogeneities. In the first waves of change, African Americans moved out from the central city. More recently, there has been a dramatic increase in the refugee population, bringing people from a myriad of nations, including Bosnia, Vietnam, Liberia, Kosovo, Somalia, and Sudan. In 1980, out of 4,539 residents, 149 were foreign born. In 2000, out of 6,826 residents, 2,301 were foreign born. The population is now about one-third Asian, one-eighth Latin American, and almost one-third African (Bixler 2002b, E1).

Such a transition is, obviously, both rapid and remarkable. Many refugee organizations have established offices in the area, providing resettlement services and educational and socialization programs. Police and other city officials have had to rethink their assumptions about the assets and needs of their constituencies. Religiously, the changes are equally dramatic. Since the formation of the town, there have been white and black Protestant churches in Clarkston. Now there are two mosques, both of which include Islamic schools for learning Arabic. The town has a Vietnamese Buddhist temple, a Mennonite church with African members, and a variety of Christian congregations from Pentecostal to Methodist. The mainline Clarkston Baptist Church itself hosts five different ethnic congregations, four of them African and one Filipino. Instead of becoming another predictable bedroom community for Atlanta, Clarkston has become a global village, with shops filled with multiethnic products and buyers. This globalized cultural space within Greater Atlanta is emerging, a "terrain where people from many different countries are most likely to meet and a multiplicity of cultures come together" (Sassen 1998, xxx).

The International Community School

Rooted in this context, the International Community School was chartered two years ago, with funding from the federal government and the county. Four years in the planning, it was the vision of several local educators, a journalist who had covered refugee issues, and several local Christian leaders. They and others recognized how the local county school system struggled to cope with such a large influx of refugee children from many different countries. Problems with language, cultural expectations, and behavioral norms overwhelmed the system. The original organizers came together with a few refugee families and decided to create ICS. In addition to serving refugee children and families, they planned to accept local children from the county to build intentionally a multinational and multicultural space. Early publicity identified three target groups: refugee children "bringing not only gifts and talents, but the deep physical and spiritual wounds of war"; "low-income children," who "are likewise children of violence, suffering from a chronic lack of safety, poverty, and racial discrimination"; and "relatively affluent children," who "are in need of a positive multi-cultural educational experience and who are isolated from the economic and social realities of the less affluent" (International Community School Informational Packet 2003). The Avondale-Patillo United Methodist Church, which receives payment for housing the school, is a typical mainline church that has lost white membership over the years due to death and changing neighborhoods. Like Clarkston, Avondale has a range of citizens, from southern whites in its original brick and ranch-style houses to refugees and African Americans living in its newer apartment complexes. It has also become an "inside the perimeter" neighborhood, attracting professional classes who want shorter commutes and the feeling of an "older neighborhood." Children attending and parents working with the school will represent all these constituencies in both Avondale and Clarkston.

The school opened its doors in August 2002 with 125 prekindergarten, kindergarten, and first-grade students attending. There are children from Rwanda, Ethiopia, Sudan, Bosnia and Herzegovina, Congo, Afghanistan, Guatemala, Iraq, Croatia, and Palestine, along with both African and Euro-American children from the Atlanta area. Lunches are catered, and an after-school program emphasizes tutoring, homework assistance, and intercultural sharing. The school expects intentional and regular participation of all parents as part of the learning community that includes highly qualified teachers and a principal with almost thirty years' experience in international education.

In this alternative educational and civil society space, refugee children will enter into U.S. culture and society, along with their parents. In one sense, this process is nothing new, since schools are prime mediating institutions, central to the infrastructure of civil society and to any process of civic formation. U.S. public education has always been a place for formation and assimilation into national membership. However, as mentioned earlier, the children and families of ICS are participating in a place that rejects one-way assimilation into a homogeneous American culture. Instead, the school advocates and enacts an interactive formation of education, cultures, and people into a new kind of global civic life that embraces religion. It envisions mutual learning among all participants, whether born of peasant parents in a Somali village or of Euro-American middle-class parents in the county hospital.

The planning materials of the school reveal a self-conscious attempt to build a new kind of globalized community. First, the school's name, the *International Community* School ("making a world of difference," as the information material says), sends a globalized message. Second, all parents of enrolled students are required to commit themselves to volunteer work in the school not only for the good of their children but also to enable them to interact with one another. Third, the four main goals of the school include not only "academic excellence" and "service-oriented education," common in most schools, but also "community in diversity" and "family and community partnerships." Finally, the very processes that birthed the school emphasized community participation and decision making. The constant concern for ICS has been formation through cultural interaction. Every day this is played out during classroom time, in which multiple cultures and languages are studied, and after school through the Heritage Language Program, which explores "languages and cultures of different countries represented by our students... songs, art, geography and some history taught by native speakers" (International Community School Informational Packet 2003).

As our initial incident shows, respecting and sharing cultures at ICS is always also respecting and sharing religion. The school literature makes this plain when it speaks of a goal of "community in diversity," which includes learning about "the beliefs and traditions" of other students amid its goal of "family and community partnership." The school expects to provide not only educational and social but also "spiritual" services. The constant challenge is finding ways to do this that enable religious differences to coexist in constructive rather than destructive ways. This challenge can only be—and is being—solved through patient daily trial and error. However, we would like to use the rest of this chapter to explore some dimensions of the challenge that suggest ways to think theoretically and act practically to support development of globalized civic spaces where religious differences can be negotiated.

From Global to Local: The Problem of Identity
in a Globalizing World

Globally we watch religion playing a significant role in collective and personal
identity formation. Locally at the International Community School, this global
reality is not only acknowledged but also embraced. Because many students
and families at ICS have lost the physical places and spaces in which the
wholeness of their identities was acknowledged and lived out, the school
attempts to provide a safe and stable space for that wholeness to thrive again.
It creates a local space with global room that includes religion. Without an
ICS, refugees from Clarkston will find their culturally particular capacities for
self-recognition, meaning making, and action overwhelmed. Being displaced
disturbs one's ability to locate one's self internally, within one's community
and in relation to other, new communities. Recognizing that dislocation negatively affects identity stability and function, ICS decided to create intentionally a location that affirms multiple experiences and identities.

While the relationship between place and identity is never a static experience, the fluidity of this relationship has increased exponentially for vast
numbers of persons by this early part of the twenty-first century. The crisis,
therefore, facing the students and families of ICS is very real. Ulf Hannerz,
in his book *Cultural Complexity*, describes the situation as "cultural flow," in
which the inherent dynamics of identity, place, and culture in a global world
continuously move. These dynamic "flows," according to Arjun Appadurai,
are currently magnified through increases in the influences of media and
global mobility. Recognizing that place can no longer be thought of in more
traditional anthropological ways as a fixed location, ICS is trying to avoid such
a "concretizing" process, which would narrow and confine its students toward
one homogenizing identity, culture, and experience. Instead, the school attempts to reflect the realities of today's world, the complexities of cultures
struggling to define and understand home for themselves (Appadurai 1988,
38, quoted in Hannerz 1992, 216). Although all persons on this planet are
affected to a greater or lesser extent by these "flows," none perhaps are as
powerfully dislocated and reshaped as refugees, forced from a homeland that
is destroying them to a completely alien environment where everything from
language to food to living space to personal hygiene may be profoundly and
irrevocably changed. The shocking additional fluidity of culture, identity, and
spaces in their new settlement situation necessitates creation of places where
this mix of factors can begin to cohere and initially sustain their survival
(Hannerz 1992, 7). During their resettlement transition, refugees experience
the push and pull of retaining their own culture while participating in the
dominant culture at least as much as is necessary for survival (Foner 1997,

969, 970; Nwaniora and McAdoo 1996, 485). Research on immigrant experience suggests that finding spaces like ICS in which persons can more safely manage the crises and renegotiations of cultural identity enables "cultural generativity—the recreating and renovating of a culture" (Hones 1999, 189). These renovating spaces offer social relationships where "collective cultural inventor[ies] of meaning and meaningful external forms" (accessible to the senses and public) can begin to emerge and develop (Hannerz 1992, 7).

Refugees work to relocate, to find a sense of place culturally, pragmatically, and religiously. Previously this process was envisioned as a "melting pot" where old cultures "melted" into the homogenizing blend of "American." In a social order where a notion of "multiculturalism" is increasingly assumed, new cultural groups may experience multiple changes in identity— retaining some elements of the "old" culture, reworking others, and developing new possibilities. Without places that offer some sense of safety and some positive relationships, displaced people will have a more difficult time with this process of change. In such places and communities, refugees can create enough stability of place to feel safe enough to explore "where," "how far," and "to what effect" their lives can and will reshape themselves in relation to their new cultural home. These places provide safe and respectful spaces in which newly settling people can begin the work—at least to some degree according to their own choices—of reorienting themselves to their new landscape. Typically the first generation of migrants sets up a religious community, either as an independent institution or nested within an existing religious institution, within an ethnic enclave. There they can "find a haven in the architecture, statues, relics, icons, smells, rituals, language, and company of fellow countrymen [sic]," along with a variety of social supports that help ease the crises of transition (Ebaugh and Chafetz 2000, 139). Post-1965 immigrants have entered into a United States with far more explicit commitments to diversity, which may enable them to retain more of their own culture while still being able to identify as "American." Other, related changes in American life around such issues as gender status and sexuality do pose considerable challenges and places of conflict. Also, because many of these newer immigrants are not Christians, they may still feel themselves holding on to a threatened way of life (Ebaugh and Chafetz 2000, 145–48).

Changes in religious life in the town of Clarkston reflect this range of possibilities. Following the traditional model, a number of new places of worship have been formed so that refugees can continue their own ethnic-religious community. For example, two mosques have opened in the neighborhood, one serving the Bosnian community, the other serving the Somalian community. Christian refugees have two additional options. They can form their own separate community within an existing church (the example here is the First Baptist Church, which hosts five international congregations), or they can participate as individuals and families as full participants in a U.S. congregation.

Christian refugees often choose the denomination they have known at home. But the story we were told of Sudanese Presbyterians attending a local Mennonite congregation in Clarkston reflects the complexity of these decisions and relationships. These Sudanese came to this congregation after being stunned by the formality of the local Presbyterian service. Although they were converted by Presbyterian missionaries and considered themselves Presbyterians, they felt more comfortable at the Mennonite church, with its more Bible-based and emotion-filled worship. What is unusual about the ICS is that it is trying to create the thick support migrants have found in these re-created religious communities while gently moving persons into increased interaction with others, both U.S. born and foreign born, unlike themselves.

From its initial planning, the ICS intentionally communicated its vision of creating a beloved community that welcomed and respected all. Expressing this hope required a richer notion of language than was typical of many schools in order to foster a locally globalized civic life. As the language, actually languages, unfolded, the school hired many translators to communicate the evolving message and craft paths of communication and action to create this multicultural place. Additionally, language was performed through lived and shared practices among cultures, as our opening incident demonstrates. In that case, even the sparsest use of spiritual practices, spoken and performed, became a site of contestation and translation at ICS. Observing the intersections of languages and practices, we watched the community negotiate shared and unshared spaces of identification moving toward common goals and values. One example of contestation and negotiation occurred when the school discovered it had scheduled a much-anticipated field trip on Id, the feast day marking the end of Ramadan. Sister Jane told us that Muslim parents found their children begging to be able to go to school on a sacred holiday. A pragmatic point of almost universal consensus among refugees and service providers to refugees is that the only thing more important than employment for successful settlement into a U.S. context is acquisition of the English language. Sister Jane, for example, remarked in a conversation with us that the primary barrier to parent participation in ICS is parents' "shyness" about their language abilities. But what cultural transformation is part of this new linguistic skill? Because the translation process involves not only questions of moving between English and a myriad of other languages but also questions of negotiating the relation of different worlds from cultures to bureaucracies to church, change is inevitable. With forms to be filled out and information sheets to be read, signed, and abided, parents and staff are continually communicating and thereby creating new and shared languages and worlds.

But sharing is not a panacea. Communicative processes also are conflicted. At one parents' meeting for example, a Euro-American ICS volunteer spent more than an hour helping a Somalian family translate and fill out the form required for their child to receive federal lunch funding. The volunteer corrected the Somali man's expectation that his wife would bring him something to drink while he worked on the form. "You are in American now," the volunteer said. "We don't do it that way here. In America, the men get drinks for themselves." Obviously, there were issues of identity, its retention, translation, and transformation in relation to U.S. public funding for feeding certain children. But perhaps less obvious were the issues of the imposition of American ideologies of identity, which this refugee family had to negotiate while acquiring a "free lunch" for their children.

Similarly, we observed a fourteen-year-old who was translating during a parents' meeting for an entire row of Bosnian Muslims. She was dressed in up-to-date U.S. fashions and looked already quite acclimated to her new culture. As is often the case, children learn the language and the culture first because of their participation in school. They then become translators for their families, not only moving between two languages but also interpreting what to their parents may be a bewildering culture and social order. Such adaptive abilities often translate into other assumptions, including levels of freedom taken by the children in their behavior, dress, and social interaction, of which their parents may not approve (Foner 1997, 970). Recognizing that language is not simply a matter of naming objects, desires, and pragmatics, ICS approached translation as central to its communication of difference [and] respected a shared desire to learn. By shaping language creation as an inclusive process, ICS invited parents, teachers, and students to participate in and determine the direction of the school and its resources. One example of this intention was the creation of the Parents to Parents groups through which those with stronger skills in English could share their translation capacities with other members of their language group.

ICS's support for the multiplicities of language resonates with Hannerz's view that by focusing on the back-and-forth dynamic of multiple languages at a particular place, one creates a site for understanding cultural complexity. The thickness of many languages shifts back and forth with the thinness of the few that become the preferred language(s) of emerging, coherent, and yet still global space. Through the "thinning" process of languages and their meanings and values, groups that had been quite mobile and disparate begin to settle and cohere into one new group. Their media for communication become more unified. In the process, they begin to shape their emerging group identity with developing images and engagements conveying their own forms of agency and collectivity with feelings of "neighborhood," or what we might call "home"—or, in this case, school (Appadurai 1996, 6–7). Through the back-and-forth of thick and thin, peripheral to center, as Hannerz calls it, cultural and identity boundaries are crossed as languages are "appropriat[ed], penetrat[ed], and coopt[ed from] one group to another with bilingualism, multilingualism, and translation" (Hannerz 1992, 20).

At ICS, the thinning of many languages to English shapes the group identity that is emerging and will continue to emerge. This is, perhaps, a microcosm or exemplar of the challenges of forming this miniature global civic space. How thin or thick will this "English" be? How, amid this flow, will messages involving U.S. culture be shared, adjusted, inserted, and reconstructed with and through the linguistic mix of ICS? How will that shape the flow of culture(s) that becomes the place, the group identity, meaning, and values of this micro-site, ICS? What contribution will the languages of religion make to this evolving civic space?

Of course, not all of the conversation partners are refugees or those involved with refugee services. In a conversation with Joy, a member of the Avondale-Patillo United Methodist Church for thirty years and a local teacher, we heard descriptions of other kinds of translations. There was the difficult work of translating for other parishioners the importance of housing and supporting this international school. There were the languages needed to communicate with refugees. She searched for language with which she could advocate with her own church peers on behalf of the school. She told us how previous experiences with refugee youth who had damaged church property while playing soccer helped her empathize with her church peers' resistances and anxieties. She had learned to translate that fear into opportunity for church growth, since their congregation was aging, and many refugee parents in the apartment complex sent their children regularly to the church's Sunday school. She also overheard the language of the New Testament calling the church to offer its space as "the work of the gospel," no matter what the faith background of the families and children. Having grown up in the local area and seen it globalize, Joy now in her sixties, believed that cross-religious cooperation was crucial for their local future.

Through experimentation, the school is developing a very successful language of the arts. At every parents' meeting and at most workdays during breaks from painting and room preparation, some form of art is performed and/or participated in. After his opening remarks at the meeting with which we began, the principal and a member of the community from Ghana, who is building a micro-enterprise organization for refugee women in the area, led the whole room in a French song. There have been Eastern European performances of balalaika and piano, and Caribbean performances on the steel drums. The after-school program offers daily times of intercultural sharing that highlight the arts embodying and respecting values and meanings from various cultures. This art-based language exchange and integration has become part of ICS's social practices, rituals, and daily life. It is one way of creating a coherent language of mutuality and shared group identity. Sister Jane told us about an ongoing art group for women that meets at ICS. Its purpose is multiple: to create community among refugee women; to enable cross-cultural forms of expression of their experiences of crisis and transition; to offer sources of support and healing, including religion; and to enable a new relationship to and ownership of the space where their children are learning.

However, relationships and languages spoken in organizations other than the school can segment and complicate emerging dialogues. For example, we were told in a conversation about a Muslim father from Clarkston who allowed his daughters to participate in the after-school program offered by a local refugee service organization. Though agreeing to this, he was also careful to forbid participation in any parts of the program that he deemed "too American." According to Nancy, a Mennonite ESL teacher who worked with this man's daughters, he would ask if an activity was going to "Christianize" or "Americanize" his daughters. Parents from Vietnam, Somalia, and other countries shared these concerns. Speaking and other communication practices that become "too American" engender an identity transformation that for many refugees carries more the prospect of loss than of useful assimilation. Yet learning to speak and understand new languages and practices allows newcomers and locals at ICS to maintain continuity with their previous ways of life while exploring new possibilities for expanding their identities.

Feeling Our Way Forward: Some Concluding Thoughts

At the International Community School in Clarkston, we sense the emergence of a multicultural space combining a strong expectation for engagement across difference with an acceptance of cultural and religious diversity. It serves as a model in a globalizing world.. ICS presents a microcosm of intersection and reconstruction, creation and re-creation, "where, in some way and to some degree diversity gets organized" (Hannerz 1992, 22), where the thick becomes shared and thinner, where the continual fluidity of complex cultures becomes recognizable and coherent. While always struggling with forces pressing for a space dominated by the lowest (and most powerful) common denominator, this institution is slowly, painfully trying to create something different. Working together amid conflict, negotiation, and joy, identities are sustained and reconfigured as shared values for living and learning emerge.

In her study of women's projects trying to create common democratic space in communities torn apart by violence, Cynthia Cockburn (1998, 211–30) remarks on the importance of a balance of fluid identity and a sense of safety. Successful projects, she found, affirmed difference, left collective identity negotiable, and emphasized group process. She writes, "We have seen them [the women] negotiating their partial agendas, living with mixity, and learning to translate each other's languages" (229). These seem to us key factors for developing new models of localized global cultures that become shared civic spaces.

Because religions deeply contribute socially, culturally, and politically to identity and community, they are fundamental to these conversations over civic space. The emerging structures of new global civil societies, we suggest, are discovered in local settings. By participating in the processes of ICS, including sharing of religious traditions and values, we have witnessed and discovered points where religious identity is being negotiated in relationship to global and local forces for the sake of an emerging shared vision of a beloved community. Even in the early stages, religious negotiation at ICS affects and is affected by the emerging global context of those committed to the school. Because our exploration of global civil society is specific to one place, it inverts many current views of the interface of global and local, civic and religious forces. Over time, we hope that this kind of localized study will contribute to the larger theories about the relationships of religion and global civil society. We believe such studies complicate calculations about how religion does and does not, can and cannot contribute to new forms of shared values and life. By detailing more precisely the moments when religion enhances or blocks the processes of translation and re-creation of identity and community, we can develop better models of civil society in a globalized world.

NOTE

1. Names in this chapter have been changed to protect privacy.

BIBLIOGRAPHY

Abu-Lughod, Lila. 1993. *Writing Women's Worlds: Bedouin Stories.* Berkeley: University of California Press.
Anheier, Helmut, Marlies Galsius, and Mary Kaldor, eds. 2001. *Global Civil Society.* Oxford: Oxford University Press.
Appadurai, Arjun. 2001. *Globalization.* Durham, NC: Duke University Press.
———. 1996. *Modernity of Large.* Minneapolis: University of Minnesota Press.
Bergeron, Suzanne. 2001. "Political Economy Discourses of Globalization and Feminist Politics." *Signs: Journal of Women in Culture and Society* 26:983–1006.
Bhattaacharjee, Anannya. 1997. "The Public/Private Mirage: Mapping Homes and Undomesticating Violence Work in the South Asian Immigrant Community." In *Feminist Genealogies, Colonial Legacies, Democratic Futures,* edited by M. Jacqui Alexander and Chandra Talpade Mohanty, 308–29. New York: Routledge.
Bixler, Mark. 2002a. "Clampdown Delays Refugee Reunions in Georgia." *Atlanta Journal Constitution,* May 1, F5.
———. 2002b. "Influx of Refugees Makes Demands on a DeKalb Town in Transition." *Atlanta Journal Constitution,* June 19, E1.
Bourdieu, Pierre, and Loic J. D. Wacquant. 1992. *An Invitation to Reflexive Sociology.* Chicago: University of Chicago Press.
Burawoy, Michael, (editor) 1991. *Ethnography Unbound: Power and Resistance in the Modern Metropolis.* Berkeley: University of California Press.

Cockburn, Cynthia. 1998. *The Space between Us: Negotiating Gender and National Identities in Conflict*. New York: Zed Books.

Cohen, Jean, and Andrew Arato. 1992. *Civil Society and Political Theory*. Cambridge, MA: MIT Press.

Collins, Patricia Hills. 1990. *Black Feminist Thought: Knowledge, Consciousness and the Politics of Empowerment*. Boston: Unwin Hyman.

Ebaugh, Helen Rose, and Janet Saltzman Chafetz. 2000. *Religion and the New Immigrants*. Walnut Creek, CA: AltaMira Press.

Ervin, Alexander. 2000. *Applied Anthropology: Tools and Perspectives for Contemporary Practice*. Boston: Allyn and Bacon.

Foner, Nancy. 1997. "The Immigrant Family: Cultural Legacies and Cultural Changes." *International Migration Review* 31:961–74.

Freeman, Carla. 2001. "Is Local:Global as Feminine:Masculine? Rethinking the Gender of Globalization." *Signs: Journal of Women in Culture and Society* 26:1007–37.

Gallop, Jane. 1988. *Thinking through the Body*. New York: Columbia University Press.

Greenwood, Davydd J., and Morten Levin. 1998. *Introduction to Action Research: Social Research for Social Change*. Thousand Oaks, CA: Sage.

Hannerz, Ulf. 1992. *Cultural Complexity: Studies in the Social Organization of Meaning*. New York: Columbia University Press.

Hones, Donald F. 1999. "Crisis, Continuity, and the Refugee: Educational Narrative of a Hmong Father and His Children." *Journal of Contemporary Ethnography* 28:166–98.

International Community School Informational Packet. 2003.

Israel, Barbara A., Amy J. Schultz, Edith Parker, and Adam Becker. 1998. "Review of Community-Based Research: Assessing Partnership Approaches to Improve Public Health." *Annual Revue of Public Health* 19:175–202.

Kannabiran, Vasanth, and Kalpana Kannabiran. 1997. "Looking at Ourselves: The Women's Movement in Hyderabad." In *Feminist Genealogies, Colonial Legacies, Democratic Futures*, edited by M. Jacqui Alexander and Chandra Talpade Mohanty, 259–79. New York: Routledge.

Lechner, Frank, and John Boli, eds. 2000. *The Globalization Reader*. Malden, MA: Blackwell.

Levitt, Peggy. 2001. *The Transnational Villagers*. Berkeley: University of California Press.

Nwaniora, Emeka, and Mariette McAdoo. 1996. "Acculurative Stress among Amerasian Refugees: Gender and Racial Difference." *Adolescence* 31, (122): 477–86.

Pieterse, Jan Nederveen. 1995. "Globalization as Hybridization." In *The Globalization Reader*, edited by Frank Lechner and John Boli, 99–108. Malden, MA: Blackwell.

Sassen, Saskia. 1998. *Globalization and Its Discontents: Essays on the New Mobility of People and Money*. New York: New Press.

Shohat, Ella. 2001. "Area Studies, Tranationalism, and the Feminist Production of Knowledge." *Signs: Journal of Women in Culture and Society* 26:1269–72.

Troppe, M. 1994. *Participatory Action Research: Merging the Community and Scholarly Agendas*. Providence, RI: Campus Compact.

Winland, D. N. 1994. "Christianity and Community: Conversion and Adaptation among Hmong Refugee Women." *Canadian Journal of Sociology* 19:21.

10

Religious Transnationalism

Susanne Hoeber Rudolph

Churches are among the oldest of the transnationals, having long claimed a role equivalent to or transcending the political—before "nation" and "state" were even articulated concepts. On the other hand, churches were not and are not always transnational, operating above or extending across states. They have a history of being subsumed by states or collaborating with them. There have been times when the act of popes anointing kings signified the suzerainty of the sacred; there also have been and are times when states have appointed churchmen, licensed churches, and absorbed the sacred into their sovereignty. The questions I address in this chapter are the following: What are the implications for religion of the "fading of the state" (Rudolph and Piscatori 1997)? What are the prospects for the universal "ecumene" some religious leaders are attempting to build in the expanding transnational space? The term "ecumene" here refers to a community of individuals and organizations who believe that diverse religions share sufficient moral and spiritual ground to support cooperation across "civilizational" and political boundaries.

Until the sixteenth century, the unity of the Roman church's ecclesiastical organization transcended political boundaries. Regardless of political jurisdiction, the church controlled the appointment of clergy, collected church taxes from the faithful, controlled monastic lands, and exercised discipline over its priests and the faithful. But this universalism came to an end when the state or the empire contested the church's claim. From the sixteenth century onward and the rise of the absolutist state, ecclesiastical appointments, taxation, jurisdiction, administration, and discipline migrated to the hands of secular authorities. By 1523 the Spanish crown had secured the right to nominate every bishopric in Spain. Like the Chinese government today, the French king (on the basis of the Concordat of Bologna) became master of every important ecclesiastical appointment in France (Rice and Grafton 1994; Eckhom 2001). The nationalization or "state-ization" of churches in the fifteenth and sixteenth centuries coincided with the assertion of state sovereignty claims by political kingdoms. When the destructive force of religious competition between Protestants and Catholics was tamed by the principle *cujus regio, ejus religio*, the faith of the rulers of particular polities became the determinant of a country's religious dispensation, breaking the unity of a universal church. The church was superseded by many nationalized churches (Casanova 1997, 121–43). These events suggest that there is an intimate tie between forms of polity and forms of religious organization.

Nineteenth-century social thinkers saw an affinity not only between forms of polity and forms of religious organization but also between political forms and how religious phenomena are imagined. Reiterating the verities of much nineteenth-century religious scholarship, Max Weber asserted that "it is a universal phenomenon that the formation of a political association entails subordination to its corresponding god" (Roth and Wittich 1978, 1:412). He tells us that Yahweh, having begun his career as the god of a tribe, became the god of a confederation as Israelites expanded to larger areas; "political and military conquest also entailed the victory of a stronger god over the weaker god of the vanquished group" (413). Reorganization of political communities, Weber tells us, tends to entail formation of new cultic communities. He aligns the rise of monotheism with the emergence of empires, assuming a parallelism between the emergence of an imperial figure that subordinates lesser polities with the emergence of a triumphal godhead that subordinates the lesser gods of subordinate units.

I do not want to confirm or dispute the credibility of these assertions. I want to use them to raise a question fruitful for our deliberation: What is the implication for religion of the fading of sovereignty? What are the likely consequences of globalization for the structure of religion? Transnational forms of organization are growing stronger. Economic forces, multinational corporations, multilateral lending organizations; normative and legal regimes based in transnational communities of discourse, such as climate, environment, human rights, indigenous people's rights, women's issues; as well as the flow of migrants through permeable and controlled boundaries all collaborate to diminish the monopoly claim of national sovereignty assertions. Such forces encourage the transgressing and thinning of national boundaries. They lead to the creation of a transnational space in which civil society begins to form a transnational politics. This new politics is not an international politics, in which bounded states are presumed to be the actors, but a politics that transgresses borders, in which substate or cross-state expressions of civil society—such as some churches or transnational nongovernmental organizations—are the actors. It leads to the creation of transnational epistemic communities whose members share common worldviews, purposes, interests, and practices (Haas 1992, 1–35).

What are the implications of these developments for religious communities? Does such a thinning of borders and fading of states approximate the conditions of the world before the Reformation, when Charles V's weakly articulated universal empire coincided with the idea of a universal church ("Christendom")? Does the emergence of transnational civil society provide the environment for a new universal church?

I make a distinction between the possibility for a new or resurrected universal church, which I think is unlikely, and the possibility of a universal religiosity, for which current history provides some support. By universal church I mean the worldwide theological and institutional hegemony of a particular religion. Universal religiosity refers to an aggregative intellectual and social process of ecumenization, reaching across civilizational and state borders and engaging the full diversity of world religions. Such a process would be at once global and local, composed, on one hand, of intentional, transreligious hermeneutic initiatives by churchmen and churchwomen and, on the other hand, of spontaneous neighborly sharing of informal local practices by adherents of different religions. When nurtured, universal religiosity allows for the recognition that there is truth in all religions—a sentiment that is still vigorously challenged by the orthodox in the East and the West alike.

Why is religion in the new transnational space unlikely to take the form of a universal church but likely to take the form of a universal religiosity? The time for the sort of process Weber saw, in which the religion of a political hegemon could assert itself over subordinate or conquered units, is over, disrupted by the experience of colonization and the nationalist and democratic reaction against it. In the age of imperialism, Western religions migrated with the flag in ways that seemed to herald the universalization of Christian hegemony in the parts of Africa and Asia that were annexed to empires, just as the march of conquering Muslim peoples—Safavids, Afghans, Ottomans— had seemed to herald a similar hegemony. The pattern of religious diffusion has changed, however. Accelerating population movements in response to shifting labor demand, especially the migration of Middle Eastern and Asian peoples to the West, have broken the earlier coincidence of religion with geographic areas. In the age of migration, despite the best efforts of some Western nation-states to ring themselves with immigration statutes, the bearers of non-Western religions are migrating to the West, though not with large enough populations or sufficient ideological or material force to herald a counterhegemony.

Redistribution of religions has scattered faiths across the regions of the world in ways never before seen: Islam in Paris, Buddhism in Düsseldorf,

Zoroastrianism in Tokyo, Hinduism in Iowa City. To look only at one of the most conspicuous groupings: the Muslim community in the United States, approximately eight million strong, is growing vigorously, and Islam is on the verge of becoming the second-largest religion in America. Europe has fifteen million Muslims, two million in Germany alone (Afridi 2002; Fisher 2001). The fall of communism in the Soviet Union and Eastern Europe led to a brisk influx of proselytizers, notably Christian evangelicals but also representatives of minorities already in place—Catholics, Sunni, Shiite—leading to a reaction among the dominant Orthodox community, weakened by a century of repression (Witte and Bourdeaux 1999; Luxmoore and Babiuch-Luxmoore 1999; Braker and Warburg 1998). This modern territorial redistribution layers on top of an older reality, fruit of medieval migration, conquest, and preaching: Hinduism in Thailand, Islam in Nigeria, or Christianity in Korea.

Rather than generate the hegemony of a new universal church, the migratory pattern is likely to spawn multireligious arenas. Such arenas also are not altogether new. Global cities historically have been the sites for such multireligiosity. William McNeill noted in his sweeping accounts of world history that ancient cities typically had been constituted of multiple religions and that in the historical record such multiculturalism was more normal than exclusivist regimes. World cities today—Bombay, Frankfurt, New York, Cairo—are the nodal points where multiplicity of religious affiliations is incubated and whence it radiates outward (McNeill 1993, 29–39).

Multireligious arenas can generate several kinds of social and ideological outcomes: toleration/compartmentalization, expulsion and/or extermination, or creation of an ecumenical community. "Toleration" is a minimalist noun signifying something less than appreciation but a benign sort of "live and let live" settlement. "Compartmentalization" is a form of toleration that is based on discrimination: "I'll tolerate your exotic or abominable practices if you confine them to your people"; "I'll tolerate your practices as long as they are privatized and I don't have to see them." Ethnic/religious accommodation in ancient and medieval global cities or empires often rested on social toleration and compartmentalization enjoined by economic and political prudence. The Ottoman millett "system" approximated such an arrangement for a time when it developed self-regulating spheres for minority religious communities— Orthodox Christians, Armenians, Jews—on the assumption that they recognized the primacy and privileges of the Islamic hegemony (Braude and Lewis 1982). The high degree of sectarian and caste difference within Hinduism and between Hinduism and other faiths in India was rendered "tolerable" by highly institutionalized compartmentalization, enforced by rules governing interaction. The springing up of immigrant neighborhoods or gated communities in Western cities often accomplishes a similar insulation. Expulsion or extermination as an outcome hardly requires elaboration to any newspaper reader of the 1940s or the 1980s and 1990s.

Development of an ecumenical mentality—which would characterize what I am calling a universal religiosity by contrast to a "universal church"—is another possible outcome. I start with the more formal, transnational, ecumene-building aspect of a universal religiosity. Transnational epistemes are communities of outlook: persons and organizations that share common worldviews, purposes, interests, and practices, and for whom the relevant arena of communication and action transcends national jurisdictions. Ecumene refers to such an epistemic community with religious qualities. There have always been wandering religious virtuosos for whom neither political spaces nor formal religious boundaries mattered and who imagined they saw common themes in all religions. They were saints, *pirs*, and sadhus, often mystics in tension with formalized, institutionalized, high-culture religion, vowing to return to the sacred devotional oneness with God. Such were the ("Muslim") Sufis and ("Hindu") Bhakts of the Indian subcontinent, associated with popular religion, whose preachings often were indistinguishable from each other and whose message often emphasized the irrelevance of religious boundaries. What is new in transnational ecumenism is its intentional, rationalized, even bureaucratized form.

The very signs and symbols of transnational flows and arenas have been the epistemes that have sprung up around the eight world summits on topics such as the environment, population, global warming, women, and—immediately relevant to this chapter—religion. Summits have been characterized by what Stephen Toulmin called the upstairs/downstairs syndrome—a metaphor that will be understood by readers who followed the TV serial of the same name. In the serial, the rich or noble folks occupied the upstairs floors, and the active society of servants—who often ran the upstairs indirectly—occupied the basement. Summits have had an upstairs, where state representatives congregated, the ostensibly most important layer of the summit. They also have had a downstairs, where the NGOs congregated with the intent of making their voices heard and to nudge, pummel, and push the upstairs actors into proper conduct. Whereas the upstairs venues of summits demonstrated the persistence of the sovereign nation-state, the downstairs actors showed the increasing significance of transnational civil society, epistemes of nonstate sectors, in the decision process. With the growth of a transnational politics, states no longer are the only actors on the world stage. By the time the phenomenon of "downstairs" organizations moved to Beijing in 1995 for the summit on women, downstairs had become normalized and its significance acknowledged: even the Beijing hosts, who take a dim view of civil society, had to provide accommodations and facilities, albeit poor ones.

The World Peace Summit of religious and spiritual leaders that met during the wider Millennium Summit of world leaders in 2000 was one version of such a downstairs effort—a nonstate event in which religious congregations of the most diverse kind were represented. It was transnational civil society organizing itself and attempting to create consensus on goals and plans for peace to guide its own actions and those of states.

The proceedings highlighted the fact that ecumenical forces are revisiting the idea of religious universality not in the form of a universal church but in the formulation of a universal religiosity. Such a project is more likely to address moral than theological objectives—war and poverty rather than the conceptualization of the Godhead. Such reasoning characterized the summit's document placing the voice of diverse religions behind the quest for world peace, the eradication of poverty, and the protection of the environment. The document implied these goals represented the normative and spiritual common objectives of different faiths.

There have been other initiatives toward formulating some sacred universal principles, such as the ecumenical explorations of the World Council of Churches; the initiatives of the Chicago-based Council for a Parliament of the World's Religions, whose vice chairman served as secretary general of the Millennium Summit of religions; or the United Religion Initiative led by Episcopal bishop William Swing of San Francisco. Older is Pope John XXIII's Nostra Aetate (1965), which recognized the possibility of spiritual truth in all religions:

> The church therefore has this exhortation for her sons: prudently and lovingly, through dialogue and collaboration with the followers of other religions, and in witness of Christian faith and life, acknowledge, preserve and promote the spiritual and moral goods found among these men, as well as the values found in their society and culture. (Abbott and Gallagher 1966, 663)

Nostra Aetate was an important step away from claims of monopoly on religious truth and toward the discovery of common ground. A similar doctrine, which holds that "toleration alone, while desirable, is not sufficient in a world of religious pluralism," has been suggested by an influential Protestant voice, Dr. Joseph C. Hough Jr., president of Union Theological Seminary: "I would begin with the recognition that religion is something we human beings put together in an effort to give some cultural form to our faith. . . . [T]herefore we want to be careful about claiming that one religious form is the only one that is authentic or real" (New York Times, 2002).

There are challenges to such attempts to formulate a universal ground of religiosity. Some challengers argue that this new religiosity softens the sinews of faith and practice and blots out distinctions that should be observed. One provocative Internet article on the 2000 World Peace Summit observed that its organizers were the sort of morally promiscuous people who thought it made little difference "whether one worships a downed World War II airplane with a cargo cult, is a snake-handling Baptist or a Roman Catholic" (Harder 2000).

In a thirty-six-page declaration released a week after the summit, Cardinal Joseph Ratzinger, prefect of the Vatican's Congregation for the Doctrine of the Faith, rejected what he said were growing attempts to depict all religions as equally true and reasserted that salvation was possible only through Jesus Christ. About the same time, ten thousand evangelists meeting at Amsterdam under the auspices of the Reverend Billy Graham agreed with Ratzinger (Niebuhr 2000). Universal religiosity, if plausible, is not about to command consensus anytime soon. Nevertheless, the increasingly transnational nature of population flows and the increasingly multinational location of all major religions give more and more religious leaders a stake in the transnational and ecumenical dialogues.

I have said that universal religiosity refers on one hand to the product of an intentional, intellectual, and social process that builds a transnational religious episteme—an ecumene—with common vocabulary, grammar, and worldviews. It refers on the other hand to more informal, spontaneous social processes of syncretism, emulation, and exchange among people of different religious affiliations that create the audience and support base for transnational religious epistemes. Ecumenical dialogues by professional church leaders are more visible to newspaper-reading transnational observers than are quotidian, community-level ecumenical practices. Yet without the spontaneous practice of multireligiosity in increasingly multicultural societies—without the normalizing process that ordinary neighborhood-, town-, and district-level exchanges as well as mutual observation generate—transnational ecumenic dialogues have no broad constituency.

In accounts of quotidian interactions between religious communities, conflict occupies more space than peaceable regimes. Shail Mayaram, in recent work on South Asian communities of faith, has pointed out that social science scholarship has privileged the investigation of conflict and violence in the encounter of faiths. Such scholarship has virtually ignored the wide arena of thought and practice occupied by syncretism and by religious devotees whose identities are difficult to assign to conventional categories. Mayaram would have us explore this other, "normal" world more systematically: "In the South Asian context historically there was a constant movement back and forth across sects and also possibilities of multiple affiliation," as well as liminal identities. Local stories of competition and conversion are also stories of "dialogue, exchange and the self-regulation of difference" (Mayaram n.d.: see also Mayaram 1998; Ahmed 1985; Gottschalk 2001; Burckhalter-Fluckiger 1996).

Exchange and syncretism arise out of neighborly observation of each other's practices and out of the permeability of religious boundaries. The lived dailiness of overlapping moral dispositions creates common ground for moral reasoning, generating experience that may be receptive to elements of a universal religiosity articulated by transnational dialogues.

The question of universal religiosity raises the matter of universal religious freedom—an issue that is becoming increasingly intertwined with the meaning and practice of propagating faith and of conversion. Is preaching with the intent to substitute the preacher's faith for that of the listener freedom of religion or cultural and moral invasion? The notion that there are truths in all religions provides a different platform for thinking about the propagation of faith than does the idea that particular religions have a monopoly on truth. The belief that a religion can claim an ultimate and fundamental truth justifies the believers in the project of bringing the truth to those possessed of false gods—which raises the question of whether it is possible to be a robust Christian or Muslim while exercising tolerance for other religions (Madan 1997). The answer depends on what kind of Christian or Muslim one is. Mahatma Gandhi highlighted the tension between toleration and conversion when he questioned the meaningfulness of conversion to people who, like himself, thought there was truth in all religions (Parekh 1989, 84). Some of the organizers of the World Peace Summit of religious leaders advocated a ban on conversion on the same grounds—namely, that conversion challenged the idea of truth in all religions (Witte and Bourdeaux 2000). The difference, says one prominent Protestant churchman, between an attempt to convert and an attempt to bear witness is great:

> The attempt to bear witness is . . . to state honestly what you have discovered in faith in Jesus Christ. This is to share the things in your life that are of highest value to you, and I think this is an act of friendship. But this is very different from saying, "Now that I've told you this, you've got to believe as I do to experience this." The one is an opening to conversation; the other is closing conversation. (Hough 2002)

This position obviously has a connection to the possibility of a universal religiosity. Ecumenical conversation is difficult in an environment of competitive conversion. But the anticonversion doctrine has some peculiar bedfellows—including liberal Christians driven by concern about cultural invasion, and Hindu fundamentalists and Russian Orthodox Christians protecting their turf. In India, opposing the propagation of non-Hindu religions has become a favorite policy prescription by Hindu nationalists whose project is to create an exclusivist Hindu religious state. The theoretical ground on which they stand is the reverse of that motivating Gandhi, who believed there was truth in all religions. As spokesmen for the dominant faith, they would like to deny entry to others, protecting a single truth and its virtual monopoly in the face of Christian and Muslim alternatives.

Let me tie this question of religious propagation/conversion—and its affinity with questions of religious freedom—to recent U.S. initiatives in this arena. In 1998, the 105th Congress passed the International Religious Freedom

Act (IRFA), with the support of the Christian Coalition, B'nai Brith, and the Southern Baptist Convention. The act, introduced by Senators Don Nickels and Joseph I. Lieberman, requires the United States to respond to countries that persecute religious minorities by issuing anything from a diplomatic reprimand to stiff economic sanctions, while leaving the president substantial discretion. IRFA established elaborate machinery, including an annual State Department report on religious freedom in all countries, an ambassador whose charge is religious freedom everywhere, and a ten-person commission that publishes reports and recommends action to the president.

IRFA raises the question of whether its processes are likely to advance a universal religiosity or to enhazard it. To what extent will the commission be seen as constructing a transnational regime of human rights enlarging the arena of mutual respect? To what extent will it be viewed as an agent of the American nation-state appropriating the issue of transnational religious freedom for its own agendas: using religion as an instrument of national interest or to clear the way for projects of its own majority religion? The fact that the United States, at the end of the millennium, stands forth as the sole superpower enhances the credibility of the second reading.

The legislation and its apparatus are contradictory, loaded with different projects. One reason for the legislation was the eagerness of conservative Christian forces to protect their Christian coreligionists abroad and provide cover for those called to convert pagans. To that extent, IRFA represented the militant voice of an exclusivist Christianity for which the charge of cultural invasion posed no problem. On the other hand, the legislation represents a triumph of sorts for ecumenical perspectives. The commission in justifying its work interpreted the act as an ecumenical instrument of human rights: "The report [of 1999] applies to all religions and beliefs. It targets no particular country or region, and seeks to promote no religion over another. It does, however, recognize the intrinsic value of religion, even as it acknowledges that religious freedom includes the right not to believe or to practice" (Seiple 1999). The United States, as a multireligious state, cannot legitimately use its resources to protect only messengers of its majority religion. Instead, the legislation had to make the project one that promises to protect the freedom of worship of all religions, that universalizes protection. However, most ecumenically oriented Christian groups in the United States regarded IRFA as a tool of intrusive evangelicalism. Some activists on behalf of non-Christian religions—the adherents of the Dalai Lama's Buddhism and other Asian denominations—supported it (*Facts on File* 1998).

IRFA makes religious toleration and protection of religious freedoms the responsibility of sovereign states, holding them accountable not only for their own antireligious actions if any (as when China suppresses the unlicensed Catholic Church or Falun Gong) but also for the acts of their citizens, as when Hindu governments do not prevent nationalist groups from harassing and killing Christians and Muslims. The Commission for Religious Freedom each year identifies "states of special concern" (SPCs). In 1999, it identified China and Sudan, recommending that action be taken against their conduct. In October 2000, after sporadic attacks on Christians in India, the commission held hearings on India. These were roundly condemned by their potential beneficiaries as intervening in unhelpful ways into their own efforts to mobilize government protection. They also were condemned by the Catholic bishop's conference in India, by the spokesman for liberal Hinduism Swami Agnivesh, and by the widow of murdered Australian Christian missionary Graham Staynes. In 2002 the commission declared India an SPC in light of the terrible death toll in Muslim pogroms in Gujerat (*India Today* 2000).

The case of India, a secular state where religious liberties guaranteed by the constitution normally are enforced, raises some interesting specific problems by comparison with China and Sudan—countries where liberties are restricted. Should the American president intervene in a state that formally proclaims freedom for all religions and whose democratic political institutions provide minorities with significant political and legal protection? It is clear that that protection sometimes fails and that not all members of government are equally enthusiastic about religious liberties. How ought we to distinguish this case from that of the United States, which formally proclaims religious protections but fails to protect African American churches against arson, or from that of Germany or Great Britain, which sometimes fail to protect Muslims against murder?

I asked earlier whether the commission on freedom of religion was likely to enhance or enhazard the move toward a universal religiosity. IRFA appeared to challenge the sovereignty defense that national governments offer to justify their untroubled violation of civil and religious rights. Where such a challenge on behalf of religious freedom clears the ground for untroubled belief and practice, it comes in on the side of the transnationalization of the ecumenical spirit. Where it steps forward as the advance guard of competitive conversion, it "closes the conversation." Further, where the initiatives on behalf of religious freedom come from a single nation-state that appoints itself as the enforcer of universal rights, the project is compromised by the suspicion that ultimately a state interest—or at least the interest of a powerful religious constituency cloaked by the mantle of the state—is at stake. The legitimacy of the initiative is tainted by the failure to make religious freedom a shared project, an ecumenical project, detached from the interested intentions of a particular nation-state and its cultural and religious preferences.

I began this chapter by exploring the proposition that forms of polity and forms of religiosity are thought to have an effect on each other. If this is so, we should expect the thinning of state boundaries and the expansion of transnational political, social, and economic institutions and epistemes to affect forms of religiosity and the formulation of religious goals. Having excluded the likelihood that the new transnationalism would favor resurrecting a universal church, I explored the likelihood of a "universal religiosity" grounded in the principle that there is truth in all religions. The moves toward such a transnational ecumenism entail, on one hand, formal theological and ethical dialogues, in transnational settings, by religious spokespersons in pursuit of common ground. On the other hand, ecumenical culture is produced by informal interactions and exchanges among ordinary devotional persons in multireligious settings. Because conversion challenges the idea that there is truth in all religions, it is not easily compatible with the building of transnational ecumenes. If ecumenism in an era of fading states and expanding transnational institutions comes to be exploited in order to protect the hegemony of a nation-state (such as the United States) or of a civilizational region (such as the traditional arena of Judeo-Christian religiosity), a universal religiosity cannot flourish. A transnational ecumene must be a shared project sensitive to the variations in culture and politics that shape each region or religion's receptiveness. Universal religiosity must be founded in persuasion and consent, not in the exercise of power and coercion by nation-states.

BIBLIOGRAPHY

Abbott, Walter M., S. J., and Msgr. Joseph Gallagher, eds. 1966. *The Documents of Vatican Two.* New York: Guild Press.

Afridi, Sam. 2002. "Muslims in America: Identity, Diversity and the Challenge of Understanding." Working paper, Social Science Research Council, Working Group on Law and Culture, Planning Meeting, January 10–13.

Ahmed, Imtiaz, ed. 1985. *Ritual and Religion among Muslims of the Sub-continent.* Lahore, Pakistan: Vanguard.

Braker, E., and M. Warburg, eds. 1998. *New Religions and New Religiosity.* Aarhus, Denmark: Aarhus University Press.

Braude, Benjamin, and Bernard Lewis, eds. 1982. *Christians and Jews in the Ottoman Empire: The Functioning of a Plural Society.* 2 vols. New York: Holmes and Meyer.

Burckhalter-Fluckiger, Joyce. 1996. "Religious Identity at the Crossroads of a Muslim Female Healer's Practice." Paper presented at Annual Conference on South Asia, Madison, Wisconsin, October.

Casanova, Jose. 1997. "Globalizing Catholicism and the Return to a 'Universal' Church." In *Transnational Religion and Fading States*, ed. Susanne Rudolph and James Piscatori, 121–43. Boulder, CO: Westview Press.

"Daily News Briefs." 2000. *Catholic World News Service*, September 14.

Eckhom, Erik. 2001. "China Repeats Terms for Ties Pope Seeks." *New York Times*, October 26.

Facts on File. 1998. October 22.

Fisher, Ian. 2001. "Europe's Muslims Seek a Path amid Competing Cultures." *New York Times*, December 8.

Gottschalk, Peter. 2001. *Beyond Hindu and Muslim; Multiple Identity in Narratives from Village India.* New Delhi: Oxford University Press.

Haas, Peter. 1992. "Introduction: Epistemic Communities and International Policy Coordination." *International Organization* 46:1–35.

Harder, James. 2000. "Religion: U.N. Faithful Eye Global Religion." In "Insight on the News," October 2. http://www.insightmag.com/news/2000/10/02/World/ Religion.U.n.Faithful.Eye.Global.Religion-213309.shtml.

Hough, Joseph C., Jr. 2002. "Q&A: Acknowledging That God Is Not Limited to Christians." *New York Times*, January 12, B9.

India Today. 2000. September 25.

Luxmoore, Jonathan, and Jolanta Babiuch-Luxmoore. 1999. "New Myths for Old: Proselytism and Transition in Post-communist Europe." *Journal of Ecumenical Studies* 36:43–65.

Madan, T. N. 1997. *Modern Myths, Locked Minds: Secularism and Fundamentalism in India.* New Delhi: Oxford University Press.

Mayaram, Shail. N.d. "Community, Conversion and Coexistence." Unpublished paper.

———. 1998. "Rethinking Meo Identity: Cultural Faultline, Syncretism, Hybridity or Liminality." In *Islam, Communities and the Nation: Muslim Identities in South Asia and Beyond,* edited by Mushirul Hasan, 283–306. New Delhi: Manohar.

McNeill, William. 1993, December. "Project Report: Fundamentalism and the World of the 1990's." *Bulletin of the American Academy of Arts and Sciences* 47(3):29–30.

Niebuhr, Gustav. 2000. "A Bishop Works to Bridge Faith in the Cause of Peace." *New York Times,* September 23.

Parekh, Bhikhu. 1989. *Gandhi's Political Philosophy.* Notre Dame, IN: University of Notre Dame Press.

Rice, Eugene, and Anthony Grafton. 1994. *The Foundations of Early Modern Europe, 1460–1559.* 2nd ed. New York: Norton.

Roth, Guenther, and Claus Wittich, trans. 1978. Max Weber, *Economy and Society.* 2 vols. Berkeley: University of California Press.

Rudolph, Susanne, and James Piscatori, eds. 1997. *Transnational Religion and Fading States.* Boulder, CO: Westview Press.

Seiple, Robert A., ambassador at large for International Religious Freedom. 1999. Prepared testimony before the House International Relations Committee, October 6. Federal News Service. Accessed online at www.uscirf.gov/events/ cong_tesitimony/1999/.

Witte, John, Jr., and Michael Bourdeaux, eds. 1999. *Proselytism and Orthodoxy in Russia: The New War for Souls.* Maryknoll, NY: Orbis Books.

———. 2000. "A Primer on the Rights and Wrongs of Proselytism." In *Fides et Libertas: The Journal of the International Religious Liberty Association* vol. 3, 12–17.

Index